People, Power, Change:

Movements of Social Transformation

Luther P. Gerlach
Virginia H. Hine

People, Power, Change

Movements of Social Transformation

People, Power, Change
Movements
of Social Transformation

WITHDRAWN

Luther P. Gerlach

and

Virginia H. Hine

THE BOBBS-MERRILL COMPANY, INC.
Indianapolis

First Edition
Third Printing—1976
Library of Congress Catalog Card Number: 70-109434
ISBN 0–672–60613–5 (pbk)

To all those who are engaged in the painful processes of personal and social transformation.

ACKNOWLEDGMENTS

The authors gratefully acknowledge the indispensable contributions to the research on which this book is based by other members of our research team. Not only did they provide valuable information on the groups to which they were assigned, they also developed excellent working relationships with movement participants, which proved of inestimable value to the understanding of the movements. In addition, they contributed much to the regular staff meetings at which the information we were all collecting was exchanged, reviewed, and interpreted.

Research assistants included James and Karen Olila; Richard Rooth; Mel Holsteen; Gary Palmer; Kilian McDonnell, O.S.B.; Annie Baldwin; and Anthony Sorem. We also wish to thank Ursula Gerlach and Alden Hine, who made important contributions to the development of our concepts and to the establishment of rapport with movement participants.

To those participants in the movements we have studied, we are particularly indebted. Without their gracious acceptance of our presence, responses to our inquiries, and cooperation with our requests, the project would obviously have been impossible. Indeed, many of these individuals contributed significantly to the development of our interpretation of the data.

Finally, we wish to thank those who funded the research. Primary funding was provided by the Hill Family Foundation of St. Paul, Minnesota. Other support came from Ferndale Foundation of St. Paul, the Graduate Research Office of the University of Minnesota, and the McKnight Foundation of St. Paul.

Contents

Introduction

It has often been said that the one constant in human life is change. Human beings and their societies—their political, economic, social, and religious institutions—are continually changing. They usually change so slowly and gradually that they are perceived to be in a state of equilibrium. Anthropological studies of tribal societies often assume such a state of equilibrium. A typical monograph describes the ways in which the members of a society produce and exchange goods and services, govern themselves, determine family and kinship patterns, and institutionalize their religious beliefs. Anthropologists see each of these sets of behavioral patterns as subsystems, and they analyze how these systems are interrelated in such a way as to produce a condition of relative social stability. There is often one chapter at the end of the monograph on the subject of change. This is usually a brief summary of what has happened in that society since its contact with the West and of the ways by which it is adjusting to and emerging into the industrial age.

No anthropologist would assume that the "traditional" patterns and institutions of the tribal society he has studied existed unchanged through time before this contact. Gradual development is considered to have occurred through minor changes which did not upset the total equilibrium. In any society there are inconsistencies among the behavior patterns required by the different subsystems. These are viewed as potential sources of internally generated social change. Contact between societies of approximately the same level of complexity may result in the introduction of new ideas and institutional patterns. Such externally generated change could occur without the total disruption of social stability. A minor change in one subsystem would lead to compensating changes in other subsystems. Development is believed to have occurred through this type of adjustment and adaptation.

Anthropologists and other social scientists have seen, however, that the changes that came about in tribal societies after contact with the West were of a different kind—more rapid and more destructive of traditional patterns. Changes introduced by this contact were too great for the tribal mechanisms of social and psychological adjustment to accommodate. Traditional social patterns were not only changed; they also began to disintegrate.

Clearly there are at least two types of change. One we shall call developmental, the other radical, or fundamental. Developmental changes in political, economic, religious, or social structures, in customs, or in patterns of personal interaction are variations on a basic social theme. Radical, or fundamental, change in social structures, customs, or interaction patterns mark those moments in history which are later seen as significant turning points. To them can be traced a sharp change in direction, the emergence of an entirely new type of social structure, or the birth of a nation. The Protestant Reformation is the way we refer to one such change. The Boston Tea Party has become the symbol of another.

An example of an even more radical and far-reaching social change is now called the Agricultural Revolution. When small bands of hunters and food gatherers discovered how to grow crops, they began to settle down. The way was then open to the growth of towns and cities, the accumulation of wealth, and the emergence of hierarchical social classes. The Industrial Revolution and the Machine Age are terms for still another point of radical change in human history. This too was accompanied by new forms of political organization, revolutionary changes in kinship groupings, the emergence of new bases for power groupings, and entirely new economic structures and technological developments. Each of these radical changes involved new forms of religious thought and new concepts of the relationship between man and man.

From the point of view of the participants in social change, it is difficult to tell the difference between developmental and radical change. What might seem to be developmental "progress" to one is experienced by another as threatening and radical in nature. Similarly, what a visionary hails as radical change, others see as merely unpleasant disturbances.

In a discussion of social, political, or religious movements, change may be defined as radical if those who occupy positions of power in the existing social structures resist that change. Those who desire the change, therefore, must mobilize for collective power to oppose the power vested in existing structures. By this same criterion, developmental change may be viewed as change which the people in power regard as "progress." Resistance to radical change can be expected not only from members of the elite who are dominant and advantaged; there are also large groups in any society who are satisfied with their lot in the existing structure though they are not in positions of power. Even those who are severely disadvantaged in the society may fear change because it might make a bad situation even worse. All of these groups we lump together under the term "the established order." Economic, political, social, or religious elites remain in power because other groups are either satisfied with the status quo or afraid of change. Persons in positions of power are not the only ones who resist change.

Radical political, social, or religious movements are usually seen as results of or reactions to fundamental social disruption and the extreme personal disorientation associated with radical change. Participants are therefore assumed to be groups suffering from a particular form of social disorganization or from some type of deprivation in the existing order. If neither of these conditions applies, such persons are assumed to be psychologically maladjusted. In many studies of social movements, a negative evaluation of the participants is implied. In fact, if participants in a movement do not fit one of these three stereotypes, devotees of these theories are driven either to deny the fact that a movement exists or to conjure up such pseudo-theories as the "fun and games" theory of movements. An example of this is a statement made by Eric Hoffer, a member of the President's Study Commission on Violence. In one of the televised hearings at which participants in the student movements from the Berkeley campus appeared, Hoffer denied the possibility that the students were engaged in a "legitimate" social movement. Because they were affluent, well educated, and not products of social disorganization, he described their protest activities as a form of malicious play. Trapped in old analyses which justify social revolutions on the basis of the relative deprivation theory, he refused to view the students as "real" revolutionaries. "They are having the time of their lives," he said; "they are having a ball. . . . They are behaving like hoodlums." (*Minneapolis Tribune,* 24 October 1968.)

If a movement is viewed not simply as a response to drastic social change, but rather as a mechanism through which that change is shaped and directed, the analysis takes on quite a different tone. For instance, John D. Rockefeller III, in an interview reported in *Newsweek* (4 November 1968), perceived the student movement as one of "tremendous vitality" and "great potential for good if only we can understand and respond positively. . . . Instead of worrying about how to suppress the youthful rebellion, we of the older generation should be worrying about how to sustain it."

There are many social scientists who tend to view movements in this more positive light. Anthropologists have called some religious movements in African, American Indian, and Melanesian societies "acculturative." These movements are seen as mechanisms with which whole groups adapt to changed conditions. By means of such mechanisms new types of leadership are developed, new social structures created, and new values accepted and internalized. To the extent that these leadership patterns, social forms, or values are consistent with Western patterns thought to be functional in a modern age, the movements are considered "adaptive."

We take the position that movements are both cause and effect of social change. In this book we are focusing on movements as mechanisms of change rather than on the conditions of disorganization or deprivation which give rise to them.

Movements which became full-fledged revolutions and resulted in the defeat of an established political order, such as Communism in Russia and China or the eighteenth century revolutionary groups in France and the American colonies, were obviously mechanisms of lasting social change. These movements brought about social change by overthrowing, and themselves becoming, established orders. Others achieved it by establishing parallel and competing social structures. Protestantism brought about religious as well as social changes in this fashion. The Methodist denomination, for example, began as a revival movement similar to modern Pentecostalism. The religious fervor and emotionalism of early participants were incompatible with the established order of the Anglican church within which the movement arose. Its members, excluded from local parishes, created their own cell-like organizations linked by the activities of charismatic leaders. Growth rates, as is characteristic of most movements, were slow at first and then became exponential. As the number of adherents grew, gradual organizational routinization began. In this, Methodism followed a developmental sequence characteristic of all successful movements. The final result was a separate denomination which in time became so incompatible with the fervor of its own beginnings that many modern Methodists are being drawn out of it into a new religious revival—Pentecostalism. Movements have, in fact, been defined by anthropologist Igor Kopytoff as "rapidly emergent institutions" (33). It is easy to see that movements, which themselves may eventually become established orders, may be considered mechanisms of social change. In spite of their bureaucratization, they are never exact copies of the institutions they replace or parallel.

Many movements, however, rise within an established order, flourish, and then die. Religious revivals have punctuated the history of Christianity but not all have resulted in an extant denomination. Religious historians note the effects of these movements on the church as a whole, and attribute changes of varying magnitude to them. Many third-party presidential candidates in the political history of the United States have been leaders of movements which never overthrew the established order. Nevertheless, they dramatized a "crackpot" or radical stand on certain issues, some of which were later incorporated in modified form into the platforms of one of the major parties. For example, the final acceptance of the principles of social security may be credited partially to the activity of several small political movements during the nineteen thirties and to the efforts of their third-party candidates. These movements mobilized human energy in support of a shift in social values and proposed innovations in economic structures. The established order, while not overthrown or replaced, was effectively changed by these thrusts.

Social change in any society obviously involves change on the part of its individual members. There are many fruitless arguments about which causes the other. We have noted that movements are frequently mechanisms of change in social institutions. It is also true that people who become committed to a movement experience some degree of personal transformation. There are some movements, such as Communism, in which the primary purpose is social change. Committed participants, however, undergo severe personal transformation in the process. There are other movements, such as Alcoholics Anonymous, in which personal transformation is considered primary and any resultant social change is secondary. In Black Power, both change in social structures and the transformation of participants into people with pride and a sense of power are stated purposes. We would suggest that, no matter what the particular emphasis, a successful movement is the point of intersection between personal and social change.

For the purposes of our study, we have defined a movement as *a group of people who are organized for, ideologically motivated by, and committed to a purpose which implements some form of personal or social change; who are actively engaged in the recruitment of others; and whose influence is spreading in opposition to the established order within which it originated.*

An obvious problem for any student of movements is defining the point at which a group or a collective becomes a movement. Did Christianity, for instance, become a movement when Jesus stood in the River Jordan being baptized by John? When he called his first disciples? When multitudes came to listen to him? Or not until Paul and other converts began organizing churches? At what point did John Wesley's small group of concerned Christians become a revival movement? At what point did Communism stop being a topic of discussion for small groups of concerned intellectuals and become a truly revolutionary movement? When did the Civil Rights "Movement" become, in large part, the Black Power "Revolution," and what is the difference?

Our study of movement dynamics has led us to identify five key factors which are operationally significant and which we believe must be present and interacting before a collectivity of whatever size becomes a true movement. These five key factors are:

1. *A segmented, usually polycephalous, cellular organization* composed of units reticulated by various personal, structural, and ideological ties.
2. *Face-to-face recruitment* by committed individuals using their own pre-existing, significant social relationships.
3. *Personal commitment* generated by an act or an experience which separates a convert in some significant way from the established order (or his previous place in it), identifies him with a new set of values, and commits him to changed patterns of behavior.
4. *An ideology* which codifies values and goals, provides a conceptual framework by which all experiences or events relative to these goals may be interpreted, motivates and provides rationale for envisioned changes, defines the opposition, and forms the basis for conceptual unification of a segmented network of groups.
5. *Real or perceived opposition* from the society at large or from that segment of the established order within which the movement has risen.

Our approach to the analysis of movements is a result of three years of anthropological research into two modern movements—the Pentecostal Movement and the Black Power Movement. During our study of the worldwide spread of Pentecostalism, we first identified what we considered to be five key factors. Later, when we turned to the study of the rise of Black Power, we recognized the same five factors at work. We also conducted library research to find out if identification of these factors would be useful in interpreting accounts of other movements by anthropologists, sociologists, political scientists, or historians. This proved to be the case.

We have found that some persons resist the idea of comparing Pentecostalism with Black Power. Some non-participants say that Pentecostalism is not revolutionary because it envisions desired changes as of an otherworldly nature and as the result of divine intervention. It is therefore considered essentially a withdrawal from society. On the other hand, Black Power, these same individuals contend, is a worldly attempt to make revolutionary social, economic, and political changes through human initiative and effort. Some Pentecostals resist our comparison because they feel that theirs is a movement "of the Lord," and that social movements like Black Power are "of man." Black Power participants sometimes resist being compared with their counterparts in a religious movement because they view religion as something opposed to social change and as a handmaiden of the status quo.

We can only say as social scientists—and there are participants in both movements who agree with us—that in the mechanics of both movements we find the same generic characteristics. We find the same basic type of organization and the same methods by which they are spreading. We also see basic similarities in the type, if not the content, of their ideologies. Individuals in both movements are observably affected by participation in them. The fact of personal transformation, if not the direction, is the same. We will go even further and suggest ways in which Pentecostalism may be considered revolutionary, and Black Power religious.

Pentecostalism is revolutionary, first, because conversion to it involves fundamental changes in the individual. Second, it is revolutionary in terms of certain effects it has on established churches. It confronts both unbelievers and nominal Christians with the fact of a transforming experience, central in New Testament theology, but easily lost in the bureaucracy and ritual of the modern church. This has disquieting effects on officials of the Christian establishment and forces many of them to a soul-searching review of their positions. Most books on the encroaching "tongues movements" in Catholic and non-Pentecostal Protestant denominations include a chapter on "What can we learn from the Pentecostals?" Third, Pentecostalism has had social, economic, and political effects of potentially revolutionary nature in non-Western societies where it is spreading. These will be discussed in more detail in our analysis of commitment in chapter V.

There are stereotypes of religion as a pillar of the status quo, of religious movements as withdrawals from rather than confrontation with social change. To these have recently been added the assumption, popular in some scientific circles, that religion is a dependent variable, determined by the social, economic, and political structures of a society. Religious experience is considered a substitute for social action. According to this view, faith is an alternative to skill and self-reliance. Religious movements, particularly millenarian ones, are considered an alternative to direct action in the "real" world.

Many anthropologists, while accepting religion as a dependent variable in certain cases, insist that this is only half the picture. For example, Raymond Firth views religion as both affecting and being affected by social structure. It may change as social structures change, or it may produce those changes. Not only can religion reflect the existing structure of a society and provide sanctions for it, but also on occasion it can lead to radical social realignment (75).

Clearly, religious movements such as the Protestant Reformation and the rise of Islam have contributed significantly to vast social changes in the "real" world. They have, in fact, provided the ideological motivation and rationale for fundamental political, economic, and social changes. To the extent that religious faith enables believers to confront those in positions of power in an established system without fear of the consequences, it is a revolutionary force.

Our survey of Pentecostalism in the United States shows that participants tend to be politically conservative. Furthermore, the Pentecostal ethic militates against social change through social action. Although they envision radical political, economic, and social change here on earth, they expect this to be instituted through supernatural means. The social change associated with Pentecostalism, especially in non-Western societies moving toward industrialization, is largely an inadvertent consequence of personal change, but is nonetheless real. It should be noted that many of the newer converts who have remained in their non-Pentecostal churches, especially clergy and very active lay members, combine the radical personal change involved in the Pentecostal experience with a radical approach to social action on non-religious issues. Pentecostalism, we suggest, is conceptually revolutionary. It encourages an experience through which an individual believes himself to be radically changed; many converts behave accordingly in social situations.

Black Power, on the other hand, is clearly a movement which seeks to accomplish social change with entirely human means. But it is religious in the sense that it requires the commitment of the individual to something greater than self. If the term "religion" is narrowly defined as that which has as its referent a supernatural being, the Black Power Movement could not be considered religious except for those participants who are Black Muslims. But if we view as religious a commitment of oneself to something not only greater than oneself, but transcending even the body of believers, then the Black Power Movement can be viewed as religious.

The methods by which we collected our data are described in

greater detail in a concluding chapter. Our approach was one of participant observation. Other methods of data collection included interviews, both structured and informal, and a written questionnaire designed for computer processing. In considering a phenomenon as little understood as movement dynamics, the student must make a special effort to see the whole and to avoid the distortions of pre-occupation with the parts. For this reason we felt that the method of participant observation yielded the most reliable, if not the most quantifiable, data. In an article on scientific methods of study of various levels of organization from the inorganic, through the organic, to the psycho-social, Michael Polanyi wrote: "The observation of the ascending levels of organization requires a steadily increasing degree of participation of the observor in his subject matter" (377).

We are grateful to those participants in both movements who have cooperated with our research, allowed us to join their groups, and tried to help us understand their motivations, their goals, and their satisfactions in movement participation. In order to protect the identity of individuals, we have used fictitious names of persons and groups. Data concerning Black Power were collected in two mid-western metropolitan areas and one southeastern city. Pentecostal groups were studied in two metropolitan areas, one rural area in the United States, and in both city and rural environments in Haiti, Colombia, Jamaica, and Mexico.

This book will probably not appeal to the statistically minded for at least three reasons. First, we make liberal use of the words "some," "many," and "a few." Second, although we do compare the two movements we have studied, we have not found it possible to use the scientific comparative method in which all variables but those being measured are controlled. Third, we have employed the device of the "apt illustration," selecting evidence from the literature on other types of movements to illustrate our points. The proper scientific alternative would have been to make a random selection of known movements and test for presence or absence of our five factors. Unfortunately, sufficient data are not available. Either the movement is historically distant and not fully recorded for our purposes; or, if it is contemporary, it may be considered subversive, and participants are therefore not in a position to welcome scientific investigation. We consider ourselves fortunate to have had the opportunity to study even two movements at close range and to have been able to gain some impression of the entire network of each as well as detailed data on specific groups within them.

We have approached the subject of movements as social naturalists rather than as taxonomists or statisticians. Although we do have a great deal of "hard data," we have made many generalizations and presented much that is impressionistic. In those instances where we do refer to correlations between variables, our statements are based on a statistical treatment of the data described more fully in the chapter on methodology. The word "significant" in these contexts refers to a statistical probability or the null hypothesis being true of .05 or less. This book, however, has not been written for the statistician but for those who are trying to gain a broad picture of the changes that are occurring through the mechanism of social and religious movements. Like political scientist Eugene Meehan (374) and biologist Warren Weaver (386), we feel that the best scientific methodology is that which enables one to explain the phenomenon under study in such a way as to increase man's ability to cope with it successfully.

A final point in our orientation must be clarified. Most analyses of movements, scientific and popular, are based on the generating conditions which give rise to such movements. The three most common models are those of social disorganization, deprivation, and the deviant individual or psychological maladjustment model. We spent a good deal of time during the early stages of our research attempting to fit our data into one or another of these three models. We finally abandoned the why-did-it-start for the what-makes-it-tick approach for two reasons. First, too many participants in both movements we studied could not be classified as socially disorganized, even relatively deprived, or psychologically maladjusted.

Although the initial wave of Pentecostal revivals that spread across the country during the first decade of this century did appear to attract persons of low socio-economic status, the groups that are now being drawn into the movement—and are, in fact, the most fervent and evangelical—represent a wide range of socio-economic and educational backgrounds, including the highest. Our "hard evidence" for this statement is presented elsewhere (26). Other students of the movement in its present dimensions have found the same difficulty in employing the social disorganization and deprivation theories to explain the spreading of Pentecostalism (154, 177, 188). An excellent study of urban riots points to the same conclusion concerning participants in this aspect of Black Power (224).

The psychological maladjustment model has not been useful in interpreting our Pentecostal data. Recent studies specifically testing groups of Pentecostals for the psychological correlates of glossolalia and related religious experiences have been made by qualified psychologists. They revealed no difference between Pentecostals and non-Pentecostals in incidence of neuroses, psychoses, or other major psychological abnormalities traditionally assumed to be characteristic of movement participants (21, 88, 189, 201, 210).

Many sociological studies of movements assume some sort of personal inadequacy on the part of movement joiners. They are thought to be suffering from a sense of powerlessness, a lack of ego strength, or an inability to accomplish their own goals without the emotional support of a group of people with similar "problems." The fact of the matter is that social change of any magnitude at all cannot be made by individuals. To the extent that changes in existing social structures or customs must be made, an individual by himself *is* very nearly powerless.

A second reason why we found the models of social disorganization, deprivation and maladjustment inadequate is that they provide no basis on which to predict where a movement will spread or who will become involved. David Aberle, an anthropologist who has made important contributions to the relative deprivation theory, reports that any of the types of deprivation he has identified were possible bases for the occurrence of a movement. He also noted, however, that these same conditions are bases for apathy, despair, and disorganization, and that "the fact of deprivation is clearly an insufficient basis for predicting whether a movement will occur" (1).

This is not to say that conditions of social disorganization and deprivation are not associated with the rise of a movement. We are in accord with the relative deprivation school of thought in believing that the particular type of disorganization or deprivation associated with a specific movement should be analyzed. It is obvious, however, that factors other than the generating conditions, no matter how acute they may be, are responsible for precipitating the start of a movement. It is also apparent from our data that, once begun, a movement may spread into groups where the generating conditions do not and never did exist.

It is for these reasons that we have turned to an analysis of the internal dynamics of movements in the hope that this will bring clearer understanding of the phenomenon and increase the capacity to deal successfully with it.

The Pentecostal Movement

The history of Christianity has been punctuated by the appearance of millenarian or revivalistic movements. Many of them are known to have been characterized by outbreaks of religious ecstasies, by glossolalia or "speaking with tongues," by faith healings, by demon exorcism, prophecies, and visions. Such movements have generally been viewed by participants as revivals of the power of first century Christianity and by contemporary church officials as threats to the established order—social as well as ecclesiastical. Some of these movements were relatively local in impact and eventually died out, although not without discernible effects upon the established church (40). Others have resulted in the establishment of still extant sects or major denominations.

Pentecostalism, the most extensive of these movements, originated in the United States at the turn of the century. It has been exported, consistently since its inception and with remarkable success, to Europe, Latin America, and to many societies in Africa and Asia.

The cross-cultural spread of Pentecostalism as a movement differs from the spread of Christianity through the usual denominational missionary channels in that (a) Pentecostalism was begun by and to some extent still depends on denominationally independent "faith missionaries"; (b) compared with other Christian missionary efforts, it is characterized by a much larger proportion of indigenous lay

1

leadership, even in groups affiliated with American sects; and (c) it includes many large and proliferating bodies that are entirely indigenous in both origin and organization.

The type of religious behavior that characterizes the movement and sets it apart from conventional Christianity, even of the most fundamentalist type, is the practice of glossolalia or "speaking with tongues." This is described in the New Testament as an experience that accompanied conversion to Christianity; the passages most often cited are those in Acts 2, 10, 11, and 19, and 1 Corinthians 12 and 14.

Glossolalia is the utterance of streams of sounds which are unintelligible to both speaker and listener but which Pentecostals call a "heavenly language" and consider to be the Holy Spirit acting through them. Its practice is usually accompanied by a sense of emotional release, joy, and closeness to God. It may or may not be associated with "trances," "automatisms," or other apparently involuntary motor activity. Glossolalia *per se* is relatively unimportant in the eyes of participants in the movement. It is the subjective religious experience of the Baptism of the Holy Spirit which is believed to transform the life of the believer and which leads him to participate in that complex of individual behavior and social organization known as a "religious revival."

The first wave of revivals arose within that sector of Christianity known as "Holiness religion" and resulted in the gradual formation of some twenty-five or thirty national and regional associations; of these, the largest is the Assemblies of God. The Church of God in Christ, the United Pentecostal Church, and the Pentecostal Church of God are other relatively large bodies. All are Pentecostal sects described in sociological literature as those which appeal to members of socio-economically deprived groups.

A second wave, often called Neo-Pentecostalism or the Charismatic Renewal, attained sufficient proportions to make newspaper headlines during the 1950s and is still going on. It is attracting people from a wide range of socio-economic and educational backgrounds and is spreading into major protestant denominations as well as into Catholicism. The established Pentecostal churches are enjoying an increase in membership that outstrips all other denominations in the United States (*Yearbook of American Churches*, 1916-1966) as well as in Latin America (177, 191, 207).

The spread of the movement across class lines within the United States has resulted in the formation of uncounted numbers of independent groups. Some of these churches, often designated as "interdenominational," have memberships of several hundreds and meet in converted theatres. Some are comprised of a few families and meet in homes. Members of independent churches have often resigned from or been asked to leave churches of the major denominations because of their Pentecostal experiences—the Baptism of the Holy Spirit manifested by speaking with tongues and the personal evangelizing which appears to be a natural aftermath. None of these independent groups appears in the official membership statistics of Christendom's nose-counters.

In addition to the difficulty of estimating the number of the proliferating independent groups, another sector of Pentecostalism remains that is even less amenable to quantification. It is comprised of participants in the so-called tongues movements within the Episcopal, Lutheran, Methodist, Baptist, Presbyterian, Reformed, and Catholic churches (161, 168, 180, 188). Enclaves of "Spirit-filled" Christians who remain active in their non-Pentecostal churches meet regularly in homes, in church basements of sympathetic or participating clergymen, or on the campuses of those colleges and universities where there has been an "outpouring of the Spirit."

Total world membership in the movement is variously estimated at eight million by John Nichol, an historian of Pentecostalism (179); at ten million by Walter Hollenweger of the World Council of Churches (163); and at twelve million by *Time* (28 July 1967). There are no available figures that would indicate what proportion of estimated totals are in independent or indigenous churches rather than in the more highly organized and better-counted Pentecostal sects with national organizations and international missionary programs. According to one observer, forty-two percent of Brazil's two million Pentecostals are in independent or indigenous churches (191). McGavran (177) indicates that in Mexico forty percent are independent. A Neo-Pentecostal leader's unofficial estimate of the proportion of participants in the United States in independent churches or "hidden" in non-Pentecostal churches was twenty-five percent. Research into yearbook statistics yielded a figure of two million members of Pentecostal sects for the year 1966. If Hollenweger's estimate of four million American Pentecostals is correct, half of them are in independent groups (163).

The established Pentecostal sects, the independent churches, and the "hidden" groups are linked together into a single movement in several ways—experientially, ideologically, historically, and organizationally. Even the most sedate upper class Episcopalian Pentecostal recognizes an experiential tie with his brother in a Holiness storefront slum church through the same Baptism of the Holy Spirit. All groups unite ideologically in a common interpretation of this experience as the empowering gift of God described in the Acts of the Apostles and 1 Corinthians. Historically, links between the sects, the independent churches, and the hidden groups can be traced through the activities of a few key individuals (179). Organizational linkages between the groups are reticulate. Organizationally independent local churches or study groups are linked through kinship or friendship ties between lay members and between ministers and other leaders. Loyalties to one or several of the nationally or internationally known traveling evangelists form cross-linkages at large revival meetings and crusades. The geographical mobility of certain particularly charismatic lay members form regional ties between groups who invite them to speak or counsel with their members. An "age group" principle is operative in various teen-age groups that draw from several types of local churches. The Full Gospel Businessmen's Fellowship International provides similar cross-cutting ties for older Pentecostals and their wives.

The three basic types of Pentecostal groups can be ranged along a continuum with the long-established sects at one end, the independent groups of varying size and duration along the center section, and the "Spirit-filled" Christians still hidden in non-Pentecostal churches at the other end. The organizational characteristics of these types of groups provide a rough approximation of the Troeltsch-Weber theory of sect-to-church development, or the "routinization process" (81, 132, 142). The socio-economic correlates classically associated with stages in the process break down completely, however, when applied to Pentecostalism. Mean income, educational, and occupational levels are lowest at the sect end of the continuum and highest at the "hidden" end. Organizationally, however, the continuum operates in reverse. It is among the newly forming charismatic groups and the "tongues movements" within the main-line denominations that one finds the fervor, the near absence of formal organization, the spontaneity, the exponential growth rates, and the emphasis on religious experience usually associated with sects. Toward the middle of the continuum, the independent bodies of somewhat longer tenure have more formalized structure, more permanent leadership, and more bureaucratic routine. Finally, it is the so-called sects which are approaching a "steady state," developing the most rigid structure and hierarchical organization, and placing relatively less emphasis on spontaneous "leadings of the Spirit" and other charismata. In short, they approach the status of regular churches. The Troeltsch-Weber theory of the routinization process is useful in studying the Pentecostal Movement only if the movement as a whole can be regarded as a multi-strand cord with each strand institutionalized differentially. The sect-to-church development of the long-established Pentecostal bodies has been noted by Bryan Wilson (208) and by Kendrick (169); the latter predicts decreasing alienation from and opposition to main-line denominations. These bodies which are most "church-like" within the Pentecostal Movement as a whole represent the relatively lower socio-economic groups participating. The higher socio-economic groups most recently drawn in are among those which exhibit the most "sect-like" behavior.

Certain descriptive statistics support the observations with regard to charismatic phenomena at the opposite ends of our institutional continuum. Second-generation Pentecostals who are members of a better-known sect or of a long-established independent church were compared with Neo-Pentecostals, adult converts who comprise all of the "hidden" groups and the small, newly formed churches and three fourths of the older, independent churches. (Less than half of the Pentecostal sect members in our sample were adult converts.)

We found that Neo-Pentecostals speak with tongues significantly more often (at the .05 level) than do second-generation Pentecostals. We also found that the length of time a convert spent in "tarrying" (that is, trying to experience the Baptism of the Holy Spirit and to speak with tongues) was significantly shorter for the Neo-Pentecostal (at the .01 level). Charismatic experiences apparently do not come so easily or so often for the second-generation Pentecostals, as a group, as for their more recently involved and less highly organized brethren.

A description of the seven groups in which we did field work will make clear the wide variety of groups involved in the Pentecostal Movement as a whole as well as in the three broad types that we have identified—the traditional, independent, and "hidden" groups.

Holy Tabernacle, affiliated with a major Pentecostal sect, traces a direct line of descent back through schisms and mergers to the first local group established during the early days of the movement. Holy Tabernacle has moved far along in the process of institutionalization, having become a church with the usual complement of boards, committees, and youth and adult groups. There has been a shift in emphasis from religious experience to religious doctrine; great stress is now laid upon trained, professional leadership rather than on "Spirit-led" lay leaders. The charisma of the present minister, if such it can be called, is what Weber referred to as the charisma of office rather than personal charisma. Opposition to this minister's reign is summarily dismissed. Resultant schisms have reduced the group's growth to a relatively slow rate of increase. Members represent lower and lower-middle class groups, and many of them are second-generation Pentecostals. Social and moral behavior consistent with the nineteenth century Holiness code is expected. A dichotomous in-group, out-group self-image is carefully maintained, but realistic opposition from mainline denominations and society at large is a thing of the past. Although speaking with tongues is expected and required as a sign of the Baptism of the Holy Spirit, manifestations of this and other charisms are so carefully regulated as to proper time and place that it would be easy to mistake the usual church service for that of any fundamentalist sect.

The Store-Front Church, the second of our intensively studied groups, is also affiliated with one of the major Pentecostal denominations, but it is far more representative of the early stages of movement growth. It is a store-front mission church in a depressed urban area. Its present minister founded it slightly more than a year before we began our study. Fervor, emotionalism, and emphasis on ecstatic religious experience are very prominent during its services. Core group members, of whom there are twenty, are remarkably interrelated through previous kinship and friendship ties. The absolute authority of the minister over his little flock is based on the extremely charismatic quality of his own intense religious commitment. His im-

pressive knowledge of the scriptures has been gained through dedicated self-education. His reliance on the inner leadings of the Spirit is
total—often to the financial disadvantage of his family. Prepared for
the ministry by God's call rather than by formal denominational training, he came to this metropolitan center to establish the first church
of his denomination in this area at God's rather than denominational
direction. Though recognized by the denomination, which has a congregational polity, the Store-Front Church is only minimally supported by or connected with the larger body. It is typical, therefore,
of those outposts of organized Pentecostal sects which, while officially
controlled by a central organization, are for all practical purposes
nearly autonomous local groups. They are established, directed, and
on occasion dissolved by a single individual who feels led by the
Spirit to do so.

The third group chosen for intensive study, the House of Revelation and Salvation, was established about fifteen years ago by another
powerful and charismatic individual. The minister, a Negro of impos-
ing stature and bearing, was fully trained in an Assemblies of God
Bible College but has taken advantage of the entrepreneurial opportunities inherent in movement organization to break away from that
more structured segment to found his own brand of Pentecostalism.
His organization is as structured as any Assemblies of God church,
but it owes no allegiance to a higher body. He is an authoritarian
leader, capable of delegating authority to his lieutenants (who are
mostly relatives) and expecting both initiative and obedience from
them. The House of Revelation is loosely affiliated with two other
groups of similar polity and doctrine whose leaders were friends and
fellow students at Bible College. Where the Store-Front Church is
an example of the simple hub-and-spoke pattern—a single charismatic
leader exercising direct influence over a small group of devoted followers—the House of Revelation illustrates the same basic pattern
in more complex form. The leader directs two Houses of Revelation
in one metropolitan area in the United States and an extensive mission
school and orphanage complex with components located in three Caribbean countries. The home church is located in a converted theatre
in a lower class commercial area, and has a working membership of
about seventy-five people. Ninety percent of these are drawn from
lower and middle class Negro groups. Ten percent are both lower

and middle class whites. In addition to the usual complement of assistant pastors, boards, and committees, the church membership is organized into three categories. Assignment to one of these depends on the individual's degree of involvement and capacity for religious experience and power. Much of the responsibility is delegated along formal, bureaucratic lines.

Expansion of the leader's influence into the overseas mission field rests on an indeterminate number of supporters, both Negro and white, from various socio-economic and educational levels, including the most privileged. These supporters are articulated to the House of Revelation—and thereby to the Pentecostal Movement as a whole—only through their personal and private contacts with the charismatic leader of the House. Spiritual healings, marital and other types of counseling, and a faith-enhancing dynamism flow in one direction, while extremely rewarding financial support flows in the other. Growth rates and religious fervor, unimpressive in the home church, are noticeably higher on the "growing edge" in the Caribbean mission field, which we had an opportunity to observe. The House of Revelation, then, represents two stages in the routinization process, and illustrates the danger of confusing sect-to-church development with movement dynamics. As the home center becomes more routinized and financially more secure, the leader can delegate more authority, thereby allowing himself more time in which to promote conditions favorable to the rapid growth, religious excitement, and flexible organization that are characteristic of the early stages in movement growth. Role conflict is not one of the leader's problems, for he swings back and forth between bureaucratic and charismatic leadership with great versatility.

The fourth group selected was a small independent church of Neo-Pentecostals. Fellowship Church was established by a group of ten or twelve middle class families whose Pentecostal experiences resulted in their withdrawal or ejection from Lutheran, Presbyterian, and other denominational churches. The opposition of the established order to the phenomenon of commitment in Pentecostal terms was very realistic; such opposition has played a causal role in the formation of this and similar churches. The patterns of worship, theology and moral code, and the socio-economic status of Fellowship Church members are those usually characteristic of churches rather than sects.

Highly valued charismatic experiences involving glossolalia, faith healings, demon exorcism, prophecy, and visions tend to occur in informal situations or during home meetings of the Bible study or couples' groups, rather than in Sunday morning church services. Leadership in Fellowship Church, in contrast to that of Holy Tabernacle, the Store-Front Church, or the House of Revelation, is essentially democratic. The pastor, a former Lutheran minister whose ordination papers were withdrawn by his denomination after the establishment of Fellowship Church, accepts the doctrine of the priesthood of believers and behaves accordingly. Church policy requires that major organizational decisions be made through group consensus, although formal responsibility for such decisions is vested in the Board of Deacons. Considerable energy and time on the telephone are expended in group prayer for the guidance of the Spirit, and in informal discussions of the leading of the Spirit as it has been received by individuals in visions, revelations, or private prayer.

There is no formal membership of Fellowship Church. The group conceives of itself as a "way station" where people may come to receive the Baptism of the Holy Spirit and where Spirit-filled Christians can be nurtured until such time as they are led by the Spirit into various types of "ministries." Average attendance at Sunday services is around fifty people, including children of all ages. During our work with this group the core group of active participants included thirteen couples and four single individuals. Over a period of two years, four core group members left to join a larger downtown interdenominational group and were replaced by five new participants. Two of the most active men were trained by the pastor to serve as leaders of two of the three small groups which Fellowship people had helped to start in other parts of the city. A third individual came for special instruction in the Bible and theological beliefs, in order to prepare for assuming formal leadership of a group of lay people who had organized themselves independently. After our study of this group terminated, the pastor left to lead another smaller and less well-established group; the Fellowship core group members called another ex-Lutheran minister to lead them. Although the split occurred over certain ideological differences, all parties involved professed belief that the Spirit, not any particular human being, is the true leader of the group. The example of Fellowship Church illustrates only one of the variety of organizational and leadership patterns that may be found within this and other movements. It points up the inadequacy of the oversimplified concept of the charismatic prophet and the small band of followers as a prototype of movement organization. The power and initiative of ordinary "followers" committed to a movement should not be underestimated.

The fifth group chosen for study was a Prayer Group, representative of the informal but regular midweek meetings held, largely by Neo-Pentecostals, in homes. This group, in existence for many years, has a core of six or seven regular but not necessarily permanent members. In addition, it includes shifting concentric circles of members who attend for various lengths of time before drifting off to join other groups or to start their own. The Prayer Group is led by a middle-aged woman who is still officially a member of a major non-Pentecostal church but who regularly attends Spiritual Witness.

Spiritual Witness is an independent, non-denominational Pentecostal organization with impressive offices and staff located in a converted downtown theatre. It has a registered membership of approximately three hundred and an average Sunday morning attendance of twelve hundred. Our observations at services over a period of several months support these remarkable figures. Such attendance is explained by the fact that many regular participants maintain formal memberships in other churches, both Pentecostal and non-Pentecostal. Members represent a socio-economic cross-section, but the most affluent and well-educated Pentecostals of this city are to be found at Spiritual Witness at one time or another. Funds for a multiple ministry, mission stations, television programs, the building of a radio station in Alaska, summer camps, and other more usual church activities are budgeted by the staff *after* such funds have flowed in, rather than before—a practice to inspire the envy of many fund-raising clergymen. The individual who organized Spiritual Witness some twenty years ago is still its minister. He runs his church in the manner of a corporation executive and encourages organizational efforts on the part of his laymen. One such project is the Prayer Group of our study.

Glossolalia, healings, and other charisms are the order of the day at the weekly meetings of the Prayer Group. The recruitment activities of the core group often culminate in the introduction of a potentia convert to the very gracious and impressive lady who leads the group. Only the more stubborn cases fail to respond to the laying on of her hands and her resounding prayers for the Baptism of the Holy Spirit. Healings are of great importance in this as in most other home meeting groups. They can be accomplished by telephone or *in absentia*, as well as through personal contact at group meetings. Testimonies are a usual part of the agenda, and devotees are fond of referring to the home of their leader as the House of Miracles.

A sixth group represents a special phenomenon in the Pentecostal Movement—the outbreak of a revival and the outpouring of the Spirit on college campuses. At the time of our field work, the group consisted of students—graduate and undergraduate—and three members of the faculty at a large Catholic university. Organization of the campus revival was extremely informal. One young instructor and his wife were considered key individuals, but leadership at the meetings was often *ad hoc*. Such meetings were held in homes of married graduate students, or in dormitory rooms, or in more formally designed campus quarters. In addition to the usual occurrences of glossolalia and other charisms, there was a great deal of emphasis upon the use and meaning of traditional Catholic ritual; the importance of such ritual seems to be heightened by the Pentecostal experience under these conditions. Several of the early participants have sought psychoanalytic help in trying to evaluate their experiences.

A year after our study of the campus group, a doctor of theology at a Florida Catholic college who had become involved with Pentecostalism predicted that the movement on the original campus would put out enough adventitious roots to bring forth many distant branches. This prediction proved accurate. Catholic Pentecostals are no longer predominantly students. The university now holds annual meetings of "Spirit-filled" Catholics from all over the United States, during which new converts are made, new cross-links formed, and old faith renewed. Several national symposia have been held in various Catholic centers across the country. At one such conference the senior author, who had been invited as a speaker, talked with priests, monks, and nuns who had received the Baptism of the Holy Spirit and spoken with tongues. One of these participants reported the involvement of an entire convent in such Pentecostal experiences. Although there is no official opposition from the higher levels of Catholic organization, there is apparently sufficient informal opposition at the local level from non-participating Catholics to create a type of subtle conflict.

The seventh group in which we undertook participant observation was a group of "hiddens" who meet weekly in an Episcopal Church whose minister has received the Baptism and acts as group coordinator. There is no official membership; meetings may draw anywhere from twenty to a hundred and twenty participants, depending on the visiting man or woman who happens to be leading the group on a particular evening. Recruitment to the group is entirely by word of mouth, with mimeographed information mailed to those who have requested it. Participants are mostly Episcopalians of the middle or upper classes. The spirit of the organization derives only in part from devotion to a charismatic leader, although many find the minister's quiet counsel indispensable. More importantly, it arises from the many cross-ties between members who interact frequently and informally outside of meetings in dyadic or triadic relationships. Experiences are shared, prayer requested, and theology hammered out. No one at the weekly meetings knows everyone else present, but the slight overlap between small sub-groups can be traced by observing interactions at the post-session coffee or punch table. This group has been in existence for several years and maintains ties through leaders and friends or kin with several other similar groups in many other cities and towns. Personal contact between the "hiddens" and members of Pentecostal sects or other more formally organized Pentecostal churches is minimal and usually considered to be unrewarding, but the historical as well as experiential connections with these other segments of the movement are clearly recognized by Neo-Pentecostals.

It is interesting to note some of the differences in expression of opposition to the movement by various established denominations. Overt opposition to the Pentecostal experience and the practice of glossolalia has resulted in the resignation of laymen from their non-Pentecostal churches and—in some cases—the withdrawal of ordination papers of ministers who have become involved in the movement. These are the individuals who organize themselves into independent Pentecostal or so-called interdenominational churches. Among our informants, this type of open break occurred most frequently in the early stages of neo-Pentecostalism in Lutheran denominations, and in the Baptist, Methodist, and various smaller fundamentalist denominations. The type of opposition from those in positions of power in the Episcopal and Catholic churches is somewhat different —best described, perhaps, as the "big tent" approach. The glossolalic phenomenon is pronounced "entirely scriptural" and is accepted as possibly beneficial to certain types of individuals if practiced as individual prayer. The leading of the individual believer by the Holy Spirit is not denied. Then comes the crucial "but—."

The official position often taken is that the Holy Spirit works primarily through institutionalized channels. So long as the practice of glossolalia and associated experiences are consistent with the discipline of the church, they are acceptable. But if there should be any conflict between a bishop's opinion concerning any matter and the leading of the Holy Spirit as perceived by the individual, the bishop's orders are to be considered a closer approximation of the will of God in that situation. The net result seems to be that more Pentecostal Episcopalians and Catholics remain within their churches than leave, but the official solution has done little to alleviate internal opposition. Covert opposition is apparently as effective as overt opposition in terms of movement growth. The movement is growing rapidly in both churches.

Of the charismatic manifestations which characterize the Pentecostal Movement, glossolalia provides the most obvious point of departure from conventional Christian religious practice; it is easily the most controversial. A brief description of the phenomenon and of social contexts in which it occurs may be useful. For some participants, particularly in the established sects, the experience of speaking with tongues occurs only once and is considered an outward sign of the Baptism of the Holy Spirit which need not happen again. For most participants in the movement, glossolalia is a recurring experience which is felt to be significant in the spiritual growth of the believer.

Linguistic analyses of glossolalic utterances have revealed several noteworthy features. Glossolalia is not semantic in the sense that certain sounds represent specific ideas. It is, however, patterned in the same way semantic languages are. Certain sounds, or "phones," and certain combinations of sounds into "syllables" and "words" are characteristic of the tongue speech of individual glossolalics. Our impression of glossolalia as involving a limited number of different syllables and a high occurrence of alliteration and repetition seems to have been

borne out by linguistic analysis (166). Pentecostals speak of being
"given" more than one "heavenly language" on occasion. This accords
with our observations. The usual tongue speech of any individual has
characteristic sounds, sequences of sounds, and intonational patterns.
Occasionally one tongue speaker will use two or more distinguishable
sets of patterns or "languages." Changes are noticeable in such characteristics as the frequency of certain sounds, the use of more open
or more closed syllables, stress patterns, and intonation patterns.

Occurrences of xenoglossia, speech in a known language unfa-
miliar to the speaker, are widely reported, but all of the utterances
heard by our team members were examples of glossolalia. Cross-cultural linguistic analyses of Pentecostal glossolalic utterances are not
available at this writing, but there have been comparisons of the
glossolalic speech and the casual speech of the same English-speak-
ing Pentecostals. Results of such studies indicate that the sounds and
sound patterns of glossolalia are based on or resemble those of the
speaker's natural language.

Linguist William Samarin has defined glossolalia as "a meaningless but phonologically structured human utterance believed by the
speaker to be a real language but bearing no systematic resemblance
to any natural language, living or dead." He goes on to say that the
fact that glossolalia is unintelligible does not mean that it is "gibber-
ish" or that the sounds are "spewed out in a haphazard way." In each
glossa, or "language," as the Pentecostals would call it, there is a high
degree of linguistic structure and a kind of "microsegmental syntax"
similar to that of natural languages. Samarin feels that glossolalia is
both derivative (that is, similar to the sound patterns of the speaker's
natural language) and innovative. Glossolalics do use sounds that are
not native to their natural language. There is a simplification of
syllable structure and sound frequencies; and, on occasion, stress patterns may be different (194).

Glossolalia is similar to what anthropologists call spirit possession
in other cultures. It is explained as the control of speech organs by the
Holy Spirit, who speaks through the believer. Types of Pentecostal
"possession" vary widely, from semi-trance states accompanied by involuntary motor activity, to quiet prayer in tongues in which there is
no loss of conscious control and little if any dissociation experienced.

Pentecostal glossolalia may occur during church services (although this is infrequent), in small groups, or in solitude. None of the groups we visited permit unrestrained, spontaneous glossolalic utterances. The Holy Spirit, a visitor or seeker is likely to be reminded, is a gentleman and is not likely to be rude, to disrupt a group meeting, or to offend the sensibilities. In all of the formal church meetings we attended, spontaneous expression of spiritual ecstasy was subject to some variety of restraint, however informal. Entirely uninhibited glossolalia, "dancing in the spirit," or involuntary behaviors occur only in smaller groups—for example, when a person desiring the Baptism is being "prayed through" to the experience, or when someone has asked for healing, for exorcism, or for prayer for a specific problem. Such behavior usually occurs at the end of a church or revival service or during a prayer meeting called for that purpose. Small knots of people collect around individuals to be prayed over, in the front of a hall where the meeting has been held, before the altar of a church, in smaller rooms adjoining the sanctuary, or in homes. There are occasions when the whole congregation stays for the "altar call" session, but it is clear that this, not the formal service, is the appropriate time for charismatic manifestations.

During formal meetings or church services, glossolalia may occur, if at all, during group prayers. Invited by the minister, all participants pray aloud—some in English, some in tongues, some in sort of a "Jesus, Jesus" chant. The results may be noisy chaos to a newcomer, but they seem like quite private prayer to the initiate, who is walled in by anonymous sounds.

In most groups, anyone who feels led by the Spirit may utter a message in tongues. If the Spirit does not lead either this person or another to interpret it, a second message is discouraged. Interpretation of tongues is not simply a direct translation of a glossolalic utterance. It is listed in 1 Corinthians 12 and 14 as a separate gift of God, distinct from the gift of glossolalic utterance or "heavenly language." According to Paul's rules spelled out in 1 Corinthians, three prophecies, each with its "interpretation," are the maximum for an orderly meeting.

In one group we visited, "singing in the Spirit" often occurred when the congregation was invited to pray. One individual began to intone during a period of general audible prayer. Others followed, using such vowels and such musical tones as they were led to. The intoning gradually became spontaneous, and individual melody lines, which swelled to varying levels of intensity, produced interesting and pleasing harmonies. This spontaneous blending of vocal tones created a high sense of unity.

The emphasis placed on glossolalia in this and other analyses of the Pentecostal Movement constitutes a distortion of the phenomenological facts. Glossolalia is but one of nine spiritual gifts promised to believers. The others are wisdom, healing, knowledge, faith, the working of miracles, prophecy, and interpretation of tongues. The life of a "Spirit-filled" Christian may involve recurrent or sporadic experiences of any or all of these gifts, but far more importantly it is characterized by a sense of the immanent presence of and guidance by the third Person of the Christian Godhead. Glossolalia, although it plays a secondary role in the life of a Pentecostal, is the distinguishing characteristic of the movement as a whole. At the risk of distortion we must use it is an objective indicator of the phenomenon under study. For the purposes of this study, therefore, a Pentecostal group will be defined as *any group in which speaking with tongues is accepted as a manifestation of the Baptism or infilling of the Holy Spirit and in which its practice is valued or encouraged by members.*

II

The Black Power Movement

Black Power means many things to many people, both black and white. For some it means black separatism—the creation somewhere, somehow, of a separate black state. For some it simply means riots. For others it is the battle cry of violent mega-militants and connotes planned insurgency or guerrilla warfare. But the central concept of Black Power as defined by a growing number of black spokesmen, and as perceived by more and more members of the American public, implies the development by black Americans for black Americans of real economic and political power. It also implies the psychological transformation of blacks into a people proud of being black.

All of the ideological themes and the various approaches to methods of achieving Black Power goals can be traced back through the three hundred years of interracial history in America. Separatism is now advocated largely by the Black Muslims and the most radical of Black Power leaders. This approach, however, has been argued by various blacks since before the Civil War. Racial pride and solidarity have been unrealized but conscious goals of the black community since the days of slavery. Identification with an African heritage as a source of pride is more recent, and has been concurrent with the process of decolonization and independence in Africa.

Self-help is another theme running through Negro history; early in this century, it was clearly formulated in the United States by

Booker T. Washington (292). His concept of blacks earning their place in white society is associated with the idea that blacks must take responsibility for their own inadequacy. Many whites and some conservative Negroes still hold this view. They criticize rioters for losing the respect and good will that "good Negroes" have so painstakingly earned for their race.

However, a divergent ideological theme was introduced by one of the founders of the National Association for the Advancement of Colored People, W. E. B. DuBois. His argument that white racism, not black inadequacy, is responsible for existing inequalities made the NAACP a radical organization in its day (237). This same theme is now a basic tenet in Black Power ideology, and the *Kerner Commission Report on Civil Disorders* has inclined an increasing number of whites to accept it (291).

Integration, a traditional goal in Negro as well as in liberal white thought, has faded before the more radical proposals involving self-determination, racial pride, and black community. Integration implied that equality must be earned and could be charitably granted by white society to blacks who met white standards of behavior and proficiency. Black Power advocates reject the idea that self-fulfillment is possible only as blacks enter the mainstream of an unchanged white society, thereby abandoning their unique black history and heritage. There is increasing rejection of the idea that white society is automatically desirable. Even moderate blacks have come to realize that racism is not just a personal attitude but a product of social institutions as well. They are beginning to believe that the eradication of racism will require radical changes in American social, economic, and political structures.

There are three basic means by which Black Power participants seek to gain their ends. Conservative groups such as the NAACP and the Urban League believe in gradualism and legislative means. Moderates stand for non-violent direct action such as boycotts, sit-ins, and marches. More militant leaders advocate violence. All three methods have been used at various times by different Negro protest and action groups since the first slave ship arrived on American shores.

A new dimension has emerged with the focus of these themes and these means in the Black Power Movement. In the Civil Rights Movement the right to vote, the right to employment, the right to a good education, and all other benefits of desegregation were seen as goals in and of themselves. With the emergence of Black Power, civil rights have become simply the means to the further goals of economic and political power. Racial unity, also once seen as an end in itself, is now viewed as a means to communal bargaining power with the white power structure. This concept is now expressed in terms of black leadership of black groups and the relegation of white supporters to the status of followers. Previously, Negroes as individuals or in small groups obtained influence and position by cultivating white friends and patrons. Even in organizations established to benefit the black community, the leadership was originally largely white. The shift from whites to blacks in positions of power in these organizations has been accelerated by the advent of Black Power. Those groups which have come into being since that time reject white leadership, except in the case of certain individuals who are considered white radicals. Some even reject white support of any kind.

With the emergence of this emphasis on Black Power, the idea of black pride was transformed into the actual experience of pride for an increasing number of blacks. Such pride is often demonstrated by African dress, natural hair styles, and changes in terminology. Black militants reject the word "Negro" as a term of opprobrium assigned to black people by white masters. Many new terms have developed, of which "Afro-American" and "black" are among the most common.

Black Power was first advocated in a speech given by Stokely Carmichael during the march of James Meredith from Memphis to Jackson, Mississippi, in 1966 (272). The decisive break with traditional methods of protest came six years earlier with the college student sit-ins.

When Black Power was first proclaimed and affirmed across the land, it expressed a mood and a stance rather than a program. It was still a loose collection of enthusiasms and protest tactics. The movement took shape using themes from the past in its emerging ideology; black debate over that ideology is still in progress. As one black put it, "I have the feeling that the movement is going out of its righteous mind trying to find unity and a program." In spite of—or, as we shall point out in a later chapter, because of—this lack of ideological codification, black action groups of varied size, composition, and approach are springing up across the country. These groups of blacks, or of blacks and whites, have as their objective the implementation of one or another of the various themes that constitute Black Power ideology in its present form. The changing composition of each group, the backgrounds of its members, the situation it faces, and its competition with other groups for recognition, recruits, and support determine which of the major themes a particular group will emphasize. Each group reinterprets, modifies, and adds to the set of goals and means with which it was initially identified. Through this process, each group develops its own particular "style" and each "does its own thing" in its own way.

It must be stressed that these groups of which we are speaking exist at the local level. While many Americans have personally experienced manifestations of the Black Power revolt at the city, ward, or local community level, they characteristically perceive leadership, ideological direction, and method as something which emanates from some sort of central command or national mastermind. The large-scale national organizations such as the Urban League, the NAACP, the Southern Christian Leadership Conference, the Congress of Racial Equality, and the Student Non-Violent Coordinating Committee are often assumed to be monolithic entities which dictate policy from a national office to local branches. Even the *Kerner Commission Report* sometimes gives this impression. This is no more correct in the Black Power world than it is in Pentecostalism.

As in the case of the Store-Front Church described in the last chapter, local NAACP, SCLC, CORE, and SNCC groups may have considerable independence of action and may vary in attitude and stance according to local conditions and personnel. The local NAACP youth league in one of the cities we visited was extremely militant even though the national organization is commonly considered an "Uncle Tom" outfit by other militants. Another example of such local autonomy is the Black Panthers. Even the brief history of the name illustrates the rapid organizational shifts characteristic of the movement. Originally, "Black Panthers" was the name of an independent black political party in Mississippi which was assisted by black and white SNCC members and which worked for voter registration. Later, a number of groups in different parts of the country —with widely divergent goals—called themselves Black Panthers.

One was a youth group, another a black patrol, a third a West Coast militant action group. There was no organizational connection between these organizations at that time. Now, however, the name refers to the original West Coast militant organization which has developed a national structure and claims affiliated chapters in forty-five cities. However, even this attempt at unified national structure is frustrated by an intense rivalry among factions which has resulted in actual organizational splits. These countercurrents of unification and schism are characteristic of the whole Black Power Movement as well as of other movements.

Just as Pentecostalism is often assumed to be synonymous with the established Pentecostal sects, so the large-scale black organizations are sometimes assumed to encompass all of the groups identified with the Black Power Movement. We have seen that certain Pentecostal churches affiliated with one or another of the national or regional bodies can be far from representative of the Pentecostal Movement as a whole. The same is true of Black Power. Each urban center has a range of localized, locally organized and led, and locally named Black Power groups which owe no allegiance whatsoever to a higher body. Furthermore, it is often these groups which set the pace of change and manner of confrontation with the local white power structure. Branches of organizations with national reputations are often in the position of having to adjust to the pace and style set by the independent local groups. The term Black Power Movement as we use it here refers to the whole range of organizations and groups, at all levels of the Negro social structure, which are committed to the purpose of implementing Negro-enhancing social change in America.

These groups can conveniently be ranged along a continuum similar to that which we employed in discussing Pentecostal groups. In considering Black Power, the basis of our continuum is not degree of organizational routinization, as it was with Pentecostalism, but differences in goals-means orientation. The three points along the continuum may be referred to as the conservative, the moderate, and the militant stance. The more conservative civil rights organizations, such as the national NAACP or Urban League committees, may be placed at one end. The radical militant groups, such as those training for or engaging in urban guerrilla and terrorist tactics, are at the other extreme. Any other Black Power group may be placed somewhere in between. Each perceives the problems differently. For instance, to black conservatives, riots are riots. To moderates, they are rebellions. Militants see them as one aspect of The Revolution.

In one metropolitan area we studied, Negroes constitute about three percent of a total population of 480,000; most reside in two of four distinct core city areas. It is fair to say that before 1965 most of the white citizens of this urban area believed their city to be, in comparison with Chicago, New York, or the cities in the South, relatively free from racial prejudice, from slums, and from Negro unemployment. In fact, most white people in this area had little or no contact with blacks and no perception of what black citizens really thought or felt. On the other hand, blacks who moved to this urban area from elsewhere had heard from others that it was a good place for Negroes, but they found a great deal of subtle discrimination and latent hostility. Black Power developed here, as elsewhere, in the form of various groups committed to overt manifestation of anger, release of frustrations, and demands for change.

The first indications of racial "trouble" were incidents in which black youth clashed with white youth at public gatherings—especially at a monthly teen-age dance held by a large city firm for promotional and advertising purposes. There were the usual minor collisions with the police over what appeared to the public to be no more than unconnected criminal incidents.

A few militant blacks, including some at the local university, had participated in sit-ins, freedom rides, and demonstrations in the South and border states. Some liberal whites, again mostly college students, joined them in this, and a few moderate adult whites participated in the Selma demonstrations. More moderate blacks, along with various liberal white supporters, were active in the conventional programs of the NAACP and the Urban League, in several human rights commissions, and conventional social work programs.

Some blacks confronted various business establishments, landlords, real estate firms, agencies of city government, and the university with charges of racial discrimination. The means employed in these confrontations were essentially conventional legal actions in which the rules of the established order prevailed. Blacks often won such engagements, but their victories had little effect on the general public. Certainly they did not contribute much to the introduction of fundamental changes either in institutional practices or in the personal attitudes of white people.

Militant black activity picked up in this metropolitan area during 1966, especially after the long hot summer, when it began to appear that urban racial strife was becoming a new part of the American scene. Some far-seeing whites began to feel that "it *can* happen here," and some blacks not only agreed but also intimated that it would surely come to pass if remedial action were not taken at once.

Various measures were taken or contemplated in response to this threat. By the spring of 1967 a coalition of militant blacks, militant white university students, and influential white liberals developed a new type of community center in the heart of one black core area. A stated objective of this center was to "reach the unreachable"—the angry, depressed, and alienated youth of the area, both black and white. This objective reflected the prevalent and then-current white view that urban riots were caused by just such "down-and-outers" and could be prevented if only this group were "reached." Other activities and other community programs were contemplated, also reflecting a "deprivation causes riots" theory.

Then, in the late summer of 1967, this city had a civil disturbance of sufficient proportions to require the presence of National Guard units, although the disturbance involved less violence than that which gripped other northern cities that summer. Black Power activities and the formation of Black Power groups increased rapidly from this point on. White response was varied.

Some whites rushed in with offers of more jobs, more money for technical training and education for blacks, and more aid for community centers similar to the one mentioned above. Some developed programs to promote communication and understanding between white and black. Some focused attention upon the police and National Guard, pleading for more wisdom and less repressive force in dealing with the Black Power Movement. On the other hand there were some whites and a few Negroes who considered the disturbances as the rioting of delinquents and riffraff. Some saw the evil hand of Communist plotters at work. This faction demanded that the city counter rioting by punishing rather than rewarding the demonstrators. Whites taking this hard line urged the police to greater vigilance and to the use of more force in restoring "law and order." Acting out of a complex of motives, not the least of which was the desire for "fun and games," some young whites drove through the Negro areas on several occasions after the riots, shooting randomly at blacks. There have been a few other instances when whites openly sought conflict with blacks.

Since the single "breakthrough" riot of 1967, there have been additional minor clashes and confrontations, often with the police as a major target. Following the death of Martin Luther King, many whites in the city feared an outbreak of violence; tempers were running high. One response of the white power structure was to permit and to help blacks to establish their own force for what might be called parapolice activities. These are groups of blacks who patrol the black core neighborhoods to prevent the incursion of white troublemakers, to control the most militant black elements, and to reduce casual violence. Part of this force operated out of the community center already described. Another force was organized and operated from a technical school with black leadership and a predominantly black student body. Later, a third wing developed in another black community within the city.

While in theory having the same mission, the patrols compete with each other for recognition by whites as law enforcement bodies. They also compete for funds and equipment, patrol cars and radios, all donated by white individuals. A further basis for competition is the desire for recognition from conservative, moderate, and militant blacks. The three patrol groups differ in philosophy with regard to use of weapons, the degree of cooperation with whites and with police, and attitudes of hostility toward "the system." A fourth law enforcement group, composed of both blacks and whites, organized itself separately. It is a foot patrol which seeks to form a buffer between residents in the black community and white racists who have raided the area.

The development of these four independent patrol groups represents only one aspect of the proliferation of Black Power groups in this city. A brief description of some of the major organizations in this one metropolitan area will illustrate a variety of groups as characteristic of Black Power as it is of Pentecostalism.

The community center has grown since its inception, but retains its autonomy. It owes allegiance to no organization, although offers of alliance have been extended by representatives of several national organizations, both moderate and militant. The center itself has now divided, however, into a number of almost autonomous components—for example, the mobile black patrol and the integrated foot patrol mentioned above. In spite of rivalry, both groups use the center as headquarters. Among the other semi-independent sub-groups of the center is a group which teaches Afro-American history and culture, a group of very militant youths engaged in agitation and protest activities, and a group which works on drama and art. Many individuals share in the leadership of this center and focus on different aspects of the diversified activities.

There are many complex, bureaucratically organized institutions in our society which have equally diversified programs. For instance, YWCA programs and those of large churches often have leaders of various activities who know little or nothing of what other "departments" are doing. But in the YWCA or the large church, responsibility is vested in a single executive or board. There is someone who can speak for the organization. This is not true of this particular Black Power community center. Although the various sub-groups interact and are aware of each other's activities, there is no single leader who can speak for the whole group or whose decisions would be binding on all of the others.

Some of the original founders of this community center have since opened a similar center in another part of the city where blacks live. Although a kind of daughter of the first, this second center is now essentially autonomous. Its plans, programs, and leadership are independent. A third center, resembling these two in design and purpose, developed independently in a third black neighborhood in the same metropolitan area. These autonomous groups are linked only through the friendship and occasional cooperation of their leaders.

These community centers may be placed about halfway between the moderate center and the militant end of our Black Power continuum. There are forces at work within them and upon them which pull them now toward the middle, now toward the extreme of Black Power orientations. These forces include the activities and financial support of liberal whites and the activities of the angry black youths who participate in these centers. These youths constantly challenge the center leaders not to appear to be turning into "Toms."

There are still newer groups which are more militant than the centers. One of these units is composed of some core members of the local city planning and organizing committee for the Poor People's March. Blacks lead this group, but some whites participate. One of its objectives has been to unite poor people, both black and white, in common purpose. It has also proposed the formation of black representation in Washington which could appeal to various African countries for assistance in condemning racism in America.

There are several militant groups of high school and university students who meet for discussion and who are continually prepared to engage in protest activities. They are capable of rapid situational response to any statement, policy decision, or action of the establishment, and are adept at exploiting racial undertones. One group spearheaded opposition to a police handcuffing rule. This involved a demonstration which resulted in their being handcuffed. They threatened continued demonstrations to force arrest. Other Black Power groups protested in other ways. Eventually the rule was revoked. Sit-ins in the mayor's office, before police stations, and in front of police cars were other tactics used by these student groups to force police to abandon use of a controversial weapon. Changes in university and high school curricula, black studies programs, and administration policies remain favorite targets for these groups.

A common pattern in the Black Power Movement in all parts of the country is the initiation of protest action by black youth, followed by the consolidation of gains and continued activity by adult groups organized for this purpose. Black youth also function as gadflies to keep older, more established black organizations moving toward ever more radical goals.

The most militant group of all in the metropolitan area under study advocates violence for its own sake. They follow the manifesto of Frantz Fanon, a black Algerian psychiatrist, who describes violence as a cleansing force, one which frees the black from his inferiority complex, restores his self-respect, and invests his character with positive and creative qualities (242). Some of the members of this local group have armed themselves and talk about practicing urban guerrilla warfare.

These more militant groups are in considerable developmental flux. There is informal exchange of membership among them, leadership tends to shift, and they change rapidly in mission and composition. By the time this book appears in print, many groups such as those we observed will have disappeared and others come into existence.

Standing just to the left of the moderate middle of our continuum are a number of very small groups and certain independent individuals who consider the promotion of various forms of sensitivity training and interracial communication to be their major mission. These groups have formed in response to the statements of bewilderment on the part of whites who realize that they do not understand the problems or the orientations of black Americans. Some groups teach white groups about Afro-American history and culture. Others train whites to treat blacks in business and industry with more understanding. One group has developed around the production of a television series about blacks, their demands, and their ideas. These groups are cooperating with the white establishment, but they have a kind of vested interest in communicating the sentiments of black militants—hence, they must maintain a militant stance.

A more moderate position in this spectrum of Black Power groups is taken by a large technical training center. Its primary mission is the education and technical training of needy blacks and whites, so that they can obtain employment. Black staff members operate the center and teach in it, although some whites play important roles. Much of the money comes from influential white businessmen. Some of the students, faculty, and administrative personnel of this center are nonparticipants in the Black Power Movement. Others are interested but conservative. Still others speak out quite boldly in favor of revolutionary change. One of the key staff members is recognized as a leading militant spokesman. Some of his black militant rivals have labeled him a "Tom" for his willingness to work with conservatives, but the conservative members of the staff regard him as a local "Stokely." With its various stances, this group is a micro-continuum of Black Power. It also has loose links with similar training centers in other cities.

Another organization situated in the moderate middle of the continuum is a rumor control center staffed largely by blacks. One of the black patrol units shares its headquarters with this group. It represents an effort on the part of certain blacks and influential whites to provide a channel for community information about all pertinent activities in the metropolitan area. The rumor control center also represents an attempt at centralization of both Black Power groups and white positive response groups or "task forces." This function puts it in direct competition with the local Urban Coalition, which is attempting to do the same thing. For this reason, plus the autonomous nature of Black Power groups, the hope of centralization of efforts seems dim. At this writing (1968), three different national Black Power organizations are each trying to set up as the central information center for groups of all types across the country. Each holds national and regional meetings intended to unify the Black Power Movement. The very nature of the organizational autonomy observed in both the Pentecostal Movement and the Black Power Movement, however, would seem to militate against this hope for structural unity.

Toward the conservative end of the continuum observed in this particular city are the Civil Rights groups, the NAACP, and the Urban League. Certain individuals in local branches of these organizations are becoming quite forceful, but the general stance remains more conservative than militant. Also on the conservative end is a center designed to teach whites and blacks about Africa. One of its founders is a black professional man. The other is an African student attending the local university.

Perhaps the most conservative group in the city is one which endorses the advancement of the black cause but which also actively opposes militant extremism. In a sense it was founded in order to counter what its members considered to be the excesses of the community center previously described. Especially disturbing was the teaching, at the community center, of black youths to hate whites and to challenge the authority of their conservative black parents. Members of this conservative group are chiefly people of middle age who are in or moving into the middle class. Many are parents of the young people active at the community center. Some are white, most are black, and blacks are its chief spokesmen. Although it is regarded by many moderate and militant blacks as an "Uncle Tom" organization, it is in fact contributing to the Black Power Movement in various ways. It has organized previously isolated "integrated" blacks as a pressure group for the black cause. This pressure group, in turn, attracts moderate whites and exposes them to Black Power ideology. In spite of their more conservative stance, these blacks accept the long-range goals of Black Power. By interpreting such goals to other conservative blacks, however, members of this group tend to draw previously unorganized individuals closer to participation in the movement. Such groups appeal to blacks who have been integrated as individuals or as families into the white community.

It should be noted that the placement of these particular groups we have described along our conservative-militant continuum may not be the same by the time this book is published. The stance of any particular group is subject to change depending on local incidents or national events and upon shifts in leadership or membership within the group. The overall picture of such a continuum, however, and the variety of groups that may be ranged along it at any point in time will remain a fair description of the movement as a whole.

In addition to the relatively permanent Black Power groups, there are a great number of *ad hoc* groups of short duration and limited mission. These *ad hoc* groups are usually small, although on one occasion nearly all of the blacks in the entire metropolitan area were mobilized into one such group. In this way *ad hoc* groups sometimes constitute a structural cross-group linkage of temporary duration. These temporary groups come into being in response to specific incidents involving racial tension. They are not simply "spontaneous eruptions," for individuals step forward to take control and provide a minimum of organizational structure. On occasion an *ad hoc* group will become a permanently organized group under the initial or subsequent leader.

The pattern of the Black Power Movement in this metropolitan area includes, then, the following elements:

— a great variety of organizationally autonomous groups which work to implement various themes, use different means to achieve their goals, and often display rivalry and a spirit of competition;
— a conservative-moderate-militant continuum;
— certain ideological tenets that are common to all, even the most disparate groups; and
— shifting *ad hoc* alliances resulting in both fission and fusion.

This same pattern was evident in the two additional metropolitan areas we surveyed—one in the Midwest, one in the Southeast. Black Power groups in these and other cities are linked through the activities of traveling spokesmen-evangelists and organizers. Martin Luther King was such an evangelist and organizer for SCLC groups. Members of many local Black Power groups in a particular city came together to hear his speeches in the same way that Pentecostals from various types of churches and groups will come together for a revival meeting. An equally well-known traveling spokesman was Stokely Carmichael of SNCC. He also functioned as a traveling organizer among voter registration workers in southern states. Such groups supported efforts of southern blacks to register and to exercise their voting rights. They also organized mutual aid groups to protect black voters against the traditional means of white retaliation.

It would be misleading to describe the Black Power Movement even sketchily without mentioning the parallel development of what we will call white positive response groups. White response is as varied as the approaches to Black Power, ranging from enthusiastic acceptance of the concept of Black Power to total rejection. Some whites campaign militantly for Black Power groups while other whites prepare to repel the black advance. A characteristic middle-of-the-road response is based on the "I agree with your goals but cannot accept your means" orientation.

In the metropolitan area where we studied both Black Power and white response groups in some detail, the general community direction is toward significant social change. Both established white institutions and newer institutions such as the Urban Coalition argue the need for changes, but the shape of the changes or the means by which they will be made is far from clear.

It has become increasingly apparent that the conventional responses of white institutions are not effective and do not bring about the kinds of change that are necessary. The initiative for change is thus shifting to a host of small grass roots groups which are springing up in response to specific local situations and problems. These groups are as varied in goals and means as those within the Black Power Movement. In some cases they even overlap so that one is tempted to classify them as Black Power groups or as "white auxiliaries." While Black Power has achieved full status as a movement, the white response groups may be considered an incipient or proto-movement.

A very brief list of examples drawn from several metropolitan areas will serve to indicate the nature of the white response groups:

— two black and two white housewives met and started to recruit others in an attempt to start cross-racial communication;
— discussion groups of whites formed to discuss racial issues and explore their own reactions;
— a group of wealthy businessmen took trucks into the ghetto area and collected garbage because city schedules tended to neglect this area;
— one group was organized to collect clothing, food, and supplies for participants in the Poor People's March from their area;
— one couple volunteered their home as a collection center for whites who believed all guns should be turned in as a demonstration of commitment to white non-violence;
— concerned clergymen organized to recruit participants for various demonstrations;
— several groups organized to provide shelter and collect food, clothing, household equipment, and medical supplies for blacks who were hurt or homeless after the riots;
— groups of white university students organized to support blacks in their demands for black studies programs;
— several lawyers organized to provide voluntary legal aid for blacks;
— one group had "stamp out racism" buttons made and sold them. They also put "white racism must go" signs up in their yards and recruited others who were willing to do likewise;
— one individual started a very successful "buy black" campaign which will be described in greater detail in a later chapter;
— one young couple who had formerly owned an import business helped a black couple set up channels for importing African items, and turned over to them all their address lists and similar business information.

There is some question as to whether the Black Power Movement, the white positive response groups, and even the student campus rebellions are all part of the same social movement. We take the position here that although they may all be part of a single social revolution, at least for purposes of analysis Black Power may be identified as a separate movement. For the purposes of this study, a Black Power group will be defined as *any group (a) which accepts and attempts to implement the goals of black economic and political power, black unity, black self-determination, and racial pride for blacks, and (b) in which the locus of decision-making power, control of funds, and ownership of property is in, or is shifting to, the hands of blacks.*

III

Organization

One of the most significant and least understood aspects of a movement is its organization, or "infrastructure." We have found that movement organization can be characterized as a network—decentralized, segmentary, and reticulate. Most people, even those participating in movements, are not able to imagine an organization of this type. There is a marked tendency in our society to identify an organization as something which has clear-cut leadership and which is centrally directed and administered in a pyramidal, hierarchical pattern. It is assumed that a well-defined chain of command ties the whole organization together from top to bottom. People may sense that a popular mass movement may not have all of the bureaucratic administrative machinery that such formal organizations have, but they still feel that it must possess central direction. If there is no observable bureaucratic organization, a single charismatic leader or a very small elite is assumed to be controlling the movement.

In the minds of many, the only possible alternative to a bureaucracy or a leader-centered organization is no organization at all. Most Americans have looked at the Black Power Movement from one or another of these two perspectives. There are those who believe that the movement, or at least its militant sector, is a vast conspiracy under some kind of central directorate. They also see this central direction as essentially covert, submerged from the public view. A few would attribute the leadership to Communists or other anti-American interests. Such individuals view riots and other acts of insurgency as part of a calculated nationwide plot. For example, a growing organization of whites, members of which we have interviewed, go so far as to believe that behind the black leaders of this "subversive" movement are white American Jews led by a Jew in the pay of the Communists.

On the other hand there are those who argue that the Black Power revolt, including the associated violence, is a spontaneous eruption from the grass roots. They do not believe that there is any organization at all, even at the local level. In fact, they are more likely to feel that the greatest problem the black community faces is that it cannot unite and is essentially atomistic. According to this view, riots are "breaking out all over" because of individual pent-up frustrations and anger. Others attribute the "epidemic" to the publicity given to militants or "outside agitators" by the press, radio, and television.

The same alternative views of the Pentecostal Movement are held by those who have not considered the movement as a whole. Some assume it to be a collection of Pentecostal sects with regional, national, or international organizations linked by centralized polities similar to those of the Methodist, Presbyterian, or Congregational systems. Others see only randomly distributed "outbreaks" of tongues in various churches or denominations quite unrelated to each other or to the older Pentecostal sects.

We have found, through our field observation of the Pentecostal and the Black Power Movements, as well as in studies of other movements, that there is a third type of organization characterized by decentralization, segmentation, and reticulation.

Decentralization has to do with the decision-making, regulatory functions of the movement.

Segmentation has to do with the social structure—the composition of parts that make up the movement as a whole.

Reticulation has to do with the way these parts are tied together into a network.

Decentralization

The term used in social anthropology to describe those societies or tribes which do not have a leadership hierarchy is "acephalous," which means without a head, or headless. Such a tribe i... tural, and ethical entity, yet its segments are politically a... ically autonomous. In this type of structure there is no ... decision-making authority above the level of the local comm... localized clan or lineage of kinsmen. Furthermore, political ...rol even at the local level is often diffused and quite flexible. Power and authority tend to be distributed among a council of wise and able men, of whom one is recognized to be just a bit more able than the others. He is *primus inter pares.* The concept of "first among equals" is extremely difficult for the Western mind to grasp unless it has been experienced. It is a type of group interaction that maintains genuine egalitarianism while utilizing individual initiative and leadership capacity. It also has built-in controls over attempts to usurp authoritarian power. Political unity in such tribes is a function of external opposition. The possibility of attack by other tribes is the basis on which the autonomous segments unite under a temporary paramount leader; conceptually, they become one people. As soon as the external threat subsides, tribal unity dissolves again into acephalous segmentation.

The movements we are discussing are not societies, nation-states, or tribes, and they are certainly not "primitive" in their mode of organization. But they do have organizational structures which can best be described as acephalous—or, better, polycephalous (many-headed). Relationships between their leaders and followers are of the *primus inter pares* type. The kinship terms used in both Pentecostal groups and Black Power groups are an expression of this. Pentecostals are brothers and sisters in Christ. Black Power participants are "soul" brothers and sisters. There are certainly Pentecostal groups in which the leader is highly authoritarian. There are also certain Black Power leaders such as Malcolm X, Eldridge Cleaver, or Martin Luther King whom their followers revere—to King, especially, were attributed almost Christ-like qualities. Yet such men are still "brothers"—conceptually and emotionally equal with the humblest new convert. The powerful and almost dictatorial quality of leadership in some Pentecostal ministers must not be mistaken for centralized organizational patterns. And it should be remembered that such leaders in both movements can exercise this dominance only over their own groups.

Neither the Pentecostal nor the Black Power Movement has a single leader. In Pentecostalism there are widely recognized leaders such as David du Plessis, Derek Prince, Demos Shakarian, Oral Roberts, David Wilkerson of Teen Challenge, and, among Episcopalians, Dennis Bennett. Many others are equally well known to all Pentecostals. All Black Power participants recognize the powerful influence of the late Martin Luther King and Malcolm X, of Floyd McKissick, of Stokely Carmichael, H. Rap Brown, Eldridge Cleaver, and James Forman. To outsiders, these men often appear to be the key individuals without whom the movement would grind to a halt. But not one of them could be called the leader of the movement in which they work. A current list of influential leaders would have to be updated several times a year, for at least five reasons.

First, such leaders quite clearly disagree upon matters of theological emphasis; or, in Black Power, upon the short-range goals of the movement and the methods by which such goals should be achieved.

Second, none of these leaders in either movement has a roster of, or even knows about, all the groups who consider themselves to be participating in the movement.

Third, none of them can make decisions binding on all of the participants in the movement, and none can speak for the movement as a whole. They may articulate basic beliefs to which all members may subscribe, but they can direct actions only in that sector of the movement of which each happens to be the organizational as well as the ideological leader.

Fourth, and this is most frustrating for representatives of the established order, none of these leaders in either movement has regulatory powers over the movement. Even if Dennis Bennett were to have complied with Bishop Pike's suggestion that there be no laying on of hands for the purpose of the Baptism of the Holy Spirit by lay Christians, the members of his own church might have ceased, but it would have had little effect on Episcopalian groups in other churches or cities. By the same token, city officials are upset when well-known leaders of the Black Power Movement who incite a riot cannot control it even when they are obviously working sincerely and tirelessly to do so. Representatives of the established order must then assume either that the leader is not sincere in his efforts to stop the riot he started, or that it got "out of hand" and beyond his control. The fact of the matter is that riots are but one form of Black Power activity, and no single leader has regulatory powers over such activities, riotous or otherwise, except those carried out by his own local group.

A fifth manifestation of the polycephalous nature of these two movements is the fact that there is no such thing as a "card-carrying" member. Various organizations involved in either movement have memberships in which rights and/duties are defined to varying degrees. But there is no membership in the movement as a whole. It is for this reason that we have used the word "participant" rather than "member" of the movements. Participation in the Pentecostal Movement is based on whether or not the individual has received, is seeking, or is interested in the Baptism of the Holy Spirit and the spiritual gifts. Whether or not any individual meets this "requirement" is a matter of consensus. A leader might introduce a stranger to his group as a "Spirit-filled" Christian, but the group will make its own judgment on the basis of the stranger's testimony and the quality of his interaction with the group. Pentecostals are not fooled by the presence of glossolalia alone. This proves nothing. As one participant pointed out, "the devil can speak in tongues too." "Spirit-filled" Christians recognize each other on the basis of criteria born of a common experience, not because a leader announces that so-and-so is a participant in the movement.

By the same kind of criteria, participants in the Black Power Movement recognize each other. Sometimes the phrase "having soul" denotes this. No single leader has the right or the power to decide who does or does not "have soul." The phrase has far wider implications than mere participation in the Black Power Movement (215, 232), but it constitutes an interesting parallel to the Pentecostal concept of being "Spirit-filled." We are *not* suggesting that "having soul" is the same as being "Spirit-filled." We found that when one of our most "Spirit-filled" Pentecostal friends met one of the most dedicated "soul" brothers, they disagreed about many things, but there was a distinctive quality in each that the other recognized, understood, and respected. The point here is that membership in both movements is based on a subjective experience and is not a matter of objective requirements. There is no leader, therefore, who can even determine who is or is not a member of the movement, let alone direct, regulate, or speak for that movement. The same polycephalous or decentralized organization can be seen in other movements, even though observers and scientific analysts often assume the existence of central leadership.

Peter Lawrence's detailed account of the Cargo Cult in the Madang District of New Guinea (326) includes a diagram of the political organization, led by a man named Yali, when the movement was at its height. The diagram looks much like the organization chart on the wall of a corporation executive's office. Scattered through the text, however, are references to Yali's lack of control over his organization. Even in his own immediate area he could not guarantee that his orders would be carried out. "Boss boys" in the rural areas where transportation is by air or by foot were, of necessity, almost autonomous local leaders. Yali had little control, and variations on his ideological themes were disseminated without his consent or approval. He was even "persuaded" by certain supporters to become involved in secret pagan rituals. Australian administrators and missionaries, threatened by the rapid spread of the Cargo Cult in their area, decided it was a product of brilliant organization, run by personally appointed "henchmen" whom Yali directed from a central headquarters. (The same sort of invisible but hierarchical organization is often assumed for other movements successful in opposing an established order.)

As Lawrence points out, the movement developed in a "fortuitous fashion." Strong leaders of Cargo Cult believers in other areas moved in to organize and recruit, take actions, and spread doctrinal innovations inconsistent with Yali's scheme for "rehabilitation." Yet Yali "did nothing" to stop this. Observers interpreted his inactivity simply as the failure of a native leader to operate his supposedly monolithic organization in a proper bureaucratic fashion. Yali himself, imbued with the spirit of Westernization, thought of his system of "boss boys" as a bureaucratic chain of command. But it was never "efficient." It was, in other words, an essentially decentralized organization with an ideological but not an administrative leader.

Leadership in this type of decentralized or acephalous organization is based on personal charisma rather than on the fulfillment of bureaucratic training requirements and progression up through ranked positions.

Charisma, a term first used in sociology by Max Weber, means literally "a gift of divine or spiritual origin." As we shall point out in chapter VI, charisma is, among other things, a product of total personal commitment. This quality endows an individual with the power of persuasive influence over others and inspires dependent faith and personal loyalty in his followers. The usual model of the charismatic leader is that of the hub of a wheel with the spokes as inner circle disciples and the rim as the larger circle of followers. Too many studies of movement dynamics have been hindered by the limitations of this model, which attributes the success of a movement to a single charismatic leader.

Dorothy Emmet (361) makes an important addition to Weberian theory and one essential to the understanding of leadership in Pentecostalism, Black Power, and other movements. She distinguishes between (a) the leader who possesses an almost hypnotic power of personal authority inspiring devoted obedience, and (b) the "charismatist" who strengthens those he influences, inspiring them to work on their own initiative. The heightening of this inner power, she maintains, can be conveyed from one charismatist to another.

In both movements we have studied, the charismatic leadership is primarily of the second type. Even in the most leader-dominated group a kind of secondary or communicable charisma is generated.

To study the Pentecostal Movement is to be subjected constantly to the phenomenon of charisma. The minute the charismatic leader of a group leaves the room, the visitor is immediately taken in hand by any member happening to be close by and the charismatic bombardment goes on. There are, of course, some Pentecostals who engage in the uninspired type of "canned" fundamentalist dogma-spouting. These persons are found primarily in the long-established sect churches which are well on their way to full denominational status. But the majority are effective evangelists in the true sense of the word. Individual Pentecostals are charismatic to the degree that they believe they have been granted the "power to witness for the Lord," and to the degree that others come to believe them to be agents of the divine will.

Conversation with a Pentecostal, particularly if you are an avowed student of the movement, is likely to include his testimony. This is simply the story of how he came to receive the Baptism of the Holy Spirit, the conditions of his life situation before the event, the nature of the experience itself, and the effects on his life since that time. Even an outsider who is not a potential convert can feel the charismatic nature of these face-to-face testimonies. The directness and candor with which Pentecostals are able to describe their feelings inspire respect, if not a desire to share in such experiences. There is a temporary eloquence which transcends the particular indivdual's abilities when he talks about other subjects. One can feel the power of persuasion even if one is not persuaded. The difference between leader and follower in such a movement does not depend on the presence or absence of charisma, but on the relative degrees of that quality exhibited by the various participating individuals.

A recent series of revival meetings of some three hundred Neo-Pentecostals provided appropriate illustration of the above point. At each session during three days and evenings of meetings, the main speaker was preceded by two or three spellbinders from the audience. These men and women delivered fifteen to thirty minutes of extemporaneous, always moving, and often hilarious testimony. All were followers in their own local groups. After the meetings, small groups clustered around these laymen as well as around the five or six visiting speakers and the two out-of-town lay people called "counselors." On-the-spot prayer sessions sometimes led to plans for extended prayer-partnership interactions. Devotion to one highly charismatic leader or layman, then, does not prevent simultaneous devotion to another. Nor does it prevent the layman from forming and exercising regular influence over his own group of devoted followers. Secondary charisma enhances the humblest member's leadership potential, and contributes to the viability of decentralized organization.

The same is true in Black Power. Some individuals become Black Power leaders because they conform somewhat to rules for obtaining status through the bureaucratic channels of the white power structure. For example, some are hired by the Office of Economic Opportunity or by city governments to undertake certain duties in behalf of the "black community." Certain human rights and Civil Rights commissions at city and state levels are staffed in part by government appointees who have met specific establishment requirements. There are similar positions on Urban Coalition staffs. It is well known, of course, that blacks who have been appointed by the establishment to official positions dealing with the movement are often called "Uncle Toms" or "house niggers." To rise above this is difficult enough. To rise high enough to be considered leaders in the movement, or even to be considered brothers, they must demonstrate that they have charisma.

A majority of Black Power leaders, in our opinion, have risen from the grass roots of the movement. Starting as followers in other Civil Rights or Black Power groups, they experience a deepening commitment to the cause. Accompanying this comes the initiative and the necessary personal charisma to organize a group around an issue or a specific action. The group then continues after the originating stimulus is dealt with. Black students create campus organizations to demand scholarships, courses in African culture, and more black faculty members. One member of a Black Power community center who had charge of youth activities organized a black community patrol—a parapolice force. In this case a crisis in the city precipitated his rise to a more powerful position in the movement. In another instance, the arrest of an elderly black woman brought about a demonstration. One black youth stepped forward to take *ad hoc* leadership of the situation. Since then, a hard core of this spontaneous group now remains organized under his leadership.

This rise to leadership through crisis is familiar in African segmentary societies and is called "building a name" (381). Such leaders are typically ill equipped to deal with organizational problems of an established group. This is partial explanation for the rapid shift in leadership in the Black Power Movement. A few individuals develop the capacity to tolerate this role conflict, however, and remain in positions of organizational leadership over a longer period of time. These problems are typical of leadership in other movements as well.

Segmentation

By describing a movement as segmentary, we mean that it is composed of a great variety of localized groups or cells which are essentially independent, but which can combine to form larger configurations or divide to form smaller units. Both processes, fission and fusion, occur in Black Power and Pentecostalism. All social systems are composed of parts or cells, but in a bureaucratically centralized society the segments are always subordinated to a center and operate according to a prescribed chain of command. Furthermore, new segments are formed in accordance with the rules and at the decision of or at least with the approval of the central administration. In contrast, in a segmentary system fission and proliferation of cells take place independently, unrelated to any central decision making. Very often each segment or cell tends to recruit from different parts of the total societal population. Each tends to develop a kind of "style" of its own, each "does its own thing," each has its own specific goals and means.

In a segmentary system, each unit has different ideas about how to achieve the more general objectives of the movement, and each interprets the movement ideology in its own way. New cells are formed from the splitting of an old cell, from proliferation by the gathering of new members under new leaders, and from combinations and permutations of these. This constant rearrangement adds a dynamic to movements which can be confusing to outside observers. It can also be disconcerting to members of the movement if they somehow decide that their movement should have the kind of stable, centralized structure characteristic of establishment organizations.

All of this leads us to ask what produces cell formation and segmentation in the first place. And why do segments vary in means goals, and patterns? We have identified four basic, interrelated way by means of which segmentation in movement organization occurs (a) an ideology of personal access to power; (b) pre-existing social personal or geographical cleavages; (c) competition; and (d) ideological differences.

Ideology of personal access to power. Participants in the Pentecostal Movement, in Black Power, and, for that matter, in the studen rebellions, operate on the assumption that individuals in the move ment have direct personal access to knowledge, truth, and power This is most clearly expressed in Pentecostalism. The Baptism of the Holy Spirit is an empowering gift of God. It enables the believer to receive spiritual gifts and it increases his sensitivity to God's will. An "Spirit-filled" Christian, layman or pastor, can preach the word o God effectively. In short, there is direct individual access to the sourc of spiritual power, wisdom, and authority. The concept of "the priest hood of believers" is basic to all Christian theology, but the Pente costals take it more seriously than do members of most conventiona denominations, and they act upon it.

A similar concept known as *Ijtihad*, "personal striving in the path of the Lord," was characteristic of Islam in its early days of expansion. This concept, similar to the Christian idea of "the priesthood of believers," and the Black Power idea of "doing your own thing" or "having your own bag," gives people the courage to make their own judgments. They decide what is the will of God for them, and take the initiative in implementing their beliefs. This attitude contributes to the segmentation, egalitarianism, and decentralized nature of movement organization.

Pentecostals who have broken from one group and joined or initiated another invariably say they have been "led of the Lord." Black Power participants do not formulate theories about the sources of their knowledge and power as Pentecostals do. Nevertheless, they have a rhetoric of individual initiative, independent action, and personal responsibility. This provides an ideological basis for the formation of new groups and the fission or segmentation of existing ones. It also produces widely divergent views of goals and methods.

One Negro professional, for instance, who was called a "house nigger" by black militants, tried his best to identify with white middle class standards and values. Originally he scorned black militancy and endorsed the concept of integration and submergence of racial differences. After the death of Martin Luther King, he began to talk about Africa, and rejected the words "black" and "Negro" as inappropriate to an individual of his racial and cultural heritage. Instead, he selected the term Afro-American. He has now teamed up with a university student from Africa to establish a Center for African Cultural Studies; the two of them are assisted by a group of blacks and whites. One of the center's major aims is to contribute to the understanding of and pride in the African heritage. To those black militants who claim that he is still far too oriented to the white man's world, that he still plays their game to get money and other aid, he replies that he is only doing what he knows is right for him. He now perceives himself, as do his followers and some other groups, as a participant in the Black Power Movement. Such is the nature of movement organization that no one can say him nay. He is simply one more variant on the basic theme.

Pre-existing personal and social cleavages.   Movements remake men and societies. They establish new allegiances and tear down others.

But they cannot erase at once all pre-existing social relationships. In fact, as we shall see, recruitment to a movement follows the lines of pre-existing social relationships; a cell is often composed of people who were close friends or relatives before the movement encompassed them. But, by the same token, pre-existing cleavages, factionalism, rivalries, and conflicts continue to influence the development of the movement's organization and activities.

Extra-movement differences in socio-economic and educational background as well as religious upbringing have influenced segmentation in the Pentecostal Movement. As pointed out in the preceding chapter, one can arrange the different types of Pentecostal groups along an organizational continuum and find regular differences in income, occupational status, and level of education. This is simply the result of the segmentation process. As the movement spreads across class or cultural boundaries, new "Spirit-filled" Christians characteristically seek established Pentecostal sect churches in their cities, intending to join them in their worship services and to talk about the experience of Baptism. The established Pentecostals eagerly welcome such converts, of course, interpreting their presence as a sign that the movement is indeed growing. But both groups generally discover that a truly rewarding association is hindered by differences not only in educational and socio-economic background, but also in theological orientations. Repeatedly we have seen how newly Baptized Pentecostals tend to withdraw and form their own independent groups; or, if they are Episcopal or Catholic groups containing sympathetic or participating clergymen, they simply meet regularly in their own churches with members of other non-Pentecostal churches who have had the Pentecostal experience. Thus pre-existing social cleavages tend to segment the movement organizationally.

Many Neo-Pentecostals find this distressing, since unity in Christ should somehow prevent such cleavages. Yet they admit honestly their awareness of Pentecostalism's lower-class origins, and its reputation as a religion of down-and-outers. They know about and do not want to be identified with the common "Holy Rollers" stereotype. Many even refuse to call themselves Pentecostals because of this stereotype. Instead, they refer to themselves as participants in the charismatic revival. We have found that when we brought together Pentecostals of widely different backgrounds for purposes of discussing our research, they were often uncomfortable together, and the meetings were awkward. On certain occasions differences in dress and hair style or different views on the use of alcohol and tobacco caused mutual discomfort, not only because of the obvious social cleavages, but also because these differences in taste also represent deep theological differences which are of great importance, particularly to the more fundamentalist Pentecostals.

On the other hand, one well-educated Lutheran Pentecostal who described how uncomfortable he had been with the people, theology, and type of worship services of a Pentecostal sect said that if he had to be set adrift in a lifeboat with two or three others, he would rather be with the Pentecostals with whom he had no social rapport than with people in his own church and social group who had not experienced the Baptism of the Holy Spirit. "We'd know how to pray together," he said, "and in a crisis that's what counts."

The fact that pre-existing social cleavages are forcing the establishment of thousands of independent churches and "hidden" groups within non-Pentecostal churches may disappoint participants who would prefer to find organizational unity in Christ; but it does facilitate the spread of the movement, for reasons which will be discussed presently.

Segmentation and formation of new groups based on pre-existing class and occupational lines are very apparent in Colombia, Haiti, and Mexico. There is one notable Pentecostal group in Bogota composed of a leading banker, several members of the government, a lawyer, and several influential businessmen. In the same city there are also a number of Pentecostal churches serving the emerging urban middle class, and a larger number whose members come from the urban working class. In Mexico City, members of the largest Pentecostal church are generally of the urban middle class. Working-class Pentecostals are found in other city churches. In Port-au-Prince, the two churches we studied drew members from two quite different socio-economic strata, but each church was internally homogeneous.

Segmentation along socio-economic lines in these countries occurs not only because of the members' backgrounds, but also because of pre-existing cleavages among various missionaries from the United States. They arrive periodically, come to strengthen existing groups and initiate new ones. Two such evangelists visiting in Port-au-Prince during our field work there were American Negroes with large followings in Haiti. Another was a white evangelist who commands a large source of funds. He considered giving financial assistance to one of the Negro missionaries, but finally decided to channel his funds through another white leader whose views about the "white Pentecostal's burden" were more compatible with his own.

A large-scale missionary effort in Colombia, supported by both money and personnel from the United States, also segmented and for a time ran aground on the reef of factionalism. Some of the cleavages were along differences in age, socio-economic class, and cultural heritage of the several score lay and professional evangelists and assistants gathered for the crusade. A major split occurred between the North American evangelists and the Cuban and Colombian members of the team.

One other major cause for segmentation and proliferation of cells in a movement is what we have decided to call "geographical peel-off." Members of one cell will move to another city for extra-movement reasons—usually jobs or family connections. Unless they find a compatible Pentecostal group to join, these individuals will often initiate a new cell and begin converting local residents. This is very common in Haiti, where Pentecostals in Port-au-Prince tend to return to rural villages where they have relatives. Soon a small Pentecostal group will be established there, often without the financial support or even the knowledge of the bishop in Port-au-Prince. These cells then begin to draw converts from villages ten and fifteen miles away through contacts of kinship or local market-exchange relationships. It is customary in these groups for the local minister and his lay leaders to divide the church when it has become a flourishing and financially sound center; they encourage those members who live over ten miles away to form "daughter" cells. The "mother" church will then help the new groups get started with contributions of money for buildings. Leadership is often provided by intensive tutelage in Biblical knowledge by one of the lay members who has been "raised up by the Lord" to guide the new group. Sometimes a lay leader in the "mother" church will move his family to the village of the "daughter" church to provide leadership. In time the "daughter" church reaches out through similar contacts to residents of villages ten and fifteen miles farther in the interior, and the process of cell division starts again.

Even in the United States, where it is not uncommon for members to drive many miles to church, Pentecostal groups tend to segment on the basis of distance. One small independent church in a suburban area produced three offshoots during the two years of our study. When last heard from, another was beginning. In one case, a member of the offshoot group was given intensive Bible study and interpretation by the pastor of the independent church in order that he could lead his own group. Leadership for two other offshoots was provided by lay leaders of the original church, who drove to their new flock each week.

The remarkable spread of Pentecostalism among the Otomi Indians in Mexico, many of whose churches were visited by a member of our research team, can be attributed in large part to one member of the tribe who was converted to Christ by Pentecostals during a short stay in the United States. When he returned to his mountain home, he brought his contagious brand of Pentecostalism with him, and eventually the whole tribe "caught" it.

A similar instance of the spread of the movement through geographical mobility is recorded for a remote tribe in Argentina where the rise of a "spontaneous indigenous church" resulted from the conversion to Pentecostalism of two or three young men while they were living in a large urban center for a period of wage labor (170).

A fundamental cleavage that contributes to segmentation and proliferation of Black Power groups is the well-known "generation gap." This pan-human gap has been exacerbated among black Americans by the movement. Many older Negroes stay out of the movement although their children and younger brothers and sisters are being drawn in. But those older black adults who do join the movement, or who have worked in Civil Rights groups out of which it grew, exhibit attitudes and approaches which differ sharply from those of younger participants. Most differences center around the problem of the means by which common goals should be achieved. In one city the appearance and rapid growth of a militant Black Power group with a strong youth program was followed not long after by the formation of another more moderate group, many of whose members were parents of the young people in the first group. In this case pre-existing and opposed orientations based largely on age were responsible for segmentation within the movement. In addition, the creation of a new and growing wing contributed to the growth of the movement as a whole.

Differences between the NAACP youth league in certain cities and the NAACP groups of the parents' generation exemplify segmentation based on pre-existing cleavages.

Also in Black Power, as in any movement, segmentation and proliferation of cells occurs on the basis of pre-existing personal differences or conflicts. In one of the urban centers we studied, one of the most significant lines of cleavage in the movement derives from a personal conflict between two key black militant leaders. One was a minister, the other a social worker. They competed for influence among members of the black community, especially the youth, even before the advent of Black Power militancy. Their philosophies of social change and their tactics have always been different. Their circles of friends and admiring subordinates are certainly different and this also predates the movement. Personal concerns of long standing are also involved. Although this personal conflict can be and has been temporarily shelved on occasions when the movement faces a crisis, it does coincide with a major cleavage in the Black Power Movement in this city. Each of the two rival leaders heads a different type of action group. Each has also played a significant role in factional struggles for control of a model city-urban renewal program.

Whether pre-existing cleavages are socio-economic, educational, geographical, or personal, they are still important factors contributing to the segmentary nature of movement organization.

Personal competition.   Movement members, especially those with leadership drives and capabilities, compete for a broad range of economic, social, political, psychological, and spiritual rewards. They compete for personal influence and authority over others, for positions of power, for financial support, for the recognition by others of the fact that they do have certain gifts and capabilities. They are motivated by the desire to do the will of the Lord or to further the cause of their people. The need to achieve always involves some comparison with the performance of others.

Some of this competition is essentially selfish in motive. Any movement attracts a few charlatans, self-seeking profiteers, and—as some Pentecostals call them—"Holiness con-men." Based on our re search in Pentecostalism and Black Power, we contend not only that such persons are in a small minority numerically, but also that their influence on the overall course of these movements is minimal. Certainly, we gain no understanding of these movements and no ability to predict their development by focusing our attention upon the charlatan.

Most of the competition stems from altruistic devotion to the cause or to the group. It is a blend of striving for self, for the group, and for the cause—a blend so complex that neither the competitive participant nor the observer can isolate his motives. The Pentecostal commitment experience so identifies self with Christ that both identities are served by the same act. When a Pentecostal succeeds in some struggle, spiritual or material, he "gives all the glory to God." His gain is Christ's and Christ's is his. For a Black Power participant, commitment involves a similar identification of oneself with one's people and one's envisioned goals for those people. What bestows pride, dignity, and even material rewards upon one's people also bestows such rewards upon oneself, and vice versa.

Personal striving and interpersonal competition are discussed here not in order to reduce motivation to the personal level, but to show how it causes cell segmentation and proliferation and thus may contribute to the spread of the movement.

Money, social and political power, and prestige are also available in the world of Black Power, in amounts which are more than enough to inspire considerable competition. Some Black Power money is obtained from blacks in the movement, but most of it is obtained from the white establishment. The latter has many motives for giving the money, both stated and unstated. Much giving has stemmed from white fear and guilt. Much has been provided to "pacify" the blacks. Some of the giving stems from the premise that riots and rebellion are caused by deprivation—chiefly economic deprivation; to counter the rioting, whites attempt to alleviate the economic causes. Some of the money is no more than conscience money, given to expiate guilt feelings. A small but growing portion of it is given by those who truly believe that such assistance will be used to promote social change which enriches the entire society.

Blacks are very quick to perceive these different motives for giving. Black militants find that one of the best ways to secure funds for their projects is to demand them while there are overt or covert threats of violence in the streets. Funding for hundreds of groups all over the country came after the death of Martin Luther King, when remorse, guilt, and fear were maximized.

Among the results of such competition are innovation, cell proliferation, and segmentation within the movement. For example, blacks learn that white business firms, government offices, and various clubs and associations want to receive "sensitivity training"—that is, training to make persons aware of what white racism does to blacks, training to aid whites in developing effective relationships with blacks. Part of this interest stems from a genuine desire to understand; part of it is just a kind of demonstration to the world, and to their consciences: "Look, we are trying to learn, we are trying not to be racist." Blacks also discover that most white groups are willing to pay and pay well for such sensitivity training. In one urban center blacks have formed a number of different groups to "package" programs in sensitivity training. Some blacks still give this training as loners, but most prefer to represent a militant group. A connection with such a group is almost a necessary credential for training whites in sensitivity. Astute whites have learned the difference between militants and "Uncle Toms."

In a similar manner, and often in conjunction with sensitivity training, blacks have organized to teach whites about Afro-American history and culture. Enterprising blacks, who may start as assistants in established groups of community educators, often split off to do their own teaching to their own white audiences. If successful, they soon gather their own circle of followers and assistants; eventually, this circle segments. One criteria for splitting and "doing one's own thing" is, of course, the ability to offer something new to an established audience, or to offer an established approach to a new audience. Often the ties between these black teachers and certain members of their white audiences become so strong that they form joint action groups, with the black man acting as an advisor and liaison agent with the black community. In such instances, blacks compete not only for positions of influence but also for control of funds.

Money and material aid flow even more freely in the Pentecostal Movement, but there is a major difference in the source of such backing. In Pentecostalism, movement funding is primarily internal. With few exceptions it comes from participants in the movement, not from members of the establishment, as in Black Power. The practice of tithing—giving a tenth of one's income to the Lord's work—is taken seriously by all types of Pentecostals. In one of the Episcopalian Pentecostal groups we observed, the priest often says, "If you don't tithe, you're just not with it." But there is also a good deal of supererogatory giving inspired by specific situations. Evangelists are often given free will offerings or "love offerings" after their messages at revivals or at home meetings where they have led the discussion and prayers. Such offerings may be quite substantial. Pentecostal giving of this type is personalized. A typical participant gives money in direct proportion to the non-material rewards he feels he has received from a preacher, teacher, evangelist, or missionary. Participants also give in proportion to the enthusiasm an evangelist or missionary from another part of the world can inspire for a job that could be done where "the harvest is ripe and the laborers are few." Although the believer is unable to go, his contribution enables someone else to go, so that the will of the Lord may be done. Clearly, there is competition for internally generated funds, although neither donors nor recipients may perceive it in quite this way.

Among Pentecostals, competition for followers is linked with competition for funds; both activities contribute to the proliferation of cells and to the growth of the movement. A Baptist preacher in Florida left his denomination after he received the Baptism of the Holy Spirit with tongues. He started his own church of "Spirit-filled" Christians, which flourished and stimulated the establishment of several other churches. The minister has now turned to flying evangelism, owns two airplanes, has established missionary centers in Colombia, and plans expansion into other Latin American countries. He receives support from his four Florida churches as well as from brothers across the country who have heard him talk about his work for the Lord, or who have benefited from his gifts of healing or exorcism. The more cells he establishes, the more his fame spreads, and the more additional funds flow in, enabling him to establish still newer cells. Such mutual escalation helps to explain the exponential growth rates of movements with decentralized, segmented organization.

The Pentecostal Movement obviously grows by recruiting from non-Pentecostals. But to get started, a Pentecostal leader needs a

hard core of converted participants. Sometimes he must raid another
Pentecostal group for "seed" members. This tactic was observed in
the spread of the movement in both Haiti and Colombia. A North
American Pentecostal feels a call to take the gospel to another land—
or to another part of the United States. He obtains pilot funds for his
project from certain Pentecostal supporters. In the new area he finds
that he is competing with more established evangelists and local
leaders for access to Pentecostals. He attracts the attention of local
Pentecostals who are lay leaders in their churches or prayer groups,
and helps them to promote and establish segments already broken
away from the established churches. These groups respond because
of his personal charisma or spiritual gifts, or because he offers a different theological interpretation of the Pentecostal experience, or perhaps because he emphasizes a kind of organization that some consider
more consistent with first-century Christianity. In any case, with
his "hard core" established, he can then return to the United States
with photographs of these groups, perhaps with one of his local leaders
as a companion. With this success to report, he is able to raise more
money and can return to the country of his call to focus his work on
the recruitment of non-Pentecostals.

The Pentecostal congregation that he and his followers have initially "raided" generally responds to his efforts by redoubling its
efforts to preach a particular interpretation of the gospel, to raise
more money, and to recruit more converts. Rather than attempting to
re-recruit the "defectors," the members intensify recruitment among
non-Pentecostal sources, and establish "daughter" cells more to their
liking. Thus personal competition for both followers and funds pro-
motes cell proliferation and can be viewed as useful in the service of
God.

After analyzing the methods of financing movement activities and
their consequences in Black Power and in Pentecostalism, we offer
the following observations: Pentecostals give personally to fellow
Pentecostals, believing—or knowing—that the recipient has been
called by God to do a specific work. The giver believes in this work
as deeply as the recipient, but believes that the recipient can do it
better. In turn, the recipient feels obligated to do the work well—obligated not only to the Lord and his own conscience, but to the giver
as well. A personal bond reinforces a religious purpose.

In Black Power funding, this personalized type of giving and receiving for mutually envisioned goals is still an exception rather than the rule. Too often the goal of the white givers is to stop trouble, or to expiate guilt feelings, or to express sorrow and remorse. While these goals may be valid for the givers, they do not coincide with the goals of the receivers. The latter are convinced that radical social change is needed; they may be considering goals which the typical giver does not understand and would not like. Of course, the receiver's goals may be as valid as the giver's. But because they differ, expectations about how the money is to be spent will differ. The result is often increased hostility. There is no personal bond between giver and receiver which supports the receiver's obligation to a mutual goal, or even to his own stated goal. When whites donate money and other material resources to black leaders or Black Power segments out of the realization that these receivers will accomplish the specific social changes desired by both givers and receivers, then mutual trust and far more effective use of funds will result. If the flow of funds within Pentecostalism is any indication, it is possible that a far greater supply of funds will also be made available.

Ideological differences. It is often assumed that when people in the same organization split over a theological or ideological difference, they are merely rationalizing a personal conflict or a socio-economic cleavage. This may be partially true in some cases. But there are both personal conflicts and ideological differences within any church, even the most static type, and these seldom, if ever, produce splitting, proliferation, or fluctuation in membership. Similarly, both personal conflicts and ideological differences undoubtedly existed in certain established Civil Rights organizations before the advent of Black Power, and these did not cause the explosive organizational proliferation that characterizes the Black Power Movement today.

One major source of this distinction, we suggest, is the nature of individual commitment, which often tends to magnify ideological differences of opinion. There is an important relationship between commitment and belief which will be discussed in greater detail in chapter VI. In committed individuals, ideological differences produce an intensity of involvement that most others do not feel unless their pride or their pocketbooks are under attack. In fact, differences in ideas about goals or methods can create personal conflicts in a movement as easily as pre-existing personal conflicts can produce ideological differences.

The history of Pentecostalism is one long story of organizational fission and fusion over such questions as that of the trinitarian versus the unitarian nature of the Godhead. What has become a moth-eaten issue for most Christians is a gut-level problem for a Pentecostal who has just had a personal revelation that it is "Jesus only"—that Jesus *is* God, and that the trinitarian doctrine is wrong. The passion with which this point is explained and argued goes far beyond that normally expended on personal rivalries. The initial organizational split over this ideological difference is almost fifty years old. But the vehemence of a typical recent convert to the "Jesus Only" faction makes it quite clear that ideological differences among people who have had some sort of commitment experience are highly motivating; without reference to any other type of cleavage, such differences can be viewed as an independent cause of segmentation and organizational proliferation. Other more modern, ideological issues that have caused organizational fission are concerned with the relative importance of such gifts as demon exorcism, the place of glossolalia in a "Spirit-filled" life, whether or not a "Spirit-filled" Christian should come out of the "whore of Babylon" or remain within and try to redeem her, and whether a "Spirit-filled" Christian can smoke or take an occasional drink.

Several major ideological differences in the Black Power Movement are of such crucial import that an attempt to attribute the resulting organizational schisms to personal or socio-economic determinants would be foolish. One such difference arises over the concept of separatism—the extent to which blacks should work with whites. At one extreme, some Black Power groups tolerate white participation in the drive toward movement goals. At the other, there are groups that refuse even financial support from whites, and some that would sever all relationship between the races and attempt to establish a separate state. In between are the groups that believe blacks and whites must work out a common life as one nation, but that reject white participation in the Black Power Movement. A major ideological consideration for any Black Power group is the type of relationship it will permit with white sympathizers. Many an organizational split has occurred over this issue despite the absence of personal conflicts or socio-economic differences between the factions.

We might note in passing that in one urban center, and possibly others, some Black Power segments are differentiated in part by the types of whites active in each, and by the nature of the black-white relationship. One Black Power group receives support from moderate-to-conservative whites. Another receives support from radical whites who are largely in professional occupations. A third group is supported by liberal whites who contribute money and the kind of influence necessary to manipulate the white power structure. In one Black Power group, blacks clearly dominate the white participants. In another, whites have a measure of equality. In yet another group, the role of the white participants fluctuates as ideological positions are argued and clarified.

One of the major conceptual differences which generate segmentation and the formation of new groups within the Black Power Movement concerns the means to be used in achieving common goals. Some, following Fanon, clearly advocate the use of force and violence. Others oppose this view vehemently; they insist on non-violent means, and deplore riots. Still others consider violence as an undesirable but necessary means to an end. They reject it ideologically but admit reluctantly that it has often succeeded in situations where reason and peaceful means have failed. There are also wide differences of opinion about the type of violence that should or should not be used. Each of these different views provides a point of organizational segmentation and a motive for cell formation and manpower recruitment.

Reticulation

According to Webster, something that is reticulate is weblike, resembling a network—with crossing and intercrossing lines. We have chosen this term to describe an organization in which the cells, or nodes, are tied together, not through any central point, but rather through intersecting sets of personal relationships and other intergroup linkages. We have shown how Pentecostal and Black Power groups constantly split, combine, and proliferate. Now we shall examine the way in which these nodes in the network of the movement intersect and are linked into a reticulate macrostructure. The linkages between cells are both personal and organizational; ties of various types operate at different levels of organization.

Personal ties between members. Individual members of different local groups are associated through pre-existing ties of kinship, friendship or other close relationships. More ties based on similar experiences in the movement are formed after the individual has been drawn into the movement. Both in Pentecostalism and in Black Power, individual members have personal networks of brother members in groups other than their own. Members frequently cross back and forth, participating irregularly in the activities of their friends' or relatives' groups. Some, in fact, are core group members of more than one group with different goals and functions.

A Pentecostal, for example, may attend Sunday services at one church as well as the midweek Bible study sessions or home prayer meetings of other churches or independent groups. A Black Power participant may be active in an African culture study group, in addition to serving with a black patrol force. The membership of cell groups in both movements, then, is far from static. It fluctuates as members come and go from one group to another, thereby forming personal links between numerous groups. Another type of linkage derives from personal associations between members of a "mother" and "daughter" cell who were members of a single group before the split. Frequently, ideological differences or a geographical move induces individuals to identify with a different group, but personal ties with individuals in the old group remain, serving as channels through which communication continues.

Personal ties between leaders. Similar networks of friendship or kinship ties between leaders of local groups may link a few groups into close association; or, such relationships may connect hundreds of groups across the country in loose and indirect ways. Some of these ties are used to create informal organizational linkages. Others are linked simply through periodic visits of one leader who speaks to or works with another's group for a time. This leadership exchange system often operates across community, state, and even national boundaries. The leader of one group may be a follower in another; this provides an additional type of cross-linkage between cells.

Traveling evangelists. Pentecostal evangelists hold revival meetings and prayer sessions in varying localities throughout the United States and, in some cases, the world. The network of each evangelist characteristically includes a mix of organized and established Pentecostal bodies, loosely bound independent groups, and a few personally devoted individuals who may or may not be affiliated with a group. Sponsorship and financing usually come from the same mix, with some evangelists depending chiefly upon donations from the established groups, and others relying primarily upon contributions from devoted individuals. No single evangelist or teacher appeals to all Pentecostal groups in any locality, nor would all participants in the movement in any one city forgather in one place at one time for an evangelist-led revival.

Black Power spokesmen such as Stokely Carmichael and Rap Brown, and—more recently—Dick Gregory, Ralph Abernathy, and Playthell Benjamin, travel widely to talk to various groups. Again, not all segments of Black Power in any city gather to hear any one of them, but each draws an audience from more than one wing of the movement. Recently, movement spokesmen whose activities have been circumscribed in the United States have extended the network to the Caribbean, South America, and Africa.

Other participants in both movements travel to organize rallies, crusades, demonstrations, or religious revivals, but do not share the spotlight as speakers. These may be called traveling organizational articulators and they are important links in the reticulation of the cells.

Ritual activities. The temporary groups that arrange for and gather to hear these traveling evangelists make possible another type of linkage which cuts across and binds the organizational cells of the movement. Such linkages might be called unifying events or rituals.

In Pentecostalism revival meetings—or, as Neo-Pentecostals sometimes prefer to call them, three or four day "missions"—are well known. Members of many different Pentecostal churches, informal groups, and "hidden" groups attend such meetings. Revivals emphasize movement unity. Two of the most obvious functions of such revivals are, of course, to promote religious fervor and to intensify commitment. Less obvious functions are the reporting of trials and triumphs of the movement elsewhere, requests for support for groups not otherwise organizationally connected, and the communication of ideological refinements. Movement unity is powerfully dramatized through intense group prayer for distant participants, as well as through enthusiastic singing of hymns and songs known throughout the world of Pentecostalism.

The Black Power Movement has its counterparts in rallies, marches, boycotts, demonstrations, and confrontations. Rituals include chants and songs known throughout the movement as well as symbolic gestures, attire, and signs bearing slogans. Again, the activities of the movement beyond the local scene are emphasized. Some demonstrations accomplish this by drawing participants from other cities and organizations other than the sponsoring one, even though the issue may be local—open housing in a specific neighborhood, for example. Movement linkages between cells as well as a sense of common purpose are also enhanced by the type of demonstrations that occur all over the country following an event such as the death of Martin Luther King, or the indictment of Huey Newton. Still another way of promoting movement reticulation is to invite an outside spokesman to address or advise a group involved in a purely local confrontation. Typically, this spokesman will not only report movement activities in other areas, but will also solicit support for them. Such ritual activities emphasize movement unity; they tend to lessen local factionalism by requiring the cooperation of a variety of local groups.

Such cooperation was demonstrated recently during a week-long Black Power "revival" on a university campus. The ostensible purpose was a small-scale local issue—the indictment of a few leaders of a black student group for alleged misconduct during a sit-in. Five nationally known spokesmen, three with retinues, came to speak and advise. One was a Black Panther, another a Black Muslim, the third a leader of an economic development and self-help program, and the fourth a specialist on black history and culture. The fifth was a militant labor organizer. They used the occasion to relate the local issue to activities of the brothers across the nation. The logistics of managing the week's program, including a giant march to the courthouse, required the creation of task forces on which members of different local movement groups served. The week unified the movement at the local level, and also unified the local black community.

National or regional associations.   There are several large-scale, nationally organized associations with members who are also members of local cells. These large-scale organizations may be temporary or permanent in nature.

The largest and most significant of these in Pentecostalism—and one of the most important elements in the infrastructure of the movement—is the Full Gospel Businessman's Fellowship International (FGBFI). According to Pentecostal historian John Nichol (179) this association has "conducted dinner meetings in nearly every major ballroom in this country and abroad." The two founders of the FG-BFI, men who were reared in traditional Pentecostalism and who have attained considerable educational and economic status, have been instrumental in the spread of the movement across social, economic, and denominational lines. Its meetings are attended by "Spirit-filled" Christians of all types; its members are also members of a wide variety of local churches, both Pentecostal and non-Pentecostal.

A former FGBFI stalwart recently rebelled against what he considered an attempt by FGBFI leaders to impose too many rules and regulations on the evangelistic activities of its members. He and a group of followers formed a new international association which proclaims that the time has come for those led in the Spirit to march "Beyond Pentecostalism." This association has been growing in numbers and expanding its operations into Latin America and the Caribbean. Though a rival of the FGBFI, the two organizations are linked by personal relationships among certain members. A few, in fact, consider themselves members of both groups and hold that each group has a different and complementary role in accomplishing the will of God.

The FGBFI, it should be noted, forms a type of cross-group linkage in the Pentecostal network that is different from linkages in the denominationally organized bodies such as the Assemblies of God, the Church of God, the United Pentecostal Church, the Pentecostal Holiness Church, and scores of other national or regionally organized bodies. These hierarchically organized denominations are more like super-cells in the body of the movement. All members of these bodies are members of a local church in that one denomination. Members of FGBFI, on the other hand, are members of various types of groups within the movement. They may be members of an Assemblies of God church or a Pentecostal Holiness church; they may also be members of any one of hundreds of independent churches or home meeting groups. Finally, they may be "hidden" members of non-Pentecostal churches.

A similar type of cross-linking association was reported in the Mau Mau movement by anthropologist Donald Barnett. The Kenya Young Stars Association of young guerrilla fighters cut across various territorial groups of Mau Mau participants. This provided an important basis for unity in a movement which was, in fact, polycephalous in spite of the myth of single leadership (299).

A Black Power counterpart was the Poor People's March in 1968 which drew participants from different types of local groups all over the country. The locally organized committee in one particular city, which also represents more than one local Black Power cell, continues to function as the Poor People's Liberation Committee. It is articulated to similar cell-linking groups in other cities.

Other national linking groups are CORE, SNCC, SCLC, NAACP, and the Urban League. The latter two or possibly three are comparable to the denominational bodies within Pentecostalism. They are hierarchically organized national groups which maintain local NAACP and Urban Leagues in different cities. These groups could be described as the super-cells of the Black Power Movement. They were once considered too moderate to be called Black Power groups. They were Civil Rights groups, the soil from which Black Power sprang. They are now, however, becoming increasingly articulated to the more militant movement. The 9 August 1968 issue of *Time* reported the "conversion to Black Power" of Whitney Young, executive director of the national Urban League. Militants who had previously attacked him as an arch-conservative now welcomed him as a brother. The national Urban League is now directing significant amounts of its considerable financial resources into what Young termed "Soul" or "Ghetto Power." One local Urban League publishes a newsletter providing information about the activities of a wide range of organizationally separate Black Power groups.

Ideological linkage. An additional basis for unity in a decentralized, segmented organization is ideology. Pentecostal ideology is communicated across the network by the traveling evangelists and teachers, by the discussions, lectures, and sermons that accompany the interaction of individuals and groups, and by Pentecostal radio programs and publications. The ideology undergirds the movement's ability to organize diversity. Such activities provide impressive evidence of the power of an idea which, held with conviction, effectively links groups which are organizationally disparate. The ideology is, perhaps, the key to the infrastructure of the movement. In spite of the fact that personal, organizational, and ideological differences continually split groups, the conceptual commonality of the Baptism experience and the conceptual authority of the non-human leader provide a basis for continuing interaction between the resulting splinters. United in core belief, the Pentecostals can proceed to unite against genuine opposition, or against what they believe to be opposition.

That ideology can be both a source of organizational fission and a basis for overall unity derives from a characteristic of movement ideology which will be discussed in more detail in chapter VII. At this point, we note only that certain basic beliefs are a powerful force for unity in both the Black Power and Pentecostal Movements.

Extra-movement linkages.   The structure of both the Black Power and the Pentecostal Movements depends on the reticulation formed by various types of linkages among otherwise unrelated cells or groups of cells. The spread of both movements, however, also involves some extra-movement linkages. As noted, Pentecostals come from a broad range of social, economic, political, and religious backgrounds. Many members have personal networks of friends, associates, and contacts outside the Pentecostal community. These, as we shall see, are the links through which recruitment to the movement is constantly occurring. Participants in the movement may also call upon sympathetic non-Pentecostals for financial or other aid. In turn, Pentecostals often ask fellow members within the movement to assist a non-Pentecostal friend. These extra-movement linkages do not always persuade the non-Pentecostal to become a "Spirit-baptized" participant in the movement, but we have found that they often constitute an important source of funds. One influential non-Pentecostal who had contributed financially to the movement was introduced to a group of Pentecostals by its leader not as "brother" but as "cousin—a close cousin." These "cousin" linkages tie the Pentecostal infrastructure to the overall structure of the established social system within which Pentecostalism exists; such links help Pentecostals to deal with the system to their advantage.

Obviously, most Black Power groups depend even more heavily on extra-movement linkages. Through these linkages, which are also based on pre-existing personal ties, Black Power groups are funded, communicate with whites, implement many goals, and promote social change. Extra-movement linkages are various—to certain representatives of government agencies; to private foundations; to white businesses, churches, and other civic groups; to white individuals; and to what we have described as white positive response groups.

Both intra- and extra-movement linkages provide channels not only for the flow of funds, but—equally important—also for communication. The "grapevine" communication and intelligence system, based on interlocking personal and group networks within the infrastructure, is extremely effective. For example, news of the arrest of a young Twin Cities Pentecostal convert for "disturbing the peace" by speaking in tongues on the streets at night was known within twenty-four hours by members of "Spirit-filled" groups throughout the area. Some of these were, and probably still are, quite ignorant of the existence of each other.

Another example is that of a Lutheran pastor who has been severely censured by his denomination for professing involvement in the charismatic revival. News of his "persecution" has spread to Pentecostal groups throughout the United States, Canada, and Latin America, by means of "ham" radio, traveling evangelists, letters, and word-of-mouth.

The flow of funds between Pentecostal groups has already been mentioned. While each group raises funds by fairly conventional means and by emphasis on tithing, personalized Pentecostal giving to individuals or leaders who have provided spiritual inspiration or help to an individual creates further linkages between organizationally distinct groups. Funds, which flow through the same network channels as do information and news, constitute a unifying force in a decentralized structure.

The Black Power grapevine is even more effective. Some critics feel that if it were not for the mass media, the influence of Black Power demagogues would be minimal. They also believe that press coverage of local riots incites groups in other cities or in other parts of the same city. These people do not understand the grapevine of the ghetto and of the Black Power Movement. As one participant said, "You whites, spread out in the suburbs, are the ones who have a communications gap. In the ghetto with everyone living on top of each other, there is no communication problem!" The Black Power Movement has simply extended the ghetto communication system into a nationwide network that can, if necessary, function quite independently of newspaper, radio, and television.

In a decentralized, segmented organization, the importance of the linkages which tie the whole into a network cannot be overemphasized. It is even more important to recognize the role of personal kinship, friendship, and other associational ties. In an organization where no single individual even begins to know of all of the groups involved in the movement, and where there is no central headquarters through which information and authority can be channeled, an effective and very flexible unity can be maintained through personal ties between committed individuals.

The Adaptive Functions of Decentralized, Segmented, Reticulate Structure

At first consideration, one might view organizational segmentation as a weakness, as a maladaptive characteristic for a movement—be it Pentecostalism, Black Power, or any other. Outside observers may well see in such segmentation only something amusing—a sure sign of significant deficiencies in the movement and its members. In fact, observers, even professed students of the phenomenon, may focus so much on the fact of schism that they are misled into thinking that here is no movement, but only a collection of separate enthusiasms and divided efforts. In short, they miss the forest for the trees. Or, more accurately, for the diversity of the trees. There is a certain amount of confusion evident in the view that movements "suffer from" fissiparous tendencies and schisms, yet somehow succeed in unifying previously isolated or even hostile groups on a new basis (51, 54). This "in spite of" bias was clear in an article in the 2 September 1968 *Newsweek*. Reporting on the emergence of the Palestinian Arab guerrilla force as a "political winner," the magazine observed that such a group could function effectively "despite" the traditional Arab penchant for intramural bickering. Bitter rivalries within guerrilla ranks were assumed to have a weakening effect. The group's operational successes and the respect it has gained from Middle Eastern rulers were therefore assumed to have occurred in spite of this organizational weakness.

More recently, the press reported organizational splits within the Black Panthers and the Students for a Democratic Society. The early demise of these groups was predicted with glee. It is apparent, however, that the results of their schisms have been not only a redefinition of goals and stepped-up recruitment, but also the creation of additional thorns in the flesh of the establishment. John Herbers, "veteran civil rights reporter," was reported in *Time* (6 June 1969) as surprised because the various participants and committees within the Black Power Movement display such unity of purpose "despite organizational fragmentation."

When the success of movements is reported as having occurred "because of" rather than "in spite of" organizational fission and lack of cohesion, we will have come to understand the nature of movement dynamics much more clearly. Organizational unity is functional in a steady-state social institution designed to maintain social stability and the status quo. Segmentation and "internecine dogfighting" are functional in a social institution designed for rapid growth and the implementation of social change. Anthropologist Donald Barnett clearly recognizes and illustrates the adaptive functions of this decentralized structure in his study of the Mau Mau movement, even though his main emphasis is on the disadvantages of factionalism (299).

Many members of both the Pentecostal and the Black Power Movements also share the conventional bias. They deplore organizational variation and schism, and thus reflect the bureaucratic attitude toward division as a weakness. Blacks are, perhaps, especially sensitive on this point. They recognize that whites have ridiculed, played upon, and profited by black disunity. One of the goals of the Black Power Movement is to achieve power through unity. A cultural postulate held by many Americans, regardless of movement involvement, is that it is simply inefficient to have many different organizations, with supposedly similar goals, duplicating efforts and seeming to work at cross-purposes. Instead it is felt that all efforts should be co-ordinated under some central direction. There is a certain inconsistency between this assumption and the spirit of competition and individual initiative Americans also value highly. Apparently it is felt that entrepreneurial competition is out of place in a social movement or in any concerted response to it made by the established order.

We have found, on the contrary, that these very characteristics are highly adaptive in that they promote the growth of the movement, prevent effective suppression of it, and facilitate the desired personal and social changes.

There are those in the Black Power Movement who, in spite of their sensitivity to the problem of disunity, note that militants, moderates, and even conservatives can contribute to the Black Power cause so long as they feel a common bond. Pentecostals often perceive the value of schisms even though organizational divisions seem to negate unity in Christ. They have a conceptual basis for this acceptance in Paul's image of the many and diverse members of the one Body of Christ.

We have identified four functions of this decentralized, segmented, and reticulate form of organization which are adaptive in the growth of the movement and in the accomplishment of its purpose: maintenance of security, multipenetration, social innovation, and minimization of failures.

Maintenance of security. A segmentary, acephalous organization limits the ability of the establishment to penetrate, gather intelligence about, and counteract the movement. It protects the identity of leaders; more importantly, it assures a constant supply of leaders and replacements, should any be lost. This element of security is perhaps not so important in American Pentecostalism, and probably not so crucial in Black Power as many militants believe. It is, however, very frustrating to the establishment contemplating these movements to observe such a myriad of groups without one leader. To some it seems as if they are facing, on the one hand, a spontaneous explosion at the grass roots level; and, on the other, a many-headed hydra. This has kept the movement one up on its opposition time and again.

In Haiti, Pentecostal segmentation clearly led the establishment (composed of government, Catholic, and voodoo elements) to underestimate the size and potential of the movement. What they see is not the reticulated unity of Pentecostalism, but rather the existence of scores of small, apparently struggling cells. The impression the establishment receives is one of weak, diffuse, unorganized sets of different religious sects. When we asked a government official "Is Pentecostalism growing in Haiti?" he answered, "Pentecostalism? What's that? Oh, you mean all of those little churches out there? They are nothing of concern." A Catholic priest responded in much the same fashion. Further questioning revealed that they had little idea of the growth of the movement even in their own districts. François Duvalier, dictator of Haiti, has encouraged the growth of various Protestant churches to balance against the power of the Catholics and voodoo. He feels that he can be strong only so long as he thus divides the power of his people. He might be less charitable toward Pentecostalism if he perceived the manner in which its cells interrelate and stand together.

A few American blacks, reacting to the fear that the white establishment will seek to penetrate, subvert, and crush the Black Power Movement, endorse decentralization and segmentation as a good method of survival. They feel that if they have many leaders, Whitey cannot wipe out the movement simply by eliminating a single central authority.

Whether or not they are justified in fearing such a degree of repression, it is true that decentralized, acephalous structures are more difficult to suppress. They are also more confusing to deal with. Members of the establishment are forever asking who is the leader of the rebel activity, be it Pentecostalism or Black Power. It is similar to the problem faced by early settlers in America. They searched for a leader among various essentially acephalous Indian tribes in order to make "lasting" treaties for land, or to ensure peace. The whites were subsequently surprised and angered by rebellions led by other Indian chiefs who the whites assumed were bound by the treaty. They could not conceive of a tribe or nation without a single source of authority. In similar fashion the British in Africa attempted to identify *the* leaders of various segmented and acephalous African tribes. Frequently they found that those tribes which were centralized, hierarchically organized, and culturally "advanced" were initially more difficult to conquer, for they could command a standing army. But the acephalous, segmentary tribes, while easier to subdue at first, were far more difficult to control over the long run. British administrators often felt that they were reaching in to grab the center of a bowl of jelly.

In a recent urban riot, the governor of the state called in a "traveling evangelist" representing one sector of the Black Power Movement to plead with members of local groups to put an end to violence. Local black leaders said afterward that they felt this merely made the situation worse. The apparent assumption that local groups were under the visitor's control angered these same groups.

The opposite assumption, taken by other members of the white community, was that the local riot had no connection whatsoever with a nationwide confrontation between whites and Negroes. They preferred to see the riot simply as "Negro delinquency." Both actions taken to counter the movement were obviously ineffective. This conceptual confusion about the nature of movement organization provides security for the movement as a whole, an extra protection against recognition and suppression.

In Communist insurgencies the value of cell differentiation is well recognized and utilized. The aim is to flood a country with a diversity of cells of varying types, missions, and compositions. These cells establish, or subvert to their purposes, all manner of groups and organizations, some overt, some covert.

One difference between this planned Communist structure of cell differentiation and that of the movements under consideration is that the Communist cell system is essentially an institutionalized and routinized insurgency plan. It is a result of a series of conscious acts of will and design. Similar cell differentiation occurs in Black Power, Pentecostalism, and other movements without conscious planning or centralized direction. It is inherent in movement dynamics which are, in turn, part of a larger social process. Communists have simply recognized the value of segmented movement organization, and institutionalized it. Such institutionalization succeeds because while Communism is the established order in certain nations, it is still a movement in other areas of the world. Movement dynamics, once understood, can be exploited, and to certain extent consciously directed. There is evidence that in the early stages of the growth of Communism, at least in China, cell differentiation was *not* by design, and was *not* centrally controlled.

Robert Payne (339), in his biography of Mao Tse-tung, states that while the First Congress of the Communist Party of China was meeting in the summer of 1921 in Shanghai, "other Chinese Communists, *unknown to them*, were meeting thousands of miles away." In Paris, Berlin, Tokyo, and Moscow, Chinese gathered "and on their own determined that China would become a Communist state." No monolithic, centralized control here. Payne goes on to note that even in America there were small Chinese Communist parties. "Hardly any of these parties knew of the existence of others." He considers the emergence and varied efforts of these different Communist groups as "haphazard." He notes that they were working in slow, secret, and essentially trial-and-error ways, attempting not only to determine how to take over and change China, but also to understand what Communism was and what it would become in the Chinese context. These various groups received their stimulus from a number of sources, not all of which were Russian. Even the "evangelists" from Russia *at that time* differed in their interpretation of Communism and in their ideas of what should be done. According to Payne, a "strange medley" of Russian Comintern advisors were in "violent disagreement" about both the goals and the methods of Communism in general and Chinese Communism in particular (pp. 76-79). A similar picture of the early stages of Communism in Korea has been described by political scientist C. I. Eugene Kim (personal communication).

A second significant difference between the planned Communist use of cell differentiation at the present time and that of such movements as Black Power and Pentecostalism is the nature of communication between cells. Communist movements directed from Moscow or Peking are not only centralized but essentially subversive. Therefore, they must protect themselves from counter-intelligence. They must disguise the chain of command and sever lateral communication between cells. In Pentecostal and Black Power Movements, there is an integrating structure *because* of this lateral personal contact and communication between cells. As we have noted, the reticulate structure of the movement organization depends upon such personal ties and grapevine communication.

The Communist insurgent movements cannot afford to have one cell know about another: the requirements of insurgent security do not permit it. If each cell knows only about itself, the counter-insurgency force will not be able to learn about the personnel, plans, or activities of the other cells simply by penetrating or subverting a particular cell, or getting one of its members to talk. On the other hand, if each cell knows about the others, then the counter-insurgents could round up one cell after another on the information initially gained by penetrating only one cell. The Viet Cong certainly would seem to adhere to this dictum of cell isolation. Their security in such events as the 1968 Tet offensive was superb.

But if each cell, each guerrilla band, each group of saboteurs, or each group in charge of collecting food and supplies does not know about the other cells, how can joint action in major offensives be initiated? The answer is that each cell is articulated to a central command post rather than laterally to a host of linked cells. Thus the Communist insurgent movements have both central control and segmentary structure. Communication runs along the spokes of a wheel to a nucleus rather than laterally between cells.

One way to determine whether or not a movement is Communist dominated is to find out if the cells communicate freely on a lateral basis. It is perfectly possible for certain cells within any movement to be penetrated and directed by Communists. But if the majority of cells are communicating laterally through personal ties, traveling evangelists, and grapevine communication, that movement as a whole cannot be considered a Communist front. It will in fact resist such efforts at Communist control just as it resists all centralization efforts, even those initiated by its own leaders.

Whether a movement is structured for vertical communication between cell segments and a directing center, as in the Communist infiltration model, or whether it is an acephalous organization with lateral communication between cells, the process of segmentation is its best insurance against effective suppression.

Multipenetration. The reticulate organization is especially adapted to the task of spreading the movement across class and cultural boundaries. As we have seen, segmentation within Pentecostalism, for whatever reason, results in the establishment of groups with all sorts of organizational forms. They range from the most egalitarian to the most autocratic, and include all sizes and all degrees of organizational complexity. No matter what a potential convert's predilections are in terms of role within a religious group, there exists a Pentecostal group which can provide it. The same is true of ideological variation, methods of recruitment, modes of commitment, and type of goals and means. This organizational smorgasbord enables the Pentecostal Movement to meet a broad range of psychological as well as sociological needs, and to draw adherents from the widest spread of socioeconomic, educational, religious, and cultural backgrounds. Similar variation is found in the Black Power Movement. Unless these particular movements are unique in this respect—and we maintain that they are not—the prevailing view of a movement as something which appeals only to a particular psychological type, or to a certain social class, must be challenged.

The multipenetration function of schism was illustrated by a Pentecostal mission to a Caribbean island. As news of the mission's arrival traveled along the communication grapevine, members came from various cities. Each member knew at least a few persons in the group, but no one knew everyone who had gathered. Travel arrangements, accommodations, preliminary contacts with local residents, and the designation of certain mission members as principal speakers or counselors had been efficiently handled by the "Spirit-filled" businessman whose group was sponsoring the mission. The purpose of the mission —in terms of which group of islanders were to be contacted, how they should be contacted, or when any particular action was to be taken —was left to the leading of the Holy Spirit. As a result, sharp and occasionally painful division developed within the group on all of these matters. Cleavage occurred, as might be expected, along the lines of pre-existing friendships, socio-economic and educational differences, differing sacramental orientations, and, to a certain extent, the personality types of the designated mission leaders.

If mission members had not been deeply and personally committed individuals, the result of this cleavage would have weakened the capacity of the group to act in fulfillment of its purposes. However, the shared concept of equal access to and empowering by the Holy Spirit, while it did not prevent the expenditure of emotional energy on group in-fighting, did heighten participants' desire to make contacts outside the group. Because of differences of opinion about the original purpose of the mission, some of the group focused on contacts with influential white residents on the island and with the local Anglican church. Others engaged in evangelical witnessing on side

walks and in the marketplace. One group went to a school run by a
member of the black elite. Another sought fellowship with an American missionary at a rural mission station who had experienced the
Baptism. Still others were invited to small local and rural churches
to witness. A few even decided the purpose of the mission was to
assist those mission members who were still seeking the Baptism
of the Holy Spirit, or those who had not experienced speaking with
tongues. The success with which this was accomplished within the
group itself fed the enthusiasm and commitment of all group members and provided a unifying force. Had the group been in agreement about which island residents were to be contacted, fewer
residents would have been aware of its presence. The heat generated
by dissension within the group appeared to intensify the individual
commitment to the will of God, and heightened the charisma with
which each person carried his message. This small and temporary
mission group was a microcosm in which schism functioned to increase multipenetration into different sociological "niches." The same
processes of decentralization and segmentation can be seen in the
macrocosm of the movement.

Anthropologists have examined the segmentary principle as it
operates in various African, Asian, and Middle Eastern tribal societies.
Some have seen how this type of structure, which is very adaptive as a
mechanism for predatory expansion, can enable a tribe to expand into
new territory at the expense of the inhabitants. In one instance, segments of a predatory tribe moved into and occupied small niches of
land bordering territory of a neighboring tribe. These units were
small enough not to seem a threat, and flexible enough to experiment
with exploiting the physical environment by trial and error. They
were not bound by directives from a distant political authority. But
when the neighboring tribe whose land they were infiltrating finally
became concerned over the piecemeal invasion and attempted expul-
sion by force, the scattered invading segments not only combined
but also called in reinforcements from the homeland population. Pro-
claiming common ancestry, common tribal name, and common tribal
deities, and under temporary joint leadership, these groups defeated
the neighboring tribe and took permanent possession of the disputed
land. The emergency over, they returned to their segmented structure, quarreled again among themselves, and began to split up, moving

out still farther into new territories in small, probing segments to repeat the process of predatory expansion (7, 313, 315, 317, 322, 336, 362, 371).

As we have already noted, neither the Pentecostal nor the Black Power Movement constitutes a total society; nor is their kind of organization primitive. It is similar to tribal structure only in that its segmentary nature enables participants to move into various types of social rather than physical "habitats," and to combine seemingly unrelated groups for temporary united action.

There is another aspect of multipenetration that is particularly noticeable in the Black Power Movement. It might be called escalation of effort. It usually—though not necessarily—involves personal competition between leaders. Often, after a militant segment of the movement turns to violence, a host of more moderate groups in the same city (and even throughout the country) benefit. Representatives of the establishment listen then to demands of both militants and moderates. On the grounds that they agree with the goals but not the means of the militants, members of the established order may in fact focus their positive response chiefly on the moderates. In any case, the obvious validity of at least some of the demands spurs white groups to provide money, jobs, housing, recognition, and even some political autonomy to certain segments of the black community. Because of this, black pride, moderate and militant, is fostered throughout the black community. Furthermore, there is a real increase in power for all blacks, which encourages a kind of escalation. As one segment of the Black Power spectrum goes militant and attracts public attention, others are motivated to step out and upstage it. One black community center, for example, announced certain demands which the Urban Coalition of that city would have to meet in order to avoid censure and further violence. Leaders of rival black groups immediately presented several additional demands. The leader of the group whose demands are most successful attracts to his group a number of "floaters" in the movement (those persons uncommitted to any segment) as well as members of other groups. Rival leaders must then act dramatically in order to regain a posture of dynamic leadership or of militancy. Through such constant one-upmanship, the entire movement pushes rapidly toward its common goals.

We have examined the advantages of the segmentary structure

of movements. A crucial disadvantage is that those opposed to the movement can play one segment against another, or one leader against a rival. If this occurs, critics can attempt to explain the movement away as the product of a few self-seeking entrepreneurs. But if the segments are genuinely reticulate, if they share a common ideology, and if they submerge their differences in the face of opposition when crucial issues are at stake, then the movement has great power as a result of its inner divisions.

Social innovation. Perhaps the most adaptive function of segmentation and decentralized control is the promotion of innovation in the design and implementation of social, political, economic, or religious change. Certain segments in both the Pentecostal and the Black Power Movements are content to hold old ground. They have taken over and are satisfied with traditional forms of church organization; certain Black Power adherents have borrowed military or other bureaucratic organizational patterns from the existing power structure. But many groups in both movements are experimenting with different types of social organizations. They are also experimenting with a variety of ways to achieve common goals.

One American volunteer evangelist-missionary went to Colombia "because the Lord called him there." He gave up a successful business as a contractor in a southern state and financed himself on the proceeds. Various American and Colombian Pentecostals in Colombia advised him where and how he might best serve the Lord. He followed a few of these suggestions, but none satisfied him; all were too much like what others were doing. He wanted what participants in Black Power would call "his own bag," in order to meet the drive and the desire to serve that his commitment had generated in him. He was finally "led of the Lord" to buy a farm in a rural village. He hopes to use this as a base to develop a hard core of Pentecostals who will teach the special principles in which he deeply believes. He is not particularly interested in promoting economic development along with his religious teachings. But he is terribly concerned about the intense personal conflicts which he observes dividing families and neighborhoods in the village. He seeks ways to reduce these conflicts and promote brotherly love. This is his "burden before the Lord."

In contrast, another American businessman travels extensively around the world as a crusader for his faith. He cares little about working with small handfuls of converts in a remote village. He would not even bother to notice personal conflicts. Instead, the burden the Lord has set on his shoulders is the conversion of leading figures in government and business. He has spoken to such leaders in Colombia and Haiti. In fact, he has had a private audience with Duvalier. He has prayed for the Lord's help in converting Fidel Castro and the leaders of the Soviet Union. He and a group of like-minded believers traveled to the Soviet Union and visited Cuba in the early days of Castro's take-over. This man is constantly experimenting with new ways and new avenues of approach to these "big men." One way is to continue to make money himself so that he can finance his enterprises and speak with big businessmen and government officials as an equal

A humbler Pentecostal was also called to minister to the Communists—in particular, Russian Communists. But he concentrated on school children in the play yards, people he met on the streets of Moscow, and those who came to the churches he was allowed to use as revival halls. This gentleman had three successful months in Russia and at the time of our research was home speaking to, praying with, and collecting "love offerings" from Pentecostal groups all over the United States. Government officials of the Soviet Union had granted him another five months in which to continue his work, and he was raising the funds for this endeavor. According to Nils Block Hoell's history of the movement, there are 500,000 Pentecostal converts in Russia (149).

There are many Pentecostal groups trying various types of communal living in large homes, trailer courts, or camps. They are finding practical ways to follow the example of the first Christians who "had all things common; and sold their possessions and goods, and parted them to all men, as every man had need" (Acts 2:44-45).

One young Baptist minister, soon after receiving the Baptism of the Holy Spirit, was led by the Lord to work with young drug addicts in New York. The rehabilitation center created by this explosive combination of youthful mainliners and a committed Baptist Pentecostal is now famous for its remarkable success (175, 204). It has also sparked so many similar centers in other cities across the country that it is known as a "movement within a movement."

Both Black Power groups and white positive response groups illustrate even more clearly the importance of segmentation in generating social innovation. Both kinds of groups are continually experimenting with new ways to communicate the need for change. Some have turned to mass media to accomplish this end. The educational television channel in one urban center carried a program called "It's Our Bag," which featured two masters of ceremony, one black and one white. For several weeks they attempted to provide a forum where blacks from all sectors of the black community could "tell it like it is." Through call-in questions and interviews with whites, they hoped to stimulate the needed dialogue about crises in the cities. Their approach to the program was flexible. They tried new formats and extended or cut their time according to need and response. "Black Voices" is a program of similar purpose in another large city.

One white positive response group received a large foundation grant to gather in one central data bank the best films, literature, records, television tapes, and kinescopes dealing with racism and the urban crisis. From this center, groups around the country can now draw materials for local use. Several other groups in other parts of the country arrived at the same idea quite independently and are pursuing their goals without foundation money. They have no intention of becoming subordinate to the more affluent group who received the grant, in spite of pressure for a merger.

Hundreds, perhaps thousands, of small groups of both blacks and whites are experimenting with ways to establish face-to-face communication across the "color line." Some try to do it on the basis of being "just housewives," some as members of civic groups. Some feel that the church provides a proper setting and a religious orientation, a common basis on which to attempt communication. All such efforts require social innovation, for existing institutions simply do not provide channels through which these people ordinarily meet on a face-to-face, talk-it-over basis.

"Buying black" has occurred to whites in different parts of the country as a means of fostering a greater degree of black ownership of economic resources. This takes a bit of innovating, since most white buyers who have been "converted" to this idea live in white neighborhoods and most black-owned stores are in the ghettos. One enterprising white man whose neighbors had agreed to buy black persuaded them to telephone their orders to the ghetto grocery store; he himself made the deliveries. After the enterprise had been publicized on radio and television, both he and the black owner of the grocery store found themselves flooded with orders. More innovation will be required to meet the delivery demands.

Everywhere black groups are experimenting with modes of self-government and with the creation of new types of social institutions. Some groups are attempting to develop tutoring programs to enrich an inadequate educational system which has not met community needs in the past. Demands for black studies departments and programs in universities are ubiquitous; they in turn are stimulating the development of courses and textbooks especially tailored to black needs. These demands, intersecting with those of white student movements, are generating new and effective approaches to education.

SNCC and other groups have attempted to create local political parties outside the traditional two-party system, which they believe has shut them out as a group.

Black cooperatives of various kinds are being tried on the assumption that they serve the black community's needs better than the business organization characteristic of the system which many consider to be exploitive. Youth groups in some communities are attempting to assume responsibility for family welfare problems that have been handled ineffectively by existing institutions. Youth associations, student groups, and organizations designed to police or patrol the black community are cropping up in city after city. As one black student leader said, "Sure, we'll make a lot of mistakes. We don't have a fixed blueprint for what we are doing or even for where we are going. We get along by trial and error." The latter is a disconcerting, costly, seemingly inefficient method, but it is the only alternative to overall planning.

Some of the black leaders as well as young whites engaged in student rebellions have assumed that if representatives of the established order wanted to change existing social structures, they could. It is becoming increasingly clear that even those who want change do not have any better ideas about the nature of appropriate alternatives than do the revolutionaries themselves. Even white positive response

groups have had to resort to the time-honored method of social innovation—trial and error. A bureaucratic, centrally directed organization is obviously ill adapted to this type of approach. It is within the
context of a decentralized, segmented structure that such innovation
can most easily take place.

Minimization of failures.   Innovation through trial and error results
in a variety of adaptive and successful social "mutations" which can
lead to constructive social change. It also results in a good many failures. In fact—and in this respect, social processes are analogous to
natural processes—there are many more failures than successes. Under the pressure of selective adaptation the maladaptive variant
simply passes out of existence. This can only occur on the social level,
however, with a decentralized, segmented structure. If a movement
has been centralized under the leadership and effective control of one
man, and he errs in his judgment, the whole movement is in jeopardy.
National Socialism was very successful under Hitler so long as he calculated accurately and everyone followed his directives. Decentralization and variation would have seemed disadvantageous in comparison. When Hitler made his serious mistakes, however, they were
monumental in consequence, and spelled the end of the movement as
a viable social structure. In a polycephalous movement, the errors
of one group or one leader have little, if any, effect on the others.
Group members can disband, re-form under new leadership, or simply
be absorbed into other groups, and the movement goes on. An attempt
at innovation which fails affects only those most closely associated
with it; in fact, such failure may aid others by its demonstration of
what will not work.

   To the bureaucratically minded, segmentation seems to involve a
great deal of unnecessary duplication of effort. There are those
within both the Black Power Movement and the white positive response groups who do in fact assume that a more rational design
would be one in which each segment did only one task. Presumably, a
group of decision-makers at the top could assign such tasks after careful evaluation. Technocrats and social planners still dream about rationally directed social change. The failure of one cell or segment
under these conditions, however, would seriously cripple the move-

ment as a whole. Duplication of effort provides expendability, and this is necessary in a movement, particularly one aimed at making revolutionary social changes.

Summary

A movement is neither an amorphous collectivity nor a highly centralized autocracy. It cannot be considered an imperfect bureaucracy, one which succeeds in spite of its lack of unity. Movement organization is of a different order entirely. It is a decentralized, segmented, and reticulate structure.

Leadership is charismatic rather than bureaucratic in nature. The personal commitment characteristic of movement participants results in a communicable charisma, so that effective leadership is not irrevocably tied to certain individuals. Furthermore, no single leader or group of leaders can make decisions binding on all participants or claim regulatory powers over the movement as a whole.

Segmentation and proliferation of groups within a movement occurs because of an ideology of personal access to power, because of pre-existing personal and social cleavages, because of personal competition, and because of ideological differences.

The organizational segments of a movement are linked into one reticulate structure by personal ties between members and between local group leaders, by the activities of traveling evangelists or spokesmen, by some cross-cutting organizations, and by certain basic ideological themes.

Such an organization is adaptive because these characteristic features make the movement difficult to suppress, allow it maximum penetration of different socio-economic and cultural groups, and encourage the quest for social innovation.

IV

Recruitment

A second factor which we believe to be of importance in understanding the spread of a movement is face-to-face recruitment. No matter how a typical participant describes his reasons for joining the movement, or what motives may be suggested by a social scientist on the basis of deprivation, disorganization, or deviancy models, it is clear that the original decision to join required some contact with the movement. This is such an obvious fact that it is generally overlooked in analyses of movements. As soon as we began to realize that neither the deprivation theory nor the psychological maladjustment theory was satisfactorily explaining our Pentecostal data, we began to pay more attention to the exact nature of the individual's first contact with the movement. We found few cases, either among our questionnaire respondents or in our case histories, in which the original contact was not a personal one. This contact almost always involved a significant, pre-existing relationship—a relative, a close friend, a neighbor, an influential associate of some sort with whom the new convert had had meaningful interaction prior to recruitment.

Recruitment patterns in our intensively studied groups support this observation. Examples appeared during our study of a small store-front church affiliated with a national Pentecostal sect. Of the twenty-one members, three had been brought up in a Pentecostal church and had therefore been recruited by parents. Four of the adult converts had been drawn in by a relative—a brother, a spouse, a mother, and an aunt. Five experienced their first contact with the movement through a couple whom they had all known previously and intimately in a fundamentalist religious service organization. One came into Pentecostalism because of the witness of a neighbor, one had been a friend of the pastor and his brother, and one was introduced to the idea of the Baptism of the Holy Spirit by a close friend with whom she had both worked and spent most of her leisure time. Six young people who had been a closely knit social group for several years were recruited by one of their number who lived for a time with the pastor and his family.

In another group, a larger, independent church, the sample of fifty-six represented about three-fourths of the total membership. Of these, fifty-two percent had been converted to Pentecostalism through a relative, twelve percent by friends, eight percent by an employer-employee or similar over-under relationship. Only four percent reported that they had been introduced to Pentecostalism through the radio broadcasts sponsored by the church or because they had simply wandered by the church and stopped in. Twenty-four percent reported that they had been drawn into the movement by the direct action of God.

The minister of this particular church did not like the approach taken in our interviews on this point because he felt that we were "explaining away" the action of God in human hearts. He felt we implied that he had built his church because of his family and social relationships, and not because he was God's instrument. On this issue we did not, and would not, argue. We merely pointed out our belief that God *does* use human instruments, and that our task was to determine the type of relationship most frequently used. We found, in fact, after further conversation with several of the twenty-four percent who reported conversion as a direct act of God, that significant human relationships had been involved—in their cases, relationships with relatives or friends.

Similar patterns were found in an independent church of Neo Pentecostals. Where relatives served as the recruiting channels, spouse and sibling were the most frequently mentioned. Friends or neighbors responsible for the recruitment of others were those with whom the respondent had had almost daily interaction previously. This group was established by "Spirit-filled" converts from main-line denomina tions to whom church membership had always been of importance. Church activities had involved participation of the entire family for most of them, and had been a channel through which meaningful friendships were established. Not surprisingly, most of the friends named as recruiters were of this type.

Data from our questionnaires revealed some very interesting differences in the recruitment patterns of the four main types of Pentecostal groups ranged along the institutionalization continuum. Relatives are responsible for recruiting seventy-one percent of the established Pentecostal sect members. This declines to fifty percent for the members of large independent groups of fifteen or twenty years' duration. Relatives recruited forty-two percent of those in the recently organized independent smaller groups, and only thirty-two percent of the "hiddens." Of these, parents are, predictably, the most important type of relative at the sect end of the continuum, and spouses the most important at the hidden end. Friends as recruiters increase in importance as relatives decrease. Superimposing the socio-economic differences between these groups upon the differences in recruiting relationships, it would appear that kinship ties are more significant at the lower end of the socio-economic scale, and various types of non-kin associations more important at the upper end.

These differences are also related to the fact that, with few exceptions, the second-generation Pentecostals in our sample were members of established sect churches. Second-generation Pentecostals are, almost by definition, recruited by parents. We found an interesting statistical correlation between recruiting relationships and degree of commitment to the movement (as we have defined commitment in chapter V). Pentecostals in our sample who had been brought up in a Pentecostal church, or who reported that they had been recruited by a parent, spoke in tongues significantly *less* often than Pentecostals who were adult converts recruited by a friend, neighbor, spouse, sibling, or relative other than a parent. This difference in manner of recruitment to a movement is relevant only for those movements which have been in existence long enough for there to be a second generation. The difference is very important in understanding the relationship between recruitment and commitment to the movement, as both relate to the different types of organizations within the movement.

Our field observations have convinced us that while facilitating conditions such as deprivation or social disorganization may predispose people to join a movement, close association with a committed "witness" or participant is empirically far more explanatory. We have seen the Pentecostal Movement spread by means of such relationships into groups in which, according to current theories, it should not have had the slightest chance of success.

Evidence that pre-existing recruitment relationships are more accurate indicators of movement growth than conditions of deprivation was found in the store-front Pentecostal church. In spite of the economic deprivation characterizing the area in which it is located, and in spite of the highly charismatic personality of the minister, the church was not growing at the time of our investigation. The membership already included the recruitable relatives of the original core group. Recruitment efforts, although zealous, were expended unsuccessfully upon strangers living in the vicinity. Many of them responded to the religious faith of the minister and welcomed his visits. But in terms of movement growth, recruitment did not occur.

Norman Cohn, student of millenarian movements, has said that such movements do not appeal to those who are well integrated in kinship groups or cohesive local communities (14). Other observers commonly consider any type of movement as something which attracts socially disorganized people suffering from disruption of family or small group ties. The closely knit Pentecostal church, the Communist cell group, or the Black Power community center is seen as a surrogate family or primary group, meeting the needs of converts for identity and close associations. Pentecostalism is therefore supposed to appeal especially to migrants or to dislocated rural people moving to urban centers.

We found, however, that Pentecostalism has equal appeal for lifelong urbanites whose pre-conversion family solidarity was unquestionable. We also found that the spread of the movement among supposedly lonely Puerto Ricans in New York (118) was matched by its spread among the rural villages at home in Puerto Rico where family ties were intact and village structure had not been disrupted (178). Our own observations among the Otomi Indians in the mountains outside Mexico City supported the account by Donald McGavran of conversions involving kinship and village ties. "Group decision by two and three families (and by twenty and thirty families, too) became an ordinary mode of conversion. The faith, once lit in a people, has a chance to grow soundly and rapidly along the all-important web of relationships" (177).

Observable social changes resulting from conversion to Pentecostalism indicate that conversion by groups of families or by whole villages was not simply superficial or syncretistic. There is a similar report of the rise of a "spontaneous indigenous church" in rural Argentina. A few tribesmen who had been converted to Pentecostalism while working as wage laborers in an urban center returned to introduce religious and social changes that diffused through existing family and tribal organizations (170). In such cases it is not the disruption of social ties that facilitates the spread of the movement. Those very pre-existing relationships which constitute the tribal and village structure are the means by which recruitment occurs.

Recruitment patterns in Colombia and Haiti, as we observed them, provide strong support for the importance of pre-existing social networks as the mechanism for the spread of Pentecostalism in these countries. One Haitian woman who had recruited many of her relatives thought this point was rather obvious. "Of course I bring them to the Lord," she said. "Wouldn't you share something good with your family?"

We have found not only that Pentecostalism flourishes among socially well-integrated groups, but also that Pentecostal churches, such as the store-front church, which attempt to recruit from the truly disorganized do *not* grow. We studied one urban neighborhood where American Indians were concentrated. Two Negro Pentecostal churches and one white Pentecostal church in the same area attempted to recruit Indians. None of the churches was successful. Negro Pentecostals decided that Indians were suspicious of Negroes. White Pentecostals felt that Indians did not respond to their efforts because they did not trust whites. They decided it would take an Indian to do the job, and they persuaded an Indian of mixed blood who had been in the city for a long time to witness to the Indians. She is an able person, white oriented, and well integrated in the white community. She failed. The Indians in the neighborhood said, "She's too far above us." She explained her failure on the grounds that Indian relationships are so fragmented that no one likes anyone else in the neighborhood; the Indians refuse to get together on anything. Her one convert was disliked by everyone else; in consequence, other Indians would not come to the church. Where there is, in fact, social disorganization and community disintegration, recruitment to the movement is *least* effective.

Scholars who have focused on immigrants in urban slum areas assume that social disorganization explains the spread of Pentecostalism. Studies of inner city social structures and the so-called culture of poverty make it quite clear, however, that what appears to be social disorganization may be, in fact, forms of social organization other than those characteristic of middle class America. There are many functional alternatives to the nuclear family. For instance, the primary group for an individual may be a matri-centric family, a street gang, or various types of cliques within a larger, crowded community. Powerful in-group ties and out-group hostilities exist in supposedly disorganized slums and ghettos. These are the types of pre-existing relationships through which any movement will spread in such a community.

A more careful analysis of the types of recruiting relationships utilized by different cultural or class groups participating in any movement should increase predictability of movement growth. Anthropological studies of kinship and social structures in any given society provide a rough framework for the identification of significant social relationships—those which are likely to be experienced by the individual as influential. Within that framework, sub-cultural groups differ in the type of relationships which are experienced as most significant. We might also suggest from our findings that the type of structural relationship (brother, spouse, parent, fellow church member, neighbor, patron, peer) is less important to understanding recruitment to a movement than (a) the frequency of interaction between recruiter and potential member, or (b) the effect of the relationship (positive or negative) on the potential convert.

Many of our informants in the Pentecostal Movement were recruited by siblings, but it was always those with whom the relationship had been very positive. Negative relationships, even between kin supposedly important to each other, militate against recruitment. According to our observations, marriages which were previously experienced by both partners as satisfying tended to become the recruiting relationship for one spouse if the other became converted. Other cases suggest that if previous tensions existed in a marriage, the conversion of one spouse was divisive; sometimes such conversion disrupted the marriage. At this stage of the research, we can say that, in general, recruitment to a movement occurs through pre-existing social relationships of a positive-affect nature.

Most participants in movements know this from personal experience. They will encourage an individual whom the potential convert already trusts and admires to carry the message to him. When they forget this and try to convert a family member with whom there has been a history of hostility or characteristically negative response, they generally find recruitment efforts blocked. The victory, after a period of months or years, of winning over a Pentecostal whose recalcitrant spouse, sibling, or child finally sees the light often involves the intervention of another recruiter with more positive-affect influence. Or it can result from genuinely changed behavior of the convert which, over a period of time, alters the previously negative-affect to a more positive one. This is illustrated by the conversion of Ella, Malcolm X's sister, to the Black Muslims. A pious Christian, striving to meet white middle class standards, she was appalled by Malcolm's pre-conversion behavior—heavy drinking, use of dope, hustling, and other crime. Then came his prison experience and conversion to Islam. After months of observing the drastic change in her brother's behavior, even though initially she rejected his theological reasons for changing, she was finally converted to Islam (271). Pentecostals understand this recruitment dynamic and speak of the "witness of one's life" which is a non-verbal expression of their beliefs.

Evidence for the importance of a pre-existing relationship between recruiter and potential convert in the spread of a movement can be found in accounts of various other movements. John Lofland's study of a small religious movement on the West Coast traces its spread through what he called "pre-existing friendship nets." Although he sets up a list of personality and situational prerequisites for involvement in the movement, he notes that these are "woefully inadequate" in accounting for either the emergence of the movement or the conversion of specific individuals to it. He found the same gap-filler we did—interpersonal contact between a potential convert and a participant in the movement with whom the potential convert had had a meaningful relationship of some duration (332).

Hans Toch, in his well-documented study of social movements (52), is largely concerned with predispositions, susceptibility, and type of appeal. He admits that the crux of the social psychology of social movements is the "transaction" between susceptibility and appeal, but he does not focus on the nature of the relationships by means of which this transaction occurs. We feel, as does John Lofland, that face-to-face contacts and pre-existing relationships between people are of utmost significance for theories of movement recruitment. Predispositions and susceptibilities, after all, do not "encounter" appeals. People make the encounters through which a movement spreads.

Milton Singer's account of a contemporary movement within Hinduism stresses the importance of the guru-disciple relationship in its transmission. This type of personal relationship, according to Singer, is the "lifeline" of Hindu culture and of existing social structures (347).

Peter Lawrence, in his study of the Cargo Cult in the Madang district of New Guinea (326), does not concentrate on the lines of recruitment *per se*, but in his account one can trace the spread of the cult through personal relationships between fellow villagers, within the traditional tribal and inter-tribal trade-friend alliances, between fellow soldiers in the native division of the Australian Army, and between members of Christian missions and their native "catechists" and "mission helpers." All such relationships pre-dated the rise of the cult, and all were of pre-existing significance and influence.

Robert Lee's report on the growth of Soka Gakkai, a religious movement in Japan (329), reveals that the most important channels through which Tokyo converts had initially been contacted by the movement were neighbors (35 percent), relatives (16.4 percent) and colleagues at place of work (16.2 percent). Furthermore, all of the American adherents to the movement were found to be servicemen married to Japanese women who were responsible for bringing their husbands into the movement.

Encapsulated accounts of the first conversions to Christianity and Islam include similar recruiting relationships. According to the synoptic gospels, the first four disciples called by Jesus were two sets of brothers (Matthew 4:18-21, Mark 1:16-19); in addition, the two pairs had had previous connections as partners in economic enterprise

(Luke 5:10). Mohammed's first converts were reportedly his wife, Khadija; a patrilineal cousin and adopted son, Ali; an ex-slave and adopted son, Zaid; a loyal friend and business partner who was later his father-in-law, Abu Bakr; and another patrilineal cousin, Uthman. Three of Mohammed's daughters married converts and a fourth married a non-Muslim and converted him (355: chap. 6).

Mormonism began when Joseph Smith shared his revelation with his parents, two brothers, a neighbor, the local schoolmaster who had boarded with the Smiths, and the schoolmaster's parents and brother (301).

The Autobiography of Malcolm X provides a detailed account of one man's conversion to the Black Muslims. The initial contact with the movement came through Malcolm's brother, who visited him in prison, introduced him to Black Muslim ideology, and led him through the first stages of what we call the commitment process.

Neither Omer Stewart (349, 350) nor David Aberle (296) emphasizes the type of relationships that is involved in the dissemination of the Peyote Cult among American Indian groups, but both provide ample evidence that intragroup recruitment flows along lines of kinship ties and proximity of residence. Aberle notes that transmission of the cult from the Utes to the Navahos was "facilitated" by close relationships between individuals in the two tribes in the area to be studied.

The importance of pre-existing social relationships in recruitment to a movement is recognized, in effect, by the United States government security agencies. A person being investigated for a position requiring a security clearance can be denied eligibility if his wife, brother, or even a close friend has been identified with individuals or organizations considered subversive.

During our study of the Pentecostal and the Black Power Movements, we found that the idea of movement growth through pre-existing significant social relationships is offensive to many. Participants, like many social scientists, prefer to develop ideological (or theological) reasons for a movement's success. Social scientists focus on the type of appeal and its relationship to the particular type of deprivation or susceptibility they believe is causative. Participants suggest that the movement is spreading because more and more people are coming to accept the truth of their beliefs. This we certainly would not argue. We would only point out that a truth, or even "The Truth," must be communicated to be believed. And it is our observation that truth is most successfully communicated in the context of a personal relationship in which a certain degree of rapport and trust has already been established.

Many a Pentecostal traces his conversion to a radio or television broadcast which enabled the Holy Spirit to speak to him directly. Some remember an evangelist whose words struck home. Others can show the Bible passage, the book, or the tract which suddenly "opened their hearts to the Lord." There are Black Power traveling evangelists who touch their hearers' hearts in the same way. The tables at the back of the hall, covered with books, pamphlets, mimeographed sheets and "inflammatory" tracts, are as familiar at Black Power meetings as they are at Pentecostal missions or revivals, and they have the same effect on potential converts.

Extended conversation with a movement participant who explains his conversion on purely ideological or theological grounds will usually reveal the fact that someone brought him to hear the evangelist, placed the crucial book in his hands, or listened to the broadcast with him. A biographical analysis conducted by another anthropologist for another purpose is a case in point. The anthropologist was attempting to support the deprivation theory and did not perceive the significance of various points in her own data. Like many of our informants who recount conversion experiences that happened many years ago, her informant tended to focus on the subjectively significant aspects of the experience as they are interpreted in terms of movement ideology. Many details which are of interest to the objective observer are irrelevant to the subject, and are naturally forgotten in time. During interviews with the anthropologist, the Pentecostal repeatedly explained her conversion by saying that she had been saved because God spoke to her when she was listening to a certain evangelist on a radio program. The researcher, operating with a different set of basic assumptions, and utilizing deprivation theory, interpreted this woman's testimony as an indication of psychological deprivation. Later in the interview, the informant mentioned that at the time she had heard the crucial broadcast, she was seated in the home of close friends who were also neighbors. These friends were Pentecostal; they knew the evangelist and later took the informant to meet him. In this case, the pre-conditioning of the researcher to deprivation theory and the informant's ideological pre-conditioning combined to "hide" crucial information. On the basis of this information, the conclusion that this informant's conversion to Pentecostalism can be satisfactorily explained in terms of psychological deprivation could certainly be challenged.

Our approach to the analysis does not negate what Pentecostals call the action of the Holy Spirit in bringing them into the movement. To point out the importance of the human mediator and the type of personal relationship involved is simply to point out the proximate means, not to deny the ultimate cause, of conversion.

We do not wish to be identified with the school of thought which reduces all human behavior to biological, sociological, or even psychological determinants. The motivating or causative nature of ideals, value systems, and consciously held purposes has been well defended, not only by theologians and true believers, but also by thoughtful scientists (106-110, 357, 358, 360, 377-379). A science which cannot acknowledge the possibility that an ideological formulation, a widely shared assumptive system or "world view," or an envisioned purpose may be the independent, and not the dependent, variable is out of date. Engaged in the scientific study of movements, one must allow for the motivating power of an idea, if not for an ultimate cause behind that idea. To deal with or participate in a movement successfully, however, one must also place the proper emphasis on the human mechanism through which the idea is communicated.

One of the problems with early studies of social movements and with some popular notions today is the overemphasis on the ideological appeal of a movement as an explanation for its spread. This results in most ineffective attempts to combat a movement through rational counter-appeals. The assumption that one can recruit through ideology alone prompts massive leaflet campaigns and other mass propaganda methods. When Pentecostals in our questionnaire sample were asked to rank eight factors in the order they felt these factors had influenced them to become Pentecostal, mass media were at the bottom of the list for the sample as a whole, as well as for the sample divided into the four types of organizational groups.

It has been our observation that appeals through mass media may attract the attention of some individuals, and that many may be deeply moved by a charismatic evangelist or preacher, but that actual recruitment to the movement is a product of the capacity of individual members to persuade others, by means of face-to-face encounters, to accept their beliefs. This is not to deny the effectiveness of the mass media for other purposes—which will be discussed later—in movement dynamics. Here, we only wish to stress their ineffectiveness as a means of actual recruitment.

Successful recruitment to a movement has also been explained as the result of the influence of a charismatic leader. Actions based on this premise sometimes produce notably ineffectual attempts to suppress a movement by jailing or by otherwise removing its most articulate spokesmen. In fact, such persecution only enhances their importance by making them martyrs. Moreover, leaders have no corner on the charisma market, either in Pentecostalism or in Black Power. Nor do participants assume that charisma—and the success in recruiting it often facilitates—is necessarily a permanent attribute of any individual.

In Pentecostalism, the capacity to influence or recruit is believed to come and go as the Spirit gives power. Recruitment is therefore not limited to leaders. The concept of "the priesthood of believers" makes of every convert a potential recruiter. In fact one of the most oft-cited benefits of the Baptism of the Holy Spirit is the "power to witness"—the confidence that inspires others to believe, the capacity to recruit.

Within the Black Power Movement, today's charismatic militant leader may be tomorrow's "Uncle Tom," or vice versa. The rapidly shifting relationships between participants and representatives of the established order catapults new leaders with charismatic qualities into positions of influence every day. Charisma has been defined as a special quality of personal magnetism or spiritual power which draws wide support and gives a leader influence over others. As Weber pointed out, the most valid test of charisma is the response of the followers. In this sense charisma is an interpersonal event, and therefore may not be a permanent endowment. *Ad hoc* Black Power leaders are those whose particular orientations and readiness enable them to seize leadership in an explosive local situation to which they respond with passion. Some of these leaders develop a more permanent type of charisma which is effective with large groups of people and in a variety of changing situations. But the large number of individuals at national, regional, or local levels, in both Black Power and Pentecostalism, who fit the definition of charismatic leader is an outstanding characteristic of both movements.

If one is to explain the spread of a movement in terms of the influence of a charismatic individual, one must enlarge—or dilute—the meaning of charisma, so that it also refers to the recruitment activities of the humblest of movement participants.

In both movements there is a recognition of what might be called specificity of charismatic powers. In Black Power the individual who clearly has "his own bag" is therefore able to recruit others who respond to that "bag." In Pentecostalism, there are "Spirit-filled" individuals with the ability to lead certain types of potential converts through to the Baptism of the Holy Spirit. Frequently an interested visitor is advised to get in touch with a certain local Pentecostal or to go hear a certain visiting teacher or evangelist who is known to be especially competent in removing particular intellectual or emotional blocks. Differences in socio-economic, educational, or theological backgrounds are recognized, and known to require different variations of basic Pentecostal themes and different types of persuasive appeals. The quality of the interpersonal encounter is intuitively fitted by the appropriate "Spirit-filled" individual to the perceived needs of the potential convert. Such gifted individuals tend to develop guru-disciple relationships of variable duration with their "babes in Christ." Furthermore, the "babes" often mature into fully committed and charismatic gurus who in turn attract their own small circle of converts, thereby widening the recruiting potential of the movement. Although initial contact with the movement occurs through pre-existing relationships, the recruitment process often is completed with the aid of an appropriately chosen lay leader; or, the new recruit may be directed to a certain minister or evangelist.

The size of an evangelist's or a leader's following is in proportion to the range of backgrounds and orientations he is able to perceive and respond to appropriately. There are occasions on which the sensitivity and versatility of a single individual could be classified as extra-sensory perception, by those so inclined. Pentecostals believe the spiritual gift of supernatural wisdom is granted to the leader for a particular moment, in order to provide a channel for the Holy Spirit to touch a particular seeker.

Such flexibility of recruitment appeal indicates the versatility of certain leaders; more significantly, it shows how ordinary converts tend to tailor the Pentecostal message to their own needs and therefore to those of their closest relatives and friends. Many an educated Pentecostal could have resisted the gospel indefinitely if a respected colleague in the same economic or social class had not been converted.

While all Pentecostals agree that faith is a non-rational process and that "spiritual things are spiritually discerned," they still tend to use intellectual terms to discuss their faith and to interpret their changed social and religious lives. They may also wish to bring a wide range of concerns into harmony with their faith; reasoned intellectual analysis is not irrelevant to that process. Pentecostals employ similar intellectual concepts in communicating the good news to their peers.

We have observed a particular instance in which the movement spread across what would appear to be class and even caste barriers, as a result of this very capacity to fit the message to the need. One well-educated and very able black Pentecostal wanted his employer to receive Christ. Their relationship was one of mutual respect and trust; the employer had responded positively to the commitment and faith of his employee. But the employer was a white man in a position of economic and social prominence. The employee knew, therefore, that for the employer to come to Christ (or, in scientific terms, for recruitment to be accomplished), the employer would have to meet someone in the movement with whom he could identify more completely. He would have to see that Christ appears in Pentecostal garb not only to the underprivileged and to the racially "inferior." The employee therefore waited until he was "led" through the labyrinth of Pentecostal organizational structure to the home meeting of some well-educated and prosperous "Spirit-filled" white Christians who belonged to the same non-Pentecostal denomination as did his employer. This group responded to the "call" and a series of meetings with the employer was initiated by those in the group whose orientations and background most closely approximated his. Appropriate individuals were also drawn from other local groups. As a result, the gospel was effectively communicated and the movement effectively leapt over racial, class, and socio-economic barriers.

The key to the "leap" was the acceptance of the black employee by the white middle class group. It should be pointed out that although recruitment across racial lines is rare, racial mingling within the movement is not exceptional. "Spirit-baptized" Pentecostals of different racial backgrounds recognize a bond that takes precedence over their "earthly" divisions. One sociologist noted that the followers of one Pentecostal evangelist were racially integrated although the whites involved were poor Southerners who otherwise might be expected to be segregationists. He suggests that "the intense religious fellowship of the Pentecostal groups may be capable of eradicating, at least in the religious context, concern with race" (156). This is not to say that white Pentecostals as a group are free from racial prejudice. Their complete acceptance is limited to those Negroes who have the Baptism and who are perceived as brothers and sisters in Christ. The in-group, out-group orientation implied in racism has shifted, for committed Pentecostals, to a religious rather than a racial basis. In the mixed Pentecostal congregation we studied there is an interracial couple who are accepted by both blacks and whites; their example is often cited during evangelical activities in Mexico and Haiti.

After the initial contact with the movement and its belief system is established, a rich repertoire of ideological emphases, persuasive appeals, and organizational structures is available to complete the recruitment process. The simplistic notion of the single charismatic leader and his circle of followers is not sufficient to explain recruitment to a movement the size and nature of either Pentecostalism or Black Power. Charisma that helps to bring about recruitment is found at all levels of the organizational structure, operating through the mechanisms of pre-existing relationships and persuasion tailored to the needs and backgrounds of individual converts.

Another popular assumption is that movements spread because of the dynamics of mass hysteria operating in large meetings. Most histories of the Pentecostal Movement, whether written by advocates or by critics, attribute the early spread of the movement to the large revival meetings and the miraculous events (or "mass hysteria," depending on the point of view) which accompanied them (149, 153, 161, 168, 179). Many of these same authors have noted that outbreaks of the "tongues movement" in different parts of this country, in Europe, or in Latin America can be traced to the travels of specific individuals from one country to another. However, not all of these individuals used the mass-meeting technique. Evidence in these same histories indicates that where local groups were not meeting regularly between the visits of mass-meeting evangelists, the movement did not take hold.

It is tempting to attribute recruitment of Nazis to Hitler's mass meetings or of Communists to May Day parades. Gripped by the emotional impact and drama of such rituals, observers sometimes assume that mass hysteria pulls people into the movement. As we studied and analyzed this phenomenon, however, it became obvious that the primary function of mass meetings is not recruitment. The type of enthusiasm engendered in large groups functions far more importantly to unify the movement and to heighten the loyalty and dedication of those already converted. It may also be a decisive event in the process of commitment of someone who is already recruited but still poised on the brink of full conversion. Hitler himself wrote in *Mein Kampf:*

> The mass meeting is necessary if only for the reason that in it, the individual who, in becoming an adherent of a new movement feels lonely . . . receives for the first time the picture of a greater community, something that has a strengthening and encouraging effect. (316)

In Pentecostalism, there is no correlation between the size of the group at a meeting and the strength of the outpouring of the Holy Spirit, the number of charismatic manifestations, or the proportion of new participants who receive the Baptism. Most participants in the movement, however, welcome a series of revival meetings—or "missions" as some Episcopalian and Catholic Pentecostals prefer to call them—because of the "lift of the Spirit" in a larger group. Some feel that the Spirit of God is more manifest with more people praying, and others feel that the general tone of heightened anticipation is an aid to those who may be having difficulty in experiencing the Baptism and glossolalia for the first time. When asked to rank the importance of various factors in their recruitment experience, however, our questionnaire respondents reported that attending revival meetings was the least influential factor, except for mass media appeals.

One of the most important facts about recruitment to a movement is that individuals are not recruited to a movement but to a cell within the reticulate structure of the movement. The dynamics of large groups described loosely as "mass hysteria" may facilitate a conversion experience, but such dynamics do not ensure the recruitment of the individual into the organization of the movement. Nor do they contribute to the perpetuation of attitudinal and behavioral changes that are characteristic of movement participants. Few Pentecostals conceive themselves as members of the Pentecostal Movement. They are members of a specific church, a prayer or Bible study group, or a sub-group within a non-Pentecostal church involved in the charismatic renewal of first-century Christianity. Similarly, participants in Black Power are primarily members of a community center, a specific action group, a patrol, or a student association. The term "Black Power" is a way of describing an orientation which all of the participating cells share. There are, in fact, groups in both movements who hesitate to identify themselves with other groups in the same movement. Recruitment to either movement is a process of identification with a particular cell in a much larger and diversified network. Movement between cells within this network and shifting allegiance to other cells after conversion are common. But one cannot properly speak of recruitment to Pentecostalism or to Black Power. One must more accurately speak of recruitment to a cell in the organizational network. Some converts, of course, have a clearer concept of and interest in the movement as a whole.

We have explained that participants in the two movements we studied were usually recruited by persons with whom they already had meaningful relationships. We have also mentioned that movement participants realize successful recruiting requires flexible appeals tailored to the backgrounds and needs of potential converts. It is also important to note that participants in a movement expend more time and energy trying to influence others to their way of thinking than do people who are not involved in a movement.

Any scientific attempt to describe the urge to recruit, which seems to be a natural outgrowth of commitment in a movement, must mention a hypothesis which derives from cognitive dissonance theory. According to the latter, commitment generates cognitive dissonance because it involves choice between at least two opposing sets of beliefs and a rejection of certain socially accepted assumptions or beliefs. Logical inconsistencies between the committed believer's conceptual scheme and actual events, and the conflict between the believer's values and more widely accepted cultural mores, are considered causes of cognitive dissonance. The need to proselytize is therefore seen as the attempt to reduce this dissonance by obtaining support for the chosen belief system. According to one analysis of a small religious cult, objective disconfirmation of the beliefs concerning the end of the world only served to increase proselytizing activities because of enhanced cognitive dissonance (312).

Pentecostal beliefs are not of the apocalyptic, date-setting variety that can be conclusively disconfirmed. Faith in the second coming of Christ or in the miracles experienced by Pentecostal believers can only be disproved by so-called naturalistic explanations. Such explanations are based on an entirely different set of assumptions about final causes; they constitute disproof only to the non-believer, not to the believer. However, the suspicion dogs the unbelieving social scientist that the less demonstrable (to the scientist) an individual's beliefs, the more he will need to convince others of them, and so support his belief system. Even if this were true, it explains only the motivation of the recruiter, not the response of the potential convert. In the absence of empirical evidence, it is difficult to identify charisma with cognitive dissonance. The intellectual and emotional conflict and "discomfort" that supposedly accompany cognitive dissonance should be measurable in terms of anxiety scales (50). Those psychological tests for anxiety and neuroticism which have been administered to groups of Pentecostals, however, fail to show that Pentecostals are anxious people (88). According to Festinger (312), the only evidence of dissonance is attempts to reduce it—chiefly by proselytizing. This is an obvious tautology: people recruit because they are suffering from cognitive dissonance, and one can tell they are suffering from cognitive dissonance because they are recruiting.

Some social scientists find it difficult to interpret human behavior that seems (to them) to have no positive rewards. Persistence despite negative feedback, they feel, can only be explained in terms of a fantastic process of mental gymnastics. We have found a much more satisfying and less tautological explanation of the drive to recruit or proselytize. It lies in the nature of the commitment experience and in a certain feature of movement ideology which effectively cuts out negative feedback. These factors will be discussed in greater detail in the next two chapters.

In summary, we suggest that no matter what conditions of social disorganization or social or psychological deprivation facilitate the rise of a movement, the key to its spread is to be found in the process of face-to-face recruitment by committed participants. Those who wish to deal successfully with a movement, either to promote or to inhibit its growth, will do well to remember:

— that recruitment flows along lines of pre-existing, significant social relationships of positive-affect;
— that relationships may be those of kinship, neighborhood, community, patron-client, fellow membership, or any of a variety of types of friendships, depending on the structure of the society or sub-culture in which the movement is spreading;
— that individuals are recruited to specific cells in the organizational network, rather than to the movement *per se;*
— that recruitment to a movement is largely initiated by lay members of cell groups at the grass roots level rather than by noted leaders, although such leaders may be instrumental in the consummation of the commitment process; and
— that when such evangelistic face-to-face recruitment by committed participants begins, the movement may "lift off" the pad of its generating conditions and spread into groups and areas where these conditions do not exist.

V

Commitment

Deep personal commitment is one of the most widely noted and least analyzed aspects of movement dynamics. It constitutes the point of intersection between individual and social change. People are changed, even transformed in some cases, by the experience of commitment. Societies are changed, disrupted, and sometimes transformed by movements that rise and spread within them. When millions of individuals are experiencing personal transformation within the context of a movement, then personal and social change coincide. This, we suggest, is occurring in both of the movements we have studied. In Pentecostalism, it is the emphasis on personal transformation that is the most obvious to outsiders. In Black Power, it is resulting social change. Although other factors, such as the ideology and the organization of the movement, are important, we suggest that the motive power in either movement is the personal commitment of its participants.

Most analysts of movements—social, political, or religious—note that hard core participants display a certain quality which they describe variously as "devotion," "dedication," "intensity," or "fanaticism."

Hans Toch, in his study of the social psychology of movements (52), uses the word "commitment" almost interchangeably with the word "membership" and sees degrees of commitment as a continuum from "faith to fanaticism." He tends to stress, as does Eric Hoffer (28), the negative aspects of self-suppression and sacrifice of autonomy.

Sociologist Rudolph Heberle (25) notes a factor other than ideology which gives movements strength; he describes it as devotion which "claims the entire man." J. T. Borhek (64) defines a totally committed person as one "whose role in the group exhausts the limits of his personality"; he labels such a person a "martyr." William James (89) describes religious commitment as surrender to a higher, external power. Definitions in Webster's dictionary involve similar concepts of authority confidently transferred or entrusted.

It is clear that the phenomenon of commitment is recognized as important in the analysis of social processes, and that it is taken for granted as a characteristic of movements, but the precise meaning of the term is still more implicit than explicit.

When we began our study of the Pentecostal Movement we assumed that we knew what commitment was. If we had been asked for a working definition, we would have defined it in terms of two other factors—ideology and organization. We would have described it as acceptance of Pentecostal beliefs and involvement in Pentecostal organizations. We soon discovered, however, that what an observer interprets as commitment to a set of beliefs or to an organization, a participant considers commitment to the person of Jesus Christ. Participation in the organization of the movement and even acceptance of beliefs are felt to be secondary phenomena which flow from the basic commitment to Christ.

Participants in secular movements lacking or rejecting any sort of supra-human referent still realize that they are committed to something beyond a mere organization or a set of beliefs. Many people feel that commitment to any movement is a kind of religious experience; or, as some prefer to say it, secular movements are pseudo-religions. The religious element derives from the experience of total personal surrender to something greater than the self.

One of the traveling spokesmen for the Black Power Movement who is most concerned about development and clarification of ideology said that he felt Black Power must become a religion: "Not Christianity, because Christianity is the religion that was used to justify our subservient position and to give us religious reasons for accepting it." Nevertheless, acknowledging the need for a supernatural, religious base, he was turning to "something out of our African past." This same leader has since made plans to visit the Caribbean and Africa, in search of this past. Less than a year later, another leader in the movement began to consider just such a mystical base for the sense of personal identification with the greater-than-self. He described some of the heroes of slave rebellions before the Civil War. These heroes, he said, "live on." They were in Watts, in Detroit, and in Newark. Their faith shines from the eyes of young men who are proud of their black skins and who are throwing off the yoke of the oppressor.

A third attempt to create a religious base for the movement is to be found in the theology of Black Power formulated by the Reverend Albert Cleage, of Detroit (229). He offers a reinterpretation of the Judeo-Christian tradition based on the equation of non-white with black. Jesus thus becomes a black messiah, born of a black madonna, with primary relevance to a black Israel. Salvation involves the group, and the resurrected Christ involves revolutionary social action in this world. There are certain parallels with the way the Black Muslims interpret Islamic theology. Clearly, many leaders in the Black Power Movement perceive the essentially religious nature of the commitment that could be utilized to strengthen the movement.

Our analysis of this factor in movement dynamics began with a study of the Pentecostal experience crucial to commitment in that movement. We have since found that personal commitment and the process by which it occurs has parallels in the Black Power and other movements. Though the experiences may appear to be quite different, their functions in terms of movement growth and strength are similar. An essential difference, and one of great concern to participants, is the nature of the greater-than-self to which an individual becomes committed. We would not presume to equate these referents. Rather, our task is to analyze the generic characteristics of commitment, and to discover how it functions in personal transformation and in different kinds of social transformation.

We will analyze in some detail the phenomenon of commitment among movement participants, the process by which individuals may be led to the point of commitment, and the source or generating experience of commitment.

Manifestations of Commitment

It is common observation that strongly held convictions generate an almost impervious sense of assurance. Strength of conviction is often considered synonymous with commitment. It is associated with a certain intensity, a drive, a single-minded awareness of long-range goals. It might more metaphorically be called the "lodestone orientation." Hard core members of certain movements seem to have one-track minds. All conversational roads lead to one ideological Rome.

"You just can't argue with them" is a common complaint made by critics of the Pentecostal Movement. The same comment was once made by an American hostess who entertained a delegation of Russian patriots touring with an art and culture exchange group. It has also been made by white liberals engaged in discussion with Black Power militants. Faced by opponents exhibiting such assurance, one has a slight feeling of being somehow one down.

A second aspect of commitment is the capacity for risk-taking. Phrases used by Pentecostals to describe this manifestation of commitment imply willingness to "step out in faith," to "stand on the promise of God," or to "go out on a limb for the Lord."

Contrary to the usual view that persons who accept such challenges are those who have little to lose, we have observed many families in middle and even upper income levels who were "led" to give up well-paid jobs and who set out to serve the Lord as traveling evangelists or to organize faith camps without any guarantee of compensation.

By contrast, there are those who are "made bold in the Lord" to take entrepreneurial risks and whose economic status has consequently been raised. This aspect of the risk-taking associated with commitment is particularly significant in Mexico and Latin America Here, according to Read (191), McGavran (177), and our own observations, Pentecostal commitment to Christ and faith in his support enable peasants to break through traditional patterns and make changes in agricultural methods. In these cases, the risk-taking inherent in religious commitment has resulted in economic development

There are obvious parallels in the Black Power Movement. No

all of the most committed participants are disadvantaged ghetto residents. Many a middle or upper class Negro has risked the status and economic security achieved through successful assimilation into the white community. Commitment for these individuals involves not only risking their own gains; they also may have to endure the opprobrium of their fellows who scorn them for "throwing away the goodwill so painfully won for their race by hard-working blacks."

Also, by contrast, there are those for whom commitment has provided the self-confidence and pride necessary for them to engage in entrepreneurial activities which benefit themselves as well as the movement. Like their counterparts in Pentecostalism, these committed black Americans take risks that affect their economic behavior and force breaks with cultural patterns.

Pentecostal commitment sometimes leads to a more subtle type of departure from cultural patterns, one that still involves a certain degree of risk. Many Pentecostals practice a form of financing called "living on faith." This means following the directives of the Holy Spirit as they are perceived in prayer, and depending upon what secularists would call "chance" to provide the necessary funds. Several of our informants depend for their entire support and that of their families on this type of supernatural control of ordinary business transactions. One of the tenets of this kind of faith is that "the Lord meets your needs, not your greeds." This involves a freewheeling capacity to change directions at a moment's notice. Long-range planning is not popular with those who live on faith. The Lord seldom allows the security of pre-planned budgets. If a need is not met, it means that the Lord has something else in mind for the believer to want. However, there is little value placed on austerity for its own sake. Unexpected luxuries are welcomed and enjoyed guiltlessly.

One group of Neo-Pentecostals, devoted to a charismatic ex-Lutheran minister, has been led by the Spirit to combine their families and their resources and to live communally, following the example of the first Christians. At the time of our research there were thirty people living in this "ministry center," four families with children and several single adults. Most adults spend full time going out to teach home Bible study groups, witnessing, and bringing people to the Baptism of the Holy Spirit. They were thus full-time recruiters for the movement. They did not expect their converts to join the communal group. Rather, they encouraged them to continue in their own churches, to spread the word, and to come to the weekly meetings at the center for spiritual refreshment.

The group relies for food, clothing, and shelter on the earning power of a few who work at their usual vocations. One of these is a doctor. The building which shelters them is a monument to the technique of faith financing. It is an immense, magnificent home built in the gracious style of the early 1900s. The leader of the group explains that the Lord directed him in a vision to acquire this home and its spacious grounds. The Lord also provided the initial payments in the form of gifts from well-situated admirers of the leader. Faith is put to the test each month when the mortgage payment comes due. The combined earning power of the group does not guarantee this amount, so that fairly substantial and practical answers to group prayer are constantly required. Sometimes these come in the form of unsolicited gifts from people who attend meetings and healing services held in the home. Sometimes a bit of bush-beating by the leader is required. But always there is the sense of spontaneity, of risk, and of reliance on something other than the usual patterns of economic security. This reliance has been successful for a period of four years.

Another aspect of the risk involved in commitment is illustrated by the case of a Lutheran pastor who experienced the Baptism of the Holy Spirit with tongues. He brought many of his congregation to the experience and came into conflict with synod officials who threatened to foreclose the mortgage on his church and to remove him from office. We have been able to observe how the original experience of the Baptism generated in this pastor the capacity for commitment and risk-taking. As the threats to his security were realized, the very accepting of the risks gradually increased his commitment. In fact, as the cost of his commitment rises, its strength increases. It is not difficult to imagine that this man might be capable of making the supreme sacrifice if the opposition still kept a den of lions in the basement.

A letter from a California bishop criticizing this "heresy in embryo" (187) was the official response to the enthusiastic witness of one of the first Episcopal clergymen to receive the Baptism of the Holy Spirit. His church was split in its reaction, and the minister himself was subsequently transfered to a small, nearly defunct church in another city. His new church grew phenomenally and became wholly Pentecostal in orientation. This church, generating its own charismatic leadership, now makes it possible for the minister to spend most of his time traveling around the globe bringing the Spirit to fellow Episcopalians. Despite the original opposition, the tongues movement within the Episcopal church has become one of the most successful thrusts of Pentecostalism in terms of both numbers and fervor.

Non-participants seldom understand the directly reciprocal relationship between commitment and risk magnified by opposition. Such escalation leads to seemingly unrealistic behavior as the participant fights against overwhelming odds; but, strangely enough, it often leads to success in spite of all difficulties. It has been the unhappy experience of authorities in several denominations to find that their attempts to suppress the Pentecostal Movement within their churches have only succeeded in publicizing it, and in making the committed Pentecostals more militant. Heightened commitment leads to more effective recruitment and consequently to a rise in the number of churches affected by the phenomenon.

A third manifestation of commitment is personal charisma. The effect of charisma on the organizational structure and the recruitment patterns of a movement has already been discussed. The important point here is the relationship between charisma and personal commitment.

In any movement, one can find a few individuals who display an apparently charismatic power over others but who are committed only to their own position of power or financial advantage. These are the charlatans for whom the segmented and decentralized structure of a movement provides ample scope for maneuvering. There are individuals in Pentecostalism who have been known to manipulate the religious devotion of others to their own financial gain. There are also blacks who have made eloquent use of Black Power ideology in order to feather their own nests at the expense of both whites and other blacks. Such opportunists do not possess the gift of charisma as Weber defined it. They may utilize, but they are not capable of initiating or effectively spreading, a movement.

Charisma, in the Weberian sense, involves by definition a source greater than the individual to which the individual is committed and from which he derives his power to influence others. According to the Weberian model the leader's commitment to his God, or his cause, is primary; the followers display a secondary or indirect commitment to the cause through their personal devotion to the leader. In Dorothy Emmet's expanded model (discussed in chap. III), the charismatist is able to lead others through a process of commitment during which the followers experience directly the source of the leader's commitment. The follower's commitment is then equal to, or on occasion greater than, that of the original charismatist, and quite independent of it.

Weber (141) suggests that the only valid test of charisma is the recognition of it by a leader's followers. Such recognition is commonplace among the Pentecostals. They continually credit their leaders (local or visiting) with being "truly led by the Spirit," with the capacity to "open up the scriptures" to their followers, with having unusual powers of healing, exorcism, prophecy, or spiritual knowledge. More significantly, these attributes are very frequently credited to lay members in their own or other local groups. Furthermore, the capacity to influence others and to attract followers is invariably attributed by Pentecostals to commitment to Christ, whom they believe to be working through the gifted charismatist. In Black Power, such individuals are considered by their followers to be committed to "the revolution" and to the goals of the movement as they understand them. Indeed, an individual's particular variation on the ideological theme, his sense of commitment to it, and his capacity to influence others charismatically are experientially identical.

That charisma and commitment are observably linked in movement dynamics is not surprising. It is important, however, to understand the communicability of commitment which leads to the generation of charisma in otherwise ordinary individuals. Those opposed to a movement often fall into the trap of assuming that imprisoning or otherwise removing the most obviously charismatic leaders will inhibit the spread of the movement. Quite the reverse is true.

The fourth manifestation of commitment as we have observed in both Pentecostalism and Black Power is behavioral change. It has already been shown that commitment results in behavior that affects the organization of and recruitment to the movement. To the extent that movements are mechanisms of social change, personal commit ment is a factor in such change. Commitment also generates behavioral changes that have social effects outside the movement itself.

The Pentecostal moral code contains familiar requirements—no drinking or smoking, no dancing, gambling, or even—in some cases—attending movies or other similar entertainment. There is emphasis on hard work, paid bills, serious tithing for the Lord's work, and appreciable amounts of time spent in Bible study. More noticeable in other cultures where marriage patterns differ is strict adherence to monogamous sexual behavior. In all of this, Pentecostal behavior is indistinguishable from the behavior valued in other fundamentalist Christian sects, except in one respect: Pentecostals emphasize the effortlessness of the desired behavior. They consider moral behavior a consequence of the religious experience, not a prerequisite or social duty.

It should also be noted that among Pentecostals in non-Pentecostal churches there are many who still smoke (some to excess), drink (usually moderately) and engage in the usual types of recreation and entertainment. Even among these "hidden" Pentecostals, however, who prior to conversion were accustomed to more sophisticated recreational patterns, there is an observable shift toward the behavioral code of their fundamentalist brethren. Of those in our sample who were brought up to believe that drinking, smoking, and dancing were acceptable social behavior, sixty-one percent changed in the direction of the more conservative code, after their conversion. Post-baptismal behavioral changes are remarkably similar across both class and cultural lines.

Social changes brought about by Pentecostal commitment are more noticeable in societies where norms differ from those of white middle class America. Sidney Mintz (178) reports the conversion of a Puerto Rican villager which required the "deliberate surrender of certain prerogatives that seem to be tied to valued behavior items for males in his group—swearing, drinking, dancing, gambling, extramarital adventures, violence, and the acquiring of compadres." Clearly, Mintz considers these behavioral changes lasting. In fact he seems almost to mourn the transformation of his favorite informant, a man whose "fine critical intelligence, concern with rationality and control" and enjoyment of "the local norms for masculine behavior" did not seem to predispose him to conversion.

Gordon Harper (160) reports a similar list of significant behavioral changes for Pentecostals in a Brazilian village. The changes constituted a rejection of male *machismo* patterns and a refusal to rely on traditional witchcraft practices for protection against mishaps.

We observed the replacement of *placage* (serial common law unions) with permanent church marriages among Pentecostals in Haiti. Both Mintz and Harper report similar changes in marital arrangements for converts they knew. Four Jamaican couples who had been living in consensual union were converted to Pentecostalism and had a joint wedding ceremony during the time of our survey on their island.

Charles Erasmus (157) found that the growth of a Pentecostal church in a small Mexican town was having economic repercussions; converts not only stopped drinking but also declined to participate in fiestas. The fiesta system, a variant of conspicuous-giving institutions common in closed societies, involves a reciprocal cycle of financial responsibilities and serves to redistribute wealth so that individual inequalities are lessened. Because the Western "profit motive" is thus discouraged, such practices are considered a hindrance to economic development. Converts to Pentecostalism do not set out purposefully to change the economic system. But the economic implications of their religiously motivated behavioral changes are nonetheless far reaching. By refusing to fulfill their traditional obligations in planning fiestas, converts undermine the village economic system; at the same time, by adopting values which are part of the "Protestant ethic," such converts tend to facilitate local economic development.

A Catholic observer of the Pentecostal Movement in Chile reports that its success in overcoming the "national disease" of alcoholism has transformed Chilean Pentecostals (fourteen percent of the population) into sober, hardworking men. They are sought after by management as laborers and factory workers (155).

British anthropologist Malcolm Calley (154) notes that what he terms sexual irregularities are commonplace in Jamaica, and therefore among West Indian immigrants in England. Few couples marry until the children are grown, and about seventy percent of children are born out of wedlock. Men are reluctant to undertake marital responsibilities and women depend on maternal kin for support. He

inds that "although their members are drawn from precisely the social class in which this pattern is most common, the Pentecostal sects
are even less willing to compromise on this issue than are other
churches." He considers the actual behavior of West Indian Pentecostals in England to be "very close to the ideal." As for the more
usual behavioral changes characteristic of Pentecostals the world
over—avoidance of smoking, drinking, dancing, movies, and (among
West Indians) straightening the hair—Calley says: "My observations
of the saints in their homes lead me to conclude that these taboos are
observed strictly by all of them" (154, pp. 65-66).

In all of these reports, the behavioral changes are in the direction
of the patterns widely accepted as favorable to the process of industrialization. Pentecostalism is therefore considered an "acculturative
mechanism" by the writers we have quoted. As Sidney Mintz puts it,
the Pentecostal churches "made ideological imperatives out of . . .
personal economic advancement, a time-is-money orientation, defer-
al of immediate gratification, the pre-eminence of the economic motive and the subordination of pure pleasure" (178, pp. 263-264). Emilio
Willems (205-207) also suggests that commitment to Pentecostalism
prepares people for participation in democratic institutional structures in Brazil and Chile, and that therefore such commitment has
political ramifications.

Personal behavioral transformation in the direction of somewhat
puritanical morality is associated with commitment to other types of
movements. A belt-tightening simplicity of life is reported for Communist leaders and hard core party workers in both China and North
Vietnam (310, 339). Converts to the Black Muslim movement also
exhibit behavioral changes in the direction of strict morality and rigid
self-discipline (271). The "Puritan Ethic" in these cases can hardly
be attributed to Christian theology. There may be a set of behavioral
patterns that facilitate social change in the process of industrialization
economic development. Movements which contribute to such social
change appear to provide ideological supports for these behavioral
patterns, no matter what the theological guise. In any case, the phenomenon of commitment in Pentecostalism, as well as Black Power
and other movements, is observably manifested in behavioral changes
converts.

The Commitment Process

There are seven identifiable steps in the commitment process as w
have observed it in the movements we have studied:

— initial contact with a participant;
— focus of needs through demonstration;
— re-education through group interaction;
— decision and surrender;
— the commitment event;
— testifying to the experience; and
— group support for changed cognitive and behavioral patterns.

Initial contact.   Much has been written about types of discontent
both pathological and normal, which predispose individuals to com
mit themselves to a movement. The pre-conditioning discontent mo
frequently mentioned by our informants in the Pentecostal Mov
ment was dissatisfaction with their earlier religious experiences. The
cited the meaninglessness of most church activities, a feeling th
there was "something missing" in ritual observances, a vague desi
for "a closer walk with God," or "a hunger in my heart for more of tl
Lord." Many were keenly aware of the discrepancy between tl
Christian ideals to which they gave lip service and the reality of the
interpersonal relationships in the family, in the church, or at wor
    We observed, however, that neither this discontent nor any of t
sociological or psychological determinants which might be attribut
to it were sufficient by themselves to cause an individual to becor
involved in the process of commitment to Pentecostalism. We al
noted that many of our informants did not feel any discontent unti
relative or friend experienced the Baptism of the Holy Spirit and su
ceeded in making them sensitive to it. Only a minority of our inf
mants described some sort of crisis situation in their lives which th
felt predisposed them to involvement. Even in these cases, invol
ment usually came about through personal contact with a participa
either before or during the crisis situation.
    The same is true of Black Power. Obviously the predisposing co

litions are common to all black Americans, yet not all participate in he movement. Whatever the motivation for becoming active, a participant's story invariably includes a reference to personal contact with someone already active.

Whether the predispositions are created, or existing ones are exploited, the first step in the process of commitment to either movement is contact with a participant. As we have already noted, such initial contacts develop by means of pre-existing significant social relationships.

Focus of needs through demonstration. The second step in the process of commitment involves redefining the potential convert's needs, desires, or discontents in terms of the specific ideology of the movement. This is accomplished in part by means of the demonstration effect. The potential convert to Pentecostalism sees a change in the life of someone close to him—or he meets individuals in the movement who display a sense of assurance and depth of faith that seem admirable. Often he hears testimony which describes how the painful gap between the Christian ideal and human reality has been closed. A participant joyfully reports his capacity to love more fully than ever before, and a smiling spouse confirms the testimony. Ministers observe colleagues, freed from their painstakingly prepared sermon notes, expounding the gospel eloquently and effectively and "with power." Concerned clergy and laymen alike find the enthusiastic worship, the generous flow of funds for the Lord's work, and the *esprit de corps* of Pentecostal groups a powerful demonstration of what Christian church life ought to be.

Among Mexican, Puerto Rican, and Latin American Pentecostals the economic advantage alone of reallocation of funds previously spent in drinking and entertainment often provides an impressive demonstration of God's power to reward the faithful. Very often the focus of an individual's expectations and needs comes after witnessing a healing or hearing dramatic accounts of such healing. It does not matter if this aspect of the charismatic revival is explained in terms of psychosomatic illnesses, auto-suggestion, or other convenient hypotheses. What is important is that people who feel physical distress find relief through Pentecostal practices and accept the Pentecostal interpretation of what they have experienced. We noted during our

study that Pentecostals in Mexico, Haiti, and Colombia considere
healings a demonstration of a very practical power in the real world
This is reported to be a major appeal of the movement elsewhere i
Latin America, Africa, and India. Some writers have explained thi
on the grounds that Western medicine is not available to such people
We have observed, however, that the demonstration effect of physica
healing gives Pentecostalism considerable appeal even for middl
class Americans with ready access to Western medical theory an
practice. To Pentecostals, the Great Physician may use any channe
The ultimate responsibility for the healing is attributed to him n
matter what proximate means have been used. Surrender and com
mitment to Christ are said to greatly increase therapeutic power. I
this fashion, predisposing needs, desires, and discontents are focuse
on "Jesus as the answer" and on the Baptism of the Holy Spirit as th
means to that answer.

This second step in the commitment process has parallels in othe
movements. Jan Myrdal's series of biographical sketches of residen
in a Chinese village (337) make it clear that for the individuals i
volved, joining the Communist party was perceived as a voluntar
act. Each person had been impressed by the demonstration effect
someone, usually a relative or fellow villager, who was better off f
having joined.

The *Kerner Commission Report* notes the "intensified expect
tions" among American Negroes from which the Black Power Mov
ment took shape. The report assumes the movement developed-
"ironically"—in response to the demonstration effect of successf
non-violent direct action in the South and of accompanying legisl
tion and court decisions. Seen from the point of view of a potenti
convert to a Black Power group, this development does not see
"ironic," but, rather, as something practical and necessary in his co
version. The "bait" of demonstrable power relevant to one's disco
tents is necessary for any but the most pathological individual if o
is to move toward the risks of full commitment. Che Guevara's failu
to gain support in Bolivia was due in part to the inability of his sm
band to demonstrate to rural peasants that they had the power to i
prove their lot.

Re-education through group interaction. Commitment is a soc
phenomenon. It cannot occur nor can it be maintained in a social v

ium. Even a Pentecostal for whom commitment is a highly individual and absolutely private relationship between himself and the Lord will explain that his commitment cannot be maintained outside the mystical Body of Christ. By this he does not necessarily mean any particular church or organization, but the "fellowship of the saints"—interaction with other equally committed people. One may receive the Baptism of the Holy Spirit and the gift of tongues by oneself (about one fourth of our informants reported this), but the ongoing commitment to Christ must be nourished by interaction with other "saints." Geographical distance may force one to rely on the written word, letters from living "saints," or the words of those deceased saints recorded in the Bible. But there must be contact, or commitment will wither like a branch severed from the vine.

The occasions for Pentecostal group interaction range from the small home Bible study and prayer groups, through church services and Full Gospel Businessmen's Fellowship meetings of various sizes, to periodic large revival meetings with their highly charged emotional atmosphere. As we explained in chapter V, potential converts are recruited not into the movement as a whole but into a particular local cell. Because of the linkages between cells, most potential Pentecostals attend a variety of meetings and are exposed to a variety of ideological emphases and organizational structures over a period of several weeks or months. They tend to identify, however, with one cell—usually that toward which they were first drawn, or another which they find geographically more convenient or ideologically or organizationally more to their taste.

Whatever the size or longevity of the Pentecostal group, it is characterized by a relatively high degree of warmth, welcome for the newcomer, and supportive interaction. A clue to the content of intragroup relationships is the consistent use of kinship terms between members. As mentioned in chapter IV, Pentecostal participants are brothers and sisters in Christ, while Black Power participants are often "soul" brothers and sisters. Similar sibling terminology has also spread to the student movements.

In Pentecostalism the common parent is a supra-human being before whom all believers are equal. Anthropologists have long noted the association between non-human authority, supernatural sanctions, and personalized group relationships (116, 363, 390). In spite of the overtly dominant-submissive interaction patterns in many Pentecostal groups, the presence of highly personalized relationships and a certain egalitarianism are indicated by the frequent use of the term "brother" for even the most impressive leader.

The function of the local church or Pentecostal group in the commitment process is threefold: to provide a basis for cognitive reorientation, to facilitate the development of in-group ties, and to encourage the formulation of expectations concerning the Baptism experience.

First, re-examination of the belief system begins during group interaction. Intensive study of the Bible, informal discussions relating Biblical statements to specific personal problems, and ritual reinforcement of basic values and beliefs in song and prayer are common in groups of all sizes. In this way the building blocks for new cognitive structures are provided.

Second, relationships within the group are highly supportive which tends to nurture positive in-group ties. Unless a potential convert has very strong out-group attachments which oppose involvement, these cell group ties quickly become highly significant. If out group ties are neutral or weak, cell group relationships may become central.

The third function of group interaction in the commitment process is the formation of expectations about the experience associated with the climax of the commitment process. The potential Pentecostal hears countless testimonies concerning the Baptism of the Holy Spirit and the kinds of behavior that are likely to occur during this and subsequent infillings of the Holy Spirit. He may also witness several Baptism experiences of others who "come through" before him. In some of the more routinized sect groups, potential converts are led to expect the Baptism to be manifest in almost standardized forms. In others, they hear about a wide range of experiences and behavior involving all degrees of automatisms, dissociation, or trance states. In many groups potential converts are told repeatedly that "the Lord deals with us as individuals" and that they may expect a Baptism experience consistent with their personality type. At the same time, as their expectations are forming, they learn to place a high value on the Baptism experience. It is invariably associated with the extraordinary spiritual powers which they are hearing about and witnessing.

The period between the time an individual confesses his desire for the Baptism of the Holy Spirit and the time that he experiences it is often called a time of "tarrying before the Lord." This period may be as short as a few minutes and as long as several years. We found no correlation between socio-economic status (as measured by income and occupation) and length of tarrying time. There was a significant correlation, however, with educational background. College educated Pentecostals received the Baptism more quickly than those with less education (at the .01 level of significance).

The three functions of group interaction in the commitment process—cognitive reformulation, development of in-group ties and formation of expectations about the commitment experience—are obviously interrelated.

Group interaction seems to perform the same functions in the process of commitment common to other movements. For example, John Lofland states that the difference between a "verbal convert" and a "total convert" to the Doomsday Cult he studied was intensive interaction (usually through communal living) with full participants. When such interaction was absent, the verbal convert failed to become committed. During this intensive interaction, doctrine was endlessly discussed, daily events were interpreted in relation to doctrine, and expectations about behavior of full converts were communicated by living example. Lofland's admittedly oversimplified statement about "final conversion was coming to accept the opinions of one's friends" is true. But the process leading to conversion involved the creation of those very friendships through which the individual was influenced to change.

Edgar Schein's study of brainwashing techniques (342, 343) reveals that even when torture and induced physical and psychological stress are used, the desired change does not result from the negative forms of coercion alone. Such change requires a positive-affect identification with a "more reformed cell mate," or even inverse identification with the interrogator (49).

Non-coercive Communist indoctrination programs designed for volunteers also make full use of cell group interaction (353). The special Chinese Communist training course for hard core workers involves small discussion groups of from ten to twelve members who practice self-criticism and painstakingly apply the new ideology to the smallest details of their lives, past and present. Ties to old family and social friends are simultaneously cut or loosened, so that in-group relationships become highly significant. Party doctrine is endlessly memorized, a process which supplies the components for later cognitive restructuring.

It can be argued that group interaction in the commitment process is similar to the normal socialization process. We suggest that the difference is in goals and intensity. The goals of the socialization process are internalization of existing social values, acceptance of commonly held beliefs, and learned behavior consistent with social expectations. The goals of the process leading to commitment in a movement, however, involve values and beliefs that oppose or are different from those of the society at large; the process encourages behavior that does not conform to the social norms. Human beings are social animals and tend to internalize the values and behavior standards of groups significant to them. However, the intensity of the interactions within learning groups may vary tremendously. By intensity, we mean not only frequency of interaction, but depth of self-revelation, of personal knowledge about fellow members, and of group discussion of members' significant concerns.

Comparative data are needed, but observation of the function of group interaction in the commitment process would suggest that the greater the change to be made (in held values or in behavioral patterns), the more intense the group interaction must be.

Two things which impress the student of the Pentecostal Movement are the frequency with which Pentecostals meet formally, and their tolerance of seemingly interminable services and teaching sessions. Less noticeable but even more significant is the intensity of informal interaction between members in dyadic or small group relationships. New Pentecostal converts who have recently received the Baptism and are experiencing the greatest change in orientation frequently joke about the lack of sleep and late hours. The intimacy and intensity of in-group relationships when the Spirit first invaded the Notre Dame campus were noted by a staff psychologist. Participants felt a sense of loss when they separated for Easter vacation; they expressed their urgent desire for continued communication with their fellow converts (180). Intensity of interaction appears to be far more pronounced among Neo-Pentecostal adult converts than among second-generation members of the more routinized churches where glossolalia and other differences with non-Pentecostal churches are deemphasized.

When one compares Walker's reports of the discussion and confession types of cell groups used in advanced Communist training programs with the cells reportedly set up at the village or city block level, the differences in intensity of interaction seem clear. Where the greatest personal commitment and transformation are expected, the cells are structured for more painful self-disclosure, more exhausting analysis of fellow members' experiences and ideas, more extended exposure to fellow members, and less contact with family and friends.

Lofland's Doomsday Cult members became fully committed after extremely intense group interaction in the communal living situation. This seems consistent with the "far out" nature of the beliefs and the extreme behavioral changes required of total converts, the donation of all personal property to the cult, and the acceptance of communal living as a permanent way of life.

We have observed the same three functions of small group interaction in both Black Power and white positive response groups. After large meetings of one Black Power group, participants regularly split up into small groups and stayed up most of the night "hammering things out."

It is important to note that the intense interaction that is part of the commitment process is not the type usually referred to as "mass hysteria," commonly associated with tent meetings or with conversions during the oldtime revival meetings. Furthermore, it is not associated with the inducing of dissociational states. Neither of these phenomena is essential to the commitment process. If one does occur, it performs quite different functions.

Decision and surrender. The fourth step in the process of commitment is some form of surrender of the old identity: a transfer of control to something outside the individual's consciousness. In theological terms, this is repentance and acceptance of Christ as savior. Often gradual, this part of the process blends with the previous step. In the small, closely knit church or prayer group, many Pentecostals find gradual self-disclosure possible, and the supportive acceptance conducive to progressively less defensive self-evaluation. In this manner, the capacity for confession and surrender is developed.

There are enough cases of the sudden conversion, the off-the-street-into-revival-meeting story, to indicate that capitulation can occur simultaneously with initial contact, focus of needs, and the first experience of group interaction. As Pentecostals say, however, such conversion needs a great deal of subsequent support and guidance. One of our informants experienced the Baptism of the Holy Spirit and spoke in tongues at the second meeting she attended. In her opinion, it would have been better to "come into it more gradually." She had not had time to accept the ideology with which to interpret her experience. She felt the need of stronger in-group ties, and of someone to "open up the scriptures" to her. Other group members felt responsible for initiating informal meetings with her to help fill in the gaps.

Some of the young people involved in the demonstrations in Chicago during the 1968 Democratic Convention apparently had similar experiences. Their comments to television interviewers revealed that they were unprepared for police brutality. Others had been in the student movement longer, however, and through previous small group discussion had acquired a view of the American power structure which prepared them for even this excessive display of force. We were able to discuss their experiences with several students who had been newcomers to this type of demonstration. They reported having spent long hours in intense group discussion after the event. Ideological interpretations of their experiences were resolved, some with the help of more experienced members of the movement.

When the process of commitment is consciously manipulated, as in brainwashing, the point of surrender is the point of complete psychological breakdown (49, 342, 343). The non-coercive Communist indoctrination course described by Walker involves a similar point of crisis which comes at approximately the same time for all cell members—after about six months of training. At this stage the trainee finally breaks down and decides to confess all. The experience is reportedly a deeply affective one which leads directly into what we have called the commitment event. Memorized jargon suddenly becomes meaningful in a way that appears almost as a revelation. This is followed by peace of mind, a sense of serenity, and a powerful desire to go out and bring others to the same sense of assurance. Sargant considers this point of surrender in the new Communist as "the beginning of his end as an individual."

Many thoughtful Pentecostals are aware of the parallel between the commitment process in Pentecostalism and that observed in Communism. Many have made it clear that their antipathy to Communism is based on the recognition that both "real" Christianity and "real" Communism demand total commitment from the individual and that "no man can serve two masters." They consider the conscious manipulation of the process of commitment for ends envisioned by men as a Satanic aping of God's ways.

Commitment in those movements lacking a supra-human referent involves a decision to cast one's lot with the movement as against its opponents. Peace demonstrators whose commitment has been precipitated by an experience of excessive police force describe a "giving up" of the attempt to see both sides—a surrender of faith in non-violence or in the capacity of the establishment to deal with the crisis. Reluctant recruits to Black Power report a similar type of surrender of faith in the "legitimate" means espoused by the Civil Rights Movement (214:207-218).

Whether the commitment process prior to this point has been persuasive or coercive, and whether capitulation is viewed as the loss or the fulfillment of the self, a crucial step in the process is the moment of decision and surrender. The individual may capitulate to something or someone outside of and more powerful than the self, or he may surrender faith in old goals and old means and turn to an offered alternative.

The commitment event. The experiences to which commitment can be traced differ widely according to type of movement. As we have pointed out, there is a basic functional similarity between these various events. For this reason we will analyze in detail the experiential source of commitment as it is seen in Pentecostalism. The parallels with Black Power and other movements will be presented in the last section of this chapter.

Within the ranks of Pentecostalism there are various theological positions concerning the point at which Christian commitment begins. Conversion, salvation, and sanctification are key words in most of them. Conversion is the repentance and turning away from one's former life to Christ. The phrase "decision for Christ" points up the human responsibility for this phase. Salvation is an act of God which is variously understood as saving one from a literal hell after death; ensuring the existence of one's personal soul in an afterlife; victory over the forces of evil in this life; triumph over one's own and others' sin; or, for some of the more liberal, salvation from a sense of meaninglessness. Sanctification, also an act of God, is the making holy of one's entire life. It is variously described as the infilling of the Holy Spirit, or the immersion of the self into the Holy Spirit, or the complete interpenetration of the individual self and the Holy Spirit.

Some Pentecostal groups view conversion, salvation and sanctification as simultaneous processes. They lead potential converts to expect that a decision for Christ, awareness of salvation, the Baptism of the Holy Spirit and its manifestation in speaking with tongues will constitute a single experience. Other groups hold to a more procedural model in which the steps of Christian maturity occur separately over a period of time, and commitment to Christ deepens gradually. According to this view, conversion and salvation may precede the Baptism of the Holy Spirit by months or even years. The gift of speaking with tongues may accompany the Baptism, occur later, or, in rare cases, not be experienced at all.

It is the Baptism of the Holy Spirit, either accompanied by or leading to the experience of glossolalia, which sets a Pentecostal apart from other devout Christians for whom sanctification requires no external manifestation. Even those Pentecostals who believe themselves to have been committed to Christ before the Baptism of the Holy Spirit describe this experience as the source of their increased power, charismatic and otherwise, and the reason for their participation in the Pentecostal Movement. The phenomenon of commitment in the Pentecostal Movement has its source in an experience (the Baptism of the Holy Spirit) and an act (speaking with tongues).

The nature of the experience and its significance for the Pentecostal are best conveyed by verbatim descriptions given by participants themselves.

The first is the report of a convert from a fundamentalist Southern Baptist background. He was converted to Pentecostalism during World War II while serving in the Navy. He was attracted by the fervent faith of an interdenominational group of sailors on his carrier; but, like many other adult converts, he had to overcome the feeling that the experience of the infilling was not only against his traditional training but also against his own nature:

> I had to lay aside my own ideas in order to receive the infilling of the Holy Spirit. I had to accept it on God's terms. And

God's terms for me were that I go back there with that group of loud-praying Christians. I had to humble myself and let them pray for me.

I didn't know much about the Holy Spirit. I had heard one of my buddies tell of one of the boys who was slain under the power of God and he had fallen to the deck under the power of the Spirit. I knew how hard that flight deck was, so when I finally went back to the prayer meeting that night I said, "Lord you won't have to knock me down; I am going to lie down on the deck to start with!" And I did. I may seem humorous now, but I was completely serious. In my hunger for God I did the simple act of lying down on the deck and lifting my heart and hands to the Lord Jesus.

I wasn't there long until a boy whom I had won to Christ a few months before but who had received the Baptism before I did, he came over and put his hands on me. The Lord began to pour forth His Spirit in great torrents of blessing. If I had the vocabulary of Webster it would be insufficient to explain the joy, the blessing, the new dimension of praise in worship, the new comprehension of divine truth, the new appreciation of the Cross, the increased devotion to the Christ who died for my salvation which came as a result of my infilling.

Hour after hour, it was as if a waterfall was falling on me in Spirit; it was as if liquid love penetrated me all the way through as I praised in the Spirit. I worshipped Him in a language I never learned. I felt this great liberty to praise Jesus as I'd always wanted to but never could. I felt the Holy Spirit flow through me in a divine electricity, or a divine energy current—current after current until I didn't feel like I could stand any more and yet there was no desire at all that it would stop. It was a glorious meeting—a glorious revelation that he did to my heart until about two o'clock in the morning. That was the beginning of the Spirit walk.

When we receive the Baptism, we don't jump from a buck private to a four star general overnight, but we do become officer material. The Baptism of the Spirit isn't a goal, it's only a gateway. If we walk in obedience to the captain of our salvation, He will lead us into the deep things of God.

The second story is that of a Presbyterian missionary who received the Baptism recently during his second tour of duty in an overseas mission field. He became acquainted with a Pentecostal missionary who seemed to have a certain dynamic in his life that the
Presbyterian came to admire. The latter began a private search of the
scriptures, particularly the Acts and the Epistles. In this respect he is
very typical of educated Christians who are being drawn into the
movement. They need to know that glossolalia and related phenomena are "scripturally sound." The Presbyterian had to swallow his
pride and go for spiritual help to the Pentecostal, whom he considered an intellectual inferior.

> I made it very clear to him at the beginning that I was in-
> terested in the Baptism of the Holy Spirit to give me the
> power for the job I wanted to do as a disciple of Jesus Christ,
> but that I wanted nothing to do with tongue speaking. He
> very wisely said, "All right, then, let's just forget about it."
>
> So then we went over the scriptures again together and then
> we began to pray. He laid his hands on me and suggested
> that I just relax and think, not about my sins and worried-
> ness, but about the promises of God and my rights as a son
> of God. There was no question in my mind that I felt a
> physical warmness, a mellowness of heart, a certain relaxa-
> tion and more and more I was enjoying praising God. Now
> this sounds strange, but as a Presbyterian, I had never had
> a freedom in worship. People had told me that I was a good
> preacher, but this was a result of hard work and following
> my manuscript. I had never had a real sense of *liberty* in
> the pulpit or in prayer—maybe the best way to put it is I'd
> desired a sense of intimacy with God.
>
> So I was enjoying praising and just praying without thinking
> what I was going to pray. This was all in English of course.
> And then he (the Pentecostal) suggested that I stop speaking
> in English and start letting the Holy Spirit motivate a di-
> vine language. Well, I remember thinking, "Ah, well now
> he's caught me." But I guess I decided, "Well, Lord, I have
> to accept these things on your terms and I know from scrip-
> tures that tongues did come with this for the early disciples,
> so I'm willing to be a little bit more foolish here and see
> what comes of it."

I was aware of what was going on around us. His wife was preparing a meal. I was not caught up in any ecstatic experience nor was I emotionally beside myself. I just sort of opened my mouth as if I were going to speak and tried to let go and sure enough, this language came out of me. There was no stuttering or stammering. It just came out as a language. I remember my first thought was that it sounded sort of oriental or Indian or something although I know no languages except English and Swahili and of course some Hebrew and Greek. When this language began to come it was to me a tremendously releasing experience. I really felt like I was being given the power to express my joy and worship of the Lord without any limitations in having to think about what I was going to say, so that I was really not praying. The Holy Spirit was praying in cooperation with me, taking my voice and my body—in order to formulate the words, using my muscles, but the Spirit was animating it. The *language* was divine, but there was nothing divine about the speaking itself.

I'm told this lasted about forty-five minutes. I had my arms up, which is most un-Presbyterian, during this whole period. Another physical manifestation which took place, which also was most un-Presbyterian, and completely new to me, was that I became aware of the muscles of my arms quivering—a sort of spasmodic quivering. My first thought was that I'd been holding them up too long and the blood had drained out. So I lowered my arms and realized that this didn't help at all, but as a result it began to pass into the other muscles of my body, even till it got down to my stomach muscles. I remember I opened my eyes to make sure I wasn't imagining it. The other thing which is very common with many people but very unusual for me was weeping. I had never wept, either in confessing my sins or with joy, being taught all my life that men don't cry. But the release manifested itself in tears. I didn't want to stop the tongues. I was enjoying it too much.

The joy remained with me for a whole week even though I was not able to tell anyone about this experience for something like a month afterward, except to my wife who did not accept it at all. However, three months later she did seek the experience for herself and received it in our home.

The mild involuntary motor activities accompanying the missionary's experience are very common but do not represent the most extreme forms of dissociation, trance, or coma. The sailor's reference to waves of love and currents of energy or electricity flowing through him are also common and can be found in most of the published accounts written by famous evangelists of the nineteenth and early twentieth centuries. Many of the accounts of our informants include what William James called photisms, sensations of luminescence and weightlessness, visions of various sorts, often visual and auditory perception of the person of Christ. Some time-space disorientation is reported. One individual perceived everything "as from a great height" for over a week. Many have great difficulty taking the normal scheduling of daily life seriously. Weightlessness and "walking around four inches off the floor" for several days posed a problem to one housewife who kept dropping things.

Generalizing from all of these personal descriptions of the Baptism experience, the characteristics of the state might be summarized as follows:

— a sense of the eternal—a disorientation in time and space as normally perceived—sensations of complete freedom;
— a sense of identity with all other human beings—a sense of cosmic wholeness;
— feelings of gratitude, awe, and great love;
— a sensation of surrender to and immersion in a larger reality, an experience perceived as self-fulfillment and enhancement of individuality rather than as loss of it;
— a recognition in the Aristotelian sense—a total comprehension of that which has always been true but unperceived.

Not long after we collected our first case histories, we began to notice that the phenomenon to which participants traced their commitment was more than just an ecstatic subjective state. It typically includes an overt act which sets the individual apart in some way from those who have not had the experience. Clearly the pre-Baptismal hesitancy about glossolalia and other non-voluntary behaviors, whatever else it may mean, indicates an awareness that in some way these acts constitute a point of no return.

In order to appreciate speaking with tongues as a bridge-burning act, one has only to glance at the anti-Pentecostal literature that has circulated within official Christianity, or to engage in conversation with a few of the quietly scornful critics of the movement. Introduce the topic to any gathering of churchgoers who have no personal contact with the movement, and one is likely to elicit remarks about the "lunatic fringe," "religious fanatics," "Holy Rollers," "emotional instability," and "immature faith." Adult converts to Pentecostalism are recruited mainly from groups of nominal or respectably devout Christians. To surrender oneself, without benefit of alcohol, to the excesses of uncontrolled articulation and possible involuntary motor activity, and to cap such indignities by calling it possession by the Holy Spirit, is, by middle class American standards, indecent, if not immoral or insane. Those participants who have lost their jobs, their cherished church membership, or, as in two cases in our records, their families, are in the minority. But most have experienced ridicule or criticism by family or friends. Tongue speakers who have remained active within non-Pentecostal churches are often involved in painful tensions, or in the kind of "church split" deplored by concerned churchgoers. The fact that glossolalia, for American Pentecostals, is a bridge-burning act is not to deny its significance in the spiritual life of the individual. It is emphasized here only as it functions in terms of the dynamics of movements.

We were most eager to compare our observations on this bridge-burning aspect of the commitment experience with data from other cultural settings where middle class American mores are not the rule and where trance and spirit possession concepts are not alien. It seemed likely that in such settings glossolalia *per se* would not function as a bridge-burning act. We found that in Mexico the spread of Protestantism in general and Pentecostalism in particular has on occasion brought persecution by the Catholic Church ranging from economic sanctions to stonings and hangings. This statement is supported by McGavran's study (177). Our informants explained that although extreme persecution is rare today, alliance with a Pentecostal or *Evangelico* church in a predominantly Catholic community is still enough to burn some individual social and economic bridges. We also noted that glossolalia is much less common among Mexicans who have received the Baptism of the Holy Spirit than among American

Pentecostals. We observed that Mexican and Colombian converts to Pentecostalism who were already Protestants spoke with tongues far more frequently than converts from Catholicism. This would support our view of the function of glossolalia as a bridge-burning act for those whose conversion to the movement did not involve another type of overt break with the past.

In Haiti, voodoo spirit possession, trance, and glossolalia are not only socially acceptable but are also part of the very religious patterns which Pentecostal converts must reject. In that country, although the Baptism of the Holy Spirit is generally accompanied by speaking in tongues, the act that deeply commits an individual to the Pentecostal way of life and cuts him off from past patterns is a ritual burning of the sacred objects used in voodoo ceremonies. This act often arouses the hostility of the local voodoo priest and other influential members of the convert's community and family.

Further evidence supporting this view of glossolalia as a bridge-burning act among American Pentecostals came from comparing Neo-Pentecostal groups with those churches at the more routinized end of our organizational continuum, where conflict with the established order is a thing of the past.

In comparing the frequency of glossolalic experience for any individual with type of religious background, we found that frequent tongue speakers were significantly more often (at the .001 level) from liberal than from fundamentalist or Pentecostal backgrounds. Furthermore, frequency of glossolalia is correlated (.02 level of significance) with being alone at the time of the original glossolalic experience, a characteristic that is not common among members of established sects. This would seem to support the view of glossolalia as a commitment phenomenon of greater functional importance for those least socialized to accept it.

Any bridge-burning act obviously has two effects: the cutting off from the old and the strengthening of ties with the new. A religious movement which encourages a conversion process involving any sort of unconventional behavior will elicit such behavior from people who would not, under other circumstances, exhibit it. We have suggested that one of the functions of group interaction in the commitment process is formation of expectations concerning the commitment experience. Many Pentecostals report having spoken in tongues without ever having heard anyone else do so. More, however, have ample opportunity to pattern their behavior after that of others.

The fact that behavior associated with religious ecstasy may be culturally learned poses something of a problem for Pentecostals. Several have expressed disgust with the "inducing of tongues" that may occur after the altar call at revivals or "behind the scenes" in church prayer rooms. The "Now repeat after me" technique of conversion has been cited as an offensive example of hocus-pocus and charlatanry. Opinion is divided on this score, however. One group of Episcopalian priests active in the movement believe that glossolalia can be learned, that the spiritual growth of some individuals is held back by an inability or a hesitancy to attempt speaking in tongues, and that these persons can be helped to learn how. This involves having an experienced tongue speaker pray with the new convert. He prays in English and then in tongues, and suggests that the learner simply copy the syllables he hears. In the cases we have observed, the learner quickly advanced to independent syllable patterning. The "teacher" continued to pray in his own tongue speech as the learner "took off." The learners proceeded into the religious experiences associated with glossolalia in the same fashion as other Pentecostals for whom glossolalia utterances were more easily spontaneous.

Linguists William Samarin and James Jaquith point out that glossolalia is a linguistic phenomenon which can occur independently of any particular psychological or emotional state, and that both glossolalia and accompanying behaviors are learned behavior. Jaquith even suggests that glossolalia *per se* not be classified as religious behavior (166, 194, 196). Our observations support the contention that glossolalia can occur without any altered mental state. Experienced practitioners can "turn it on and off" at will. The subjective states that accompany any convert's first glossolalic utterances, however, as well as most subsequent ones, are what motivate attitudinal and behavioral changes. It is glossolalia plus the subjective states, not the linguistic phenomenon *per se*, which is functional in terms of movement dynamics.

That glossolalia and various accompanying acts may be learned behavior in no way "explains away" what Pentecostals feel to be its supernatural content. Nor can the scientist dismiss it by labeling it as such. Most human behavior is learned behavior. This does not explain the lasting changes traceable to the phenomenon in Pentecostalism nor the social consequences of the commitment so generated.

Our data indicate no difference in terms of depth of commitment between those Pentecostals whose tongue speech was originally "induced," and those in whom it occurred more "spontaneously." In any case, whether the bridge-burning act is viewed as learned or spontaneous behavior is not so important to our analysis as its function in terms of involvement in the movement.

We have noted that Pentecostal commitment is characterized by (a) a subjective experience and (b) an overt act. It is important to determine how experience and act are related to participation in the movement. We were able to do this for the Pentecostal Movement by utilizing data collected by means of computerized questionnaires.

As a measure of degree of participation in the movement, we used information concerning the frequency with which a respondent interacts with other participants either at church services, in home meetings, or in informal contacts. Scores from one to seven were assigned, based on whether the respondent reported that he met with other Pentecostals every day, about four times a week, twice a week, once a week, once or twice a month, a few times a year, or never.

With respect to bridge-burning, we classified a respondent according to whether or not he reported a break with his family or his church because of his involvement in the movement. If a respondent reported either type of break, he was classified as High Act; if he had not, as Low Act.

The frequency with which a respondent speaks with tongues was used as a measure of the subjective experience involved. Strictly speaking, this is not a measure of the original experience to which commitment is traced. Recurrent manifestations of glossolalia are, however, a re-enactment of the original infilling of the Holy Spirit and hence a reinforcement of that initial experience. Frequent tongue speakers were defined as persons who speak with tongues daily or several times a week. Respondents who reported these frequencies were classified as High Experience. Those who speak with tongues less frequently were classified as Low Experience. Non-tongue speakers or those still seeking the Baptism were omitted from the sample for these tests.

The sample was divided into four groups: (1) High Act-High Experience; (2) High Act-Low Experience; (3) Low Act-High Experience; and (4) Low Act-Low Experience. These four groups were compared with respect to participation in the movement.

Pentecostals who are committed by both act and experience were found to participate in the movement significantly more than others (.001 level). In comparing the relative effect of commitment by act versus commitment by experience, it was found that those who were committed by act (with experience held constant) participated more than those who were not so committed (.07 level of significance).

Those who were committed by experience (with act held constant) also participated more than those not so committed (at the .04 level of significance). This might seem to indicate that commitment by experience affects participation in a movement slightly more than commitment by act. However, when the correlation between experience and participation, and act and participation, is compared with the correlation between the combination of the two and participation, it is clear that the combination is a stronger indicator of participation than either of the components.

A comparison of the four groups with respect to movement participation strengthens the view that commitment must involve both act and experience to affect participation in a significant way. High Act-High Experience subjects participate in the movement significantly more than Low Act-Low Experience subjects. Differences between the mixed groups (High Act-Low Experience and Low Act-High Experience) were not significant. Nor was the difference between these mixed groups and the Low Act-Low Experience group. Both mixed groups are significantly less involved in the movement than the High Act-High Experience group at the same level of significance as the Low Act-Low Experience group. It would therefore appear that commitment, as we have defined it here, is significantly related to participation in a movement, and that commitment by both act and experience is a better indicator of participation than is either alone.

We have described the observable manifestations of commitment in a movement, traced the steps through which individuals can be led into a commitment experience, identified two components of commitment, and found that both are significantly related to participation in the movement. Next we must try to analyze what happens to an individual who has such an experience and performs such an act.

We suggest that one characteristic of Pentecostal Baptism and other types of conversion experiences is an alteration in the individual's understanding of self. Following the profound experience of the Baptism of the Holy Spirit, Pentecostals feel themselves to be different. Descriptions of the change are cast in Biblical language. The converts are "new creatures in Christ." They believe themselves to be related to God in a new and different way—as sons rather than as servants. They perceive themselves differently in relation to their fellow men both inside and outside the Body of Christ. To members of the Body of Christ, they are related as cells in a single organism, each with a different but important function. To those who are not yet members of the Body or who choose to reject it, they are related as creatures who live "in another dimension." They think of themselves as being "in but not of" the world that others live in. Patterns of communication with these two groups are felt to be different. The first question most Pentecostals ask a new acquaintance is "Are you a Christian?" By this they mean an authentic "born-again, Spirit-Baptized" Christian, not someone born and raised in a so-called Christian country and a member of the usual lukewarm Christian church. As our informants frankly explained, "there are just some assumptions that Christians share and other people don't, and you talk about different things and in different ways."

Behavior in relation to these two groups is altered accordingly. With fellow members of the Body, Pentecostals share a reciprocal responsibility for mutual support and concern. They also feel an undirectional responsibility to bring non-members to the Lord and into the Body if possible.

An alteration in self-image affecting social behavior implies some sort of cognitive restructuring or change in belief structure. Gradual cognitive changes are considered normal in the development of an individual, but sudden changes of this sort are often considered psychologically suspect.

A familiar explanation of the Pentecostal Baptism experience and speaking with tongues is based on the theory of psychological maladjustment. Dramatic conversion experiences, even those observed in non-religious movements, are often viewed negatively as indications of some form of compensatory behavior. As noted above, several studies of the psychological correlates of Pentecostal glossolalia have been made. Psychological tests used on different groups of tongue speakers include: the California Psychological Inventory (189), the Rorschach

Test (210), the Cattell Personality Inventory, the Willoughby Test for general level of neuroticism, the Rosenzweig Picture Frustration Test (201), and the Minnesota Multiphasic Personality Inventory (21). Investigators found no evidence that tongue speakers as a group differ from the norm with respect to incidence of neurosis or psychosis. Empirical evidence made available to date would seem to indicate that conversion and commitment in Pentecostalism cannot be explained on the basis of psychological maladjustment (88).

Psychiatrists Jerome Frank (79) and William Sargant (47, 49) analyze the changes that take place during a commitment experience in terms of neuro-physiological processes. Comparing the nature of revivalistic religious experiences with the process of psychotherapy, Dr. Frank interprets the conversion experience as a mechanism through which attitudes about the self, and about others with whom the subject maintains significant relationships, can shift in such a way as to lead to permanent attitudinal and behavioral changes. Such changes stem from the reorganization of the "assumptive system" or world view that can take place during such experiences. Similar results can be obtained by means of successful psychotherapy.

Sargant concludes that experiences such as revivalistic conversions, snake handling, and glossolalia can produce an effect similar to that of electro-shock therapy: temporary cortical inhibition that breaks up previous mental and emotional patterns and frees the individual to develop new ones.

Both Sargant and Frank stress that the dynamics of revivalism—and conversion involving dissociational experiences—do not require predisposing personality characteristics or emotional maladjustments as an explanation of participation. Both men provide evidence describing the successful involvement of normal individuals not only in religious conversion but also in thought reform and brainwashing. Contrary to popular opinion, resistance to such processes can be maintained only by attaining a condition of emotional detachment, developing a pathological immunity to suggestion, or asserting a counter-commitment to some other belief or way of life that is equally obsessive. Sargant and Frank feel that the common denominator in religious conversion, some methods of psychotherapy, thought reform, and brainwashing is not a psychological but a physiological state which can be induced in any individual.

Sargant's emphasis on the physiological mechanisms of cognitive reorganization in religious conversion, thought reform, and psycho-therapy are based on his observations of the most extreme forms of these phenomena. He concentrates on the examples of extreme dissociational behavior in revivalistic religion during the nineteenth century, in which extended verbal assaults heightened guilt and anxiety, producing a type of nervous exhaustion. He uses examples of the induced physical stress and calculated disruption of expectations in brainwashing. His data on psychotherapeutic process are based on his own work with victims of war neurosis in which therapeutic recall of incidents was drug induced and resulted in complete physical collapse. According to his findings, even less violent therapy involved the same physiological processes, since there are high anxiety states attending such therapy.

Sargant used Pavlov's findings concerning physiological breakdown and cessation, alteration, and even reversal of normal brain function in dogs to explain (and treat successfully) combat exhaustion in World War II veterans. He suggests that permanent behavioral as well as attitudinal changes can result from a physiological state of the brain in which cognitive restructuring, even complete reversal of beliefs or cognitive patterns, can occur. To explain this cognitive restructuring, Sargant postulates a temporary but dramatic interruption of normal brain functioning. According to this hypothesis, the Baptism of the Holy Spirit and glossolalia would have to be viewed as temporary interruptions of normal brain functions.

In most of the Baptism experiences we observed, even though radical cognitive changes did occur, it proved difficult to find evidence for the degree of physiological breakdown of which Sargant writes. However, it is possible that the process he describes involves a greater or lesser degree of interruption of functioning, and also that there are physiological correlates of lesser intensity. In discussing physiological aspects of the Baptism experience with Pentecostals, we found some support for the theory. Most informants could describe definite physical changes that occurred during the infilling of the Holy Spirit. The two accounts presented earlier are fairly typical. Even those who did not notice involuntary motor activity accompanying the experience reported release of muscular tension, pricklings, or sensations of electric currents coursing through the body. The familiar "wave after wave of love" is not simply a poetic metaphor. The waves are experienced physiologically. Invariably these sensations are said to enhance normal physiological function both during and following the experience. Some participants noted physiological effects for a period of days or even weeks after the experience. Frequently the changes were described as the healing of specific, often chronic, ailments.

Until the biochemists provide us with more specific information on the exact relationship between emotional and mental functioning and the chemistry of physiological functioning, it is better to withhold judgment concerning the physiological causes or effects of these types of experiences.

Whether or not there are measurable physiological changes in brain functioning that regularly accompany all conversion experiences, religious or secular, it is safe to assert that there are changes, sometimes of a radical nature, in cognitive patterning, and that these affect social behavior. This phenomenon of sudden cognitive restructuring resulting in permanent behavioral changes has been noted by others.

Psychologist Abraham Maslow draws a connection between what he calls "peak experiences" and personal change. He has studied the nature and effects of peak experiences in both religious and non-religious contexts. These peak experiences are altered states of consciousness which involve disorientation in time and space and a type of cognition different from normal cognition. Visual and auditory perception may also be different. The perceptions of "peakers" as described by Maslow are very similar to those of Pentecostals during their glossolalic or Baptismal experiences. Maslow suggests such mystic experiences contribute to personality growth and self-actualization. Permanent changes sometimes come about:

> To have a clear perception (rather than a purely abstract and verbal philosophical acceptance) that the universe is all of a piece and that one has his place in it . . . can be so profound and shaking an experience that it can change the person's character and his Weltanschauung forever after. (108:59)

Anthony F. C. Wallace (140) has recognized a process by which individuals can be led to make radical changes in orientation. He calls it a "ritual learning process," and he believes it to be different in nature from the traditional learning process involving conditioning, instrumental learning, practice, and reinforcement. It depends, rather, on the "law of dissociation" by which cognitive and affective elements can be rapidly restructured. This requires excluding from the consciousness perceptual cues associated with previous learning, and presenting new and relevant cues. The permanence of the new cognition will depend, Wallace suggests, partly upon reinforcement in the conventional learning sense.

Ward Goodenough (365), in his book on directed cultural change, has also touched upon the role of identity transformation in the processes of social change—the ways in which changes in self-image are related to behavioral change and acceptance of new values. An altered sense of self can come about in many ways familiar to anthropologists. Trials of various sorts successfully completed provide an altered view of the self. Visions, hallucinations, and other intense mystical experiences have been institutionalized in many societies as an effective way to alter the self-image. Among the Plains Indians the transforming experience of the Vision Quest was the vision itself, not the ritually prescribed ordeals through which the vision was induced (102, 380).

Goodenough notes that an alteration in self-image—which can occur either in traditional rituals in stable societies or during processes of directed culture change—is often followed by an act of commitment to the changed identity. These are frequently "acts of eradication" which destroy property or persons symbolic of the old order. They may also be acts which symbolize the new identity, new role or new patterns of social behavior. The Pentecostal Baptism experience often includes both. In Haiti, as well as in many traditional and Neo-Pentecostal groups in the United States, rituals of exorcism often precede the Baptism and speaking with tongues. Demons of anxiety, pride, greed, drug addiction, sexual deviancy, and other sin are driven out in ritualized and fairly traumatic sessions. These are clearly a symbolic as well as a real freeing of an individual from old limitations—a burning of the bridges to the past. The acts associated with the Baptism or infilling by the Holy Spirit (usually including glossolalia) symbolize and initiate new patterns and "set" the new self-image.

Anthropological literature is rich with accounts of various types of experiences and acts which not only symbolize a turning away with finality from things and people associated with one's former role, but which in many cases actually provide the skills and initiate the behavior patterns expected in the new social role. Anthropologists refer to these as initiation rites or *rites de passage* (134). Our data suggest an important difference between these rites and the commitment act and experience involved in movements. The latter leads to a view of the self that is *not* in accord with social expectations. The bridge-burning act of commitment to a movement takes the individual *out* of the larger society in some significant way and symbolizes his rejection of certain social norms. An initiation rite merely marks the passage of an individual from one accepted, traditional role within the society to another equally acceptable one. The result of *rites de passage* in primitive or complex modern societies may be a changed view of self and changed role behavior on the part of the individual, but such initiation involves no change in the social system or in the individual's basic value orientation. Commitment by means of a transforming experience and a bridge-burning act, on the other hand, involves changed behavior based on a value system different from that accepted by society at large; it may involve participation in an organization opposed to established institutions.

The word "commitment" is commonly used to indicate either wholehearted support of existing norms and structures or dedicated participation in an effort to change them. At this point the search for another term would be simply proliferation of verbiage. It is enough to point out that there is an important distinction between the processes leading to and the social results of the two types.

It is now possible to identify two components of commitment in social, political, or religious movements: an identity-altering experience, and a bridge-burning act. The commitment experience may or may not involve a mystical element, but it must produce an altered view of self and some degree of cognitive restructuring. The commitment act may be a real or symbolic destruction of the old way of life, or a real or symbolic achievement of the new, or a combination of both.

Testifying to the experience. Whatever the experience or event to which an individual traces his commitment, an essential part of the process involves testifying to it. This sixth step in the commitment process is institutionalized to various degrees in the Pentecostal Movement. Persons who have recently received the Baptism of the Holy Spirit are encouraged and in some cases pressured to get up before the group and describe their experiences. Talking about a subjective experience effectively clarifies and reifies it for the individual and draws immediate reinforcement from the group. There is an important difference between testifying to the commitment experience for the first time before a group of fellow believers, and the kind of "witnessing" that we have called recruitment. This initial testifying objectifies a subjective experience and "fixes" it as a reality, both for the convert and for his group. Without this step in the commitment process, much of the transforming effect of the commitment event would be lost.

Group support for changed cognitive and behavioral patterns.   For every action there is an equal and opposite reaction. The post-Baptismal reaction is familiar to Pentecostals; they warn recent converts that a newly "Spirit-filled" Christian is subject to some of the most subtle attacks of Satan. Doubt as well as other psychological and physical trials are attributed to this source. Support from other Christians during this period is essential. Many Pentecostals report a heightened need for group interaction immediately after the commitment event. For those who are suffering opposition or ridicule from family, friends, church officials, or outside groups, such support is a particularly important part of the commitment process.

Walker reports that an additional four months of intensive training are required before new Communists who have already experienced the surrender and commitment event are judged to be strongly and safely committed to the party (353).

Movement participants and outsiders commonly observe that new converts tend to be enthusiastic participants in movement activities. Also, they realize that commitment can be renewed by actively supporting a newcomer during the commitment process. The success of Alcoholics Anonymous is predicated on this fact. Support for changed cognitive and behavioral patterns is achieved by active participation in the group of believers and by active recruitment of other

:o the group. The importance of such ongoing activities to commit-
nent would suggest that the commitment process is best viewed as
)pen-ended.

Two Components of Commitment in Black Power
and Other Movements

)ur two-component view of commitment was supported by our own
)bservations of commitment in the Black Power Movement, and by
vidence in the literature on other movements. Few accounts of the
atter include a careful analysis of the experiences of individuals in
he process of becoming committed to the movement. It is possible,
owever, to glean from these accounts some indications of the nature
f the personal commitment involved, and to find evidence of both
lentity-altering experiences and bridge-burning acts.

The Cargo Cults of Melanesia provide examples of both phe-
omena. In one such cult that developed among the Manus of the
.dmiralty Islands, entire village populations suffered "mass seizures"
'hich began with violent trembling and ended in complete loss of
1otor control. Other symptoms included visions and auditory halluci-
ations of planes and ships arriving with cargoes of Western goods.
he cognitive restructuring associated with these revelations moti-
ated the destruction of material possessions. Participants believed
ich destruction proved to the god their need for the cargo. The wide-
)read pitching of household goods and primitive garden tools into
1e sea were indeed acts that burned bridges to former patterns
f social as well as economic behavior. The commitment to change
enerated during The Noise, the mystical phase of the movement,
nded to unify not only people of separate villages but also gen-
ational groups within villages. This is not to suggest that no
hism existed within the movement. But the unity created by a com-
on experience established new cross-cleavage ties, enabling the
mmunity to accomplish new goals. Eventually, according to Mar-
ret Mead (333), the heightened sense of unity made it possible for
ople to follow more moderate leaders, to work out new patterns of
llage construction, to develop new relationships with plantation
vners, and to take new initiatives in political activity. It is interest-

ing to note that village populations not involved in the initial wave
of seizures experienced similar ecstasies several years later. These
persons were living in new villages established after the first mass
seizures and property destruction. They had broken with the old ways
and were participating in economic and political activities modeled
after the Western image. But apparently they felt the need for more
complete commitment to the changes by means of the same mystical
experience (344). This delayed phenomenon would seem to support
the view that the bridge-burning act without an identity-altering
experience is a less effective method of generating commitment.

Peter Lawrence, in his detailed history of the Cargo Cult in the
Madang District of New Guinea (326), described "shaking fits and
uncontrolled antics." During these dissociational states persons so
afflicted were thought to be in communication with spirits of the dead
or with the syncretic God Jesus-Manup; therefore, they were better
able to receive special messages about the cargo. Prophets gathered
adherents and made changes in the conceptual framework of Madang
area tribes through the mechanism of revelatory visions and prophecies received during trance states. Although many of the rituals involving dissociation were patterned on traditional religious practices,
Lawrence insists that the new rituals his informants experienced were
very different. His resumé of the significance of the Cargo Cult includes the statement that the movement was an attempt at "completely renewing the world order."

Lawrence concentrates largely on generating conditions and on
the details of the ideologies of the five phases of the movement in the
Madang area. Only very indirectly can the reader pick up clues about
the actual commitment acts involved. He cites several acts of symbolic renunciation of the old way of life: renaming the days of the
week, reorganizing the system of rights to agricultural lands and fish-
ing reefs, large-scale reshuffling of marriage partners in order to conform to the model of monogamy. The function of commitment :
spreading the movement and the ways in which commitment wa
generated are of no interest to Lawrence. Nevertheless, it is clear th
the dual aspects of intense experience leading to altered self-imag
and of bridge-burning acts committing participants to new patter:
of behavior, characterized the spread of the cult.

John Lofland's monograph on a religious cult in California (33:

describes a commitment experience which regularly precedes the bridge-burning act by several weeks or months. Although he reports no conversions involving dissociation or altered mental state, participants seem to have experienced a specific encounter (with a committed cult member) which they describe in almost ecstatic terms: "I felt a spiritual liveliness and vitality within me," "This day I desire never to forget," "Oh what joy I felt! My whole body was filled with electricity" (pp. 52-54). Lofland seems to credit the impact of these encounters to sexual attraction. In any case, they were remembered by participants with the same specificity as a Pentecostal remembers the time of his Baptism, or the Cargo Cult participants would remember the time of The Noise. Lofland distinguishes between "verbal converts," those who experienced only the significant encounter, and total converts, those who engaged in the intense communal interaction, reorganized their lives, and took the step of committing their material resources and their time to group goals. This step is indeed a bridge-burning act of considerable magnitude. Lofland also notes that "verbal converts" who could not be brought to perform the act of commitment remained peripheral participants.

Milton Singer (347) reports a movement within modern Hinduism that appears to have remarkable parallels with the experiential aspects of Pentecostal commitment. The Hindu movement also involves home meetings, emphasis on personal and spontaneous religious experience, and spirited hymn singing. Singer does not present enough case histories to enable a reader to trace the commitment process, but he does include a description of the conversion experience of one participant. The informant describes sensations of light, of the engulfing experience of Krishna love, and of being alive with a new force of spirituality." For several days after the experience, the convert was unaware of time, murmured "Sri Krishna" continually, and sang hymns about him. One is reminded of the "Jesus, Jesus, Jesus" uttered by equally transported Pentecostals.

The Mau Mau movement in Kenya provides a dramatic illustration of bridge-burning acts which precipitate an identity-altering experience. The kinds of killings required for full participation in the movement—murder of Europeans, Indians, or loyalist Kikuyu kinsmen—were designed to cut the convert off from his past life in the Kikuyu-British colonial system and leave him no choice but further involvement with the movement. In addition, the acts which accompanied the swearing of oaths violated both British colonial standards and traditional values of Kikuyu daily life. In the Mau Mau commitment process, individuals progressed through a series of increasingly traumatic oath-taking rituals. The horror which these acts inspired, not only among victims of the movement but also among participants themselves, created a powerful bond between individual members of the movement. The traumatic nature of these acts constituted an intense and transforming experience. L. S. B. Leakey (327) and Max Gluckman (314), noting the dissimilarities between these oath-taking rituals and those of traditional Kikuyu initiation ceremonies considered the Mau Mau movement as an aberrant phenomenon which was inexplicable in terms of Kikuyu culture patterns. Barnett in his more recent analysis of the movement (299), insists that traditionally such oath-taking rituals were only rarely used. In the Mau Mau movement every participant had to undergo not only one but a whole series of oath-takings. In this sense, Mau Mau oath-taking was non-Kikuyu. This, of course, is precisely the point. Such uncharacteristic behavior can be explained by a theory of movement dynamics which takes into account the function of commitment acts and ritual experiences by means of which an individual is separated from existing cultural patterns.

The purpose of Mau Mau initiation was to render participants as anti-Kikuyu as they were anti-British. Traditional Kikuyu patterns of behavior were not successful in achieving the described national independence. Mau Mau commitment acts and experiences drew adherents out of their roles in traditional and colonial society, cutting them off from both. Attempting to reintegrate former Mau Mau members into the established order, the British set up de-oathing or "cleaning" processes. These were successful only when the individuals could be brought to lead British forces against former comrades and actually shoot at them. Even in reverse, commitment requires both the experience and the act.

In the Peyote movement, the commitment experience and the bridge-burning act merge, as is often the case in Pentecostalism. Participants believe hallucinations in a sacramental setting confer feeling of personal significance" (296). Hallucinations are also explained as a source of spiritual power by which life can be lived su

cessfully outside the ritual environment (348). Drug-induced dissociation, in this case, provides an altered view of the self that has social
implications. The bridge-burning act for Peyotists—particularly pronounced when their legal right to use peyote was in question—is the
taking of the drug itself. This is the overt act which identifies an ad-
herent with the movement and commits him to the ethical standards
of the Peyote Way.

Several accounts note an identical combination of elements in the
process of conversion to Communism. Trainees in the indoctrination
program described by Walker experience a type of euphoria after the
breakdown and confession. Before this crisis, Communist jargon is
relatively meaningless: a party line to be memorized and played with
intellectually. At the point of initial commitment, the dogma suddenly becomes sharply pertinent; the words are filled with significance, almost like a revelation. This falling into place of the cognitive
building blocks painstakingly supplied in previous months has a
parallel in Pentecostalism: scriptural passages suddenly take on new
and deeper meaning and liturgical rituals come alive with portent.

Arthur Koestler's classic description of his conversion to Communism is remarkably similar to mystic experiences that accompany
religious commitment:

> By the time I had finished with *Feuerbach* and *State and
> Revolution,* something had clicked in my brain which
> shook me like a mental explosion. To say that one had "seen
> the light" is a poor description of the mental rapture which
> only the convert knows (regardless of what faith he has been
> converted to). The new light seems to pour from all direc-
> tions across the skull; the whole universe falls into pattern
> like the stray pieces of a jigsaw puzzle assembled by magic
> at one stroke. There is now an answer to every question,
> doubts and conflicts are a matter of the tortured past—a past
> already remote, when one had lived in dismal ignorance in
> the tasteless, colorless world of those who *don't know.*
> Nothing henceforth can disturb the convert's inner peace
> and serenity—except the occasional fear of losing faith
> again, losing thereby what alone makes life worth living,
> and falling back into the outer darkness where there is
> wailing and gnashing of teeth (324:19).

It is clear that Koestler's conversion experience was not a product of dissociative trance or of mass hysteria. There are obviously functional similarities between dissociational trance states, often thought to require group hypnosis, and the profound cognitive restructuring that can occur in solitude.

Accounts of the bridge-burning acts required of converts to Communism are commonplace. To engage in minor espionage against their own governments burned bridges for many European converts like Koestler in the 1930s. Public denunciation of "counter-revolutionary" kinsmen served as the act of commitment for many Chinese Communists. Red Guard commitment involves destruction of ancestral tombs and cursing ancestors and kinsmen. It appears that the final act of indoctrination of Viet Cong members often involves participation in a terrorist strike against a village in which the new convert has a kinsman.

The excellent analysis of the Oxford Group movement by Allan Eister (308) contains a description of the religious experiences of participants which parallels almost exactly the steps in the commitment process as we observed them in Pentecostalism. Participants describe the initial experience in similar phrases. The overt acts of confession and "restitution" clearly function as bridge-burning acts. The process also includes the same variety of recruitment activities and the same type of in-group interaction.

We have observed that commitment in the Black Power Movement involves the same two components: an identity-altering experience and a bridge-burning act. The identity-altering experience is probably most poetically described by Stephen Henderson (232) who speaks of it as being "baptized in blackness and informed with Soul." He also suggests that this "transfiguration of blackness" involves two distinct elements: "They are (1) the rejection of white middle class cultural values and (2) the affirmation of black selfhood, or . . . (a) the destruction of anything that stands in the way of selfhood and (b) a celebration of blackness." The revolution will be complete, he says, when "Negroes have been turned into black people, conscious and whole and powerful and proud." The connotations of a radically changed self-image are obvious. The relationship between the identity-altering experience and an overt, bridge-burning act is probably clearer in Black Power than in the other movements we have studied

Repeatedly, in published statements and during the interviews we conducted, participants explained that the "baptism in blackness," the surge of pride in being black, occurred at the very moment of confrontation with representatives of the white power structure—city or university officials or the police. For example, members of the Black Panther organization in California reported this radical change in self-image as they were being drawn into the group during its formative period. One member said, "I feel like a man and now I'm acting like a man" (272, p. 60). They believed such changes came about not because they carried guns, but because they were willing to initiate confrontation, to "meet white policemen on their own terms and face them down." Carrying guns, which was done with scrupulous concern for legality, was the method of defying taboos and ensuring confrontation. Following the first armed confrontation, police and other observers knew they had encountered something more than a group of armed blacks. The commitment was contagious; the ranks of the Panthers more than doubled that day (272, pp. 43-45).

Clearly the bridge-burning acts in Black Power which involve violence are what Goodenough has called "acts of eradication": destruction of property or of persons symbolic of the old order. Physical violence is not necessarily involved in such bridge-burning acts. There are situations in which simply wearing Afro-American dress or hair styles constitutes an irreversible break with past patterns of behavior and past relationships. In other situations refusal to say or do an expected thing constitutes such an act. The risk of commitment is relative to both the individual and the situation. As we have pointed out with regard to Pentecostalism, there are individuals in established Pentecostal churches who have been socialized to accept glossolalia and for whom it is therefore not a commitment act. C. Eric Lincoln 265) points up the important difference between the Black Muslims and conventional black religious cults such as those of Father Divine and Daddy Grace, old style Pentecostals. The difference is the risk of commitment. "The cultists," he says, "are not required to lay down their lives for their leader or his teachings."

The Autobiography of Malcolm X (271) records an interesting case of conversion to the Black Muslims in which a series of acts and experiences alternated in an increasingly intensifying way. Significantly, the process began with an act of commitment. Malcolm's brother wrote to him in prison instructing him to stop smoking and stop eating pork (symbol of Negro subordinate status) and promising that he would be shown how to get out of jail. Malcolm obeyed. The first reinforcement came with the reaction of the white prisoners. Later, Malcolm was to interpret this as the beginning of his conversion. "Unconsciously, my first pre-Islamic submission had been manifested, I had experienced for the first time the Muslim teaching, 'If you will take one step toward Allah, Allah will take two steps toward you.'" The subjective experience began with a visit from the brother, who told Malcolm, "You don't even know who you are," and proceeded to unfold the true knowledge, according to Elijah Muhammad's teaching, of who the black man is. "When Reginald left, he left me rocking with some of the first serious thoughts I had ever had in my life. . . . Not for weeks yet would I deal with the direct, personal application to myself, as a black man, of the truth. It still was like a blinding light."

Malcolm initiated a program of self-education in the prison library, and in his cell after hours, with only the corridor light to read by. Such dedication and accompanying intellectual awakening rival in intensity the more instantaneous enlightenment of a Pentecostal. Malcolm mentions one dissociational experience involving a vision, in his prison cell, of the founder of the movement, but it is not clear from the text at what stage in the total process this occurred.

This interweaving of bridge-burning acts (giving up pork and cigarettes, learning to read and write, debating his views in formal contests with white prisoners) and the intense experiences of the vision, the recognition of "who he really was," and of coming "mentally alive," resulted in a complete reversal of his life pattern. The dope addict and hustler from Harlem who had entered prison now emerged a disciplined, puritanical, and intensely committed participant in the Black Muslim movement.

Louis Lomax, in his biography of Malcolm X (269), suggests that the transformation of his subject during his prison years has been misrepresented as somewhat mystical, and that in fact it involved "no moral or intellectual magic." Lomax traces the same personality traits in the pre-conversion "Big Red" and the post-conversion Malcolm X He sees little difference between the clever Harlem hustler who preferred to outwit the system rather than succeed within it and the bril liant Black Muslim evangelist who preached separation from a doomed system. The "harsh truth," according to Lomax, is that years of confinement simply allowed Malcolm to crystallize forces that were already at work within him. This explanation of Malcolm's conversion experience may account for a troublesome mystical element, but it does not account for the radical and observable changes in behavioral patterns. Incarceration could as easily have produced a still more ingenious hustler. It is the very process which Lomax calls "crystallizing" that concerns those engaged in the study of commitment experiences. Cognitive restructuring does not necessarily imply thoroughgoing personality change. Few committed movement participants claim this. They do claim that they perceive themselves differently, that they view the world from a different frame of reference, and that they are motivated to behave in different ways. Those who feel compelled to find "natural" (usually psychological) explanations for conversion experiences forget a third alternative—the importance of a radically changed "assumptive system," as psychiatrist Jerome Frank would call it. The fact that Elijah Muhammed's version of Islamic theology was compatible with Malcolm's previous orientation to the white man does not alter the significance of the change in behavioral patterns and social alliances which occurred after he adopted this new frame of reference.

A typical story of conversion to the Black Power Movement is that told by a black university student. The young man is the son of successful middle class parents who, as he put it, "had it made." His parents are relatively well integrated into the white man's world; they accept the white man's view of the black man's status. Any observer of the American scene would have judged this young man as a member of a disadvantaged group. But he did not consider himself deprived until the initial contact with a Black Power advocate who happened to be a professor in a college he was attending. The professor's question, "How much do you know about yourself and your people?" is what the student remembers as the beginning of his awakening. The sense of shock he experienced when another view of himself was suggested (by a person he had come to respect) paralleled in many respects Malcolm X's shock after his brother's revelation of the "truth." Almost immediately the student began reinterpreting past experiences, seeing them in a new light. Things he had taken for granted as a child, such as the television cartoons of black-faced bugs playing the vaudeville stereotype of the Negro comedian, now shocked and angered him. The focus of needs, step two of the commitment process, had begun.

Soon he transferred to a larger university and met another black student who had been active in campus affairs. Together they organized an Afro-American students' club and began to study the Black Power "Bible" by Stokely Carmichael and Charles Hamilton (225).

Cognitive reorientation began with the reading program and small group discussions. The student's thoughts were cast in the terminology of his Bible, just as Pentecostal converts use scriptural passages not only as quotations but also as their source of language, one which expresses their own thoughts and feelings. He used phrases and described entire incidents which were almost direct quotes from Carmichael and Hamilton and other Black Power "scriptures." But cognitive closure had not occurred. He still saw himself as one who weighs various viewpoints, as a "moderate" in comparison with some of the other members of the group. In-group ties were developing rapidly. He had no conflicting out-group ties locally and his feelings of alienation from his middle class parents in a distant city were increasing. When his group wrote to several Afro-American groups on other campuses "to find out about their activities," it was clear that his expectations about the commitment act would soon be formulated.

Six weeks later the black student club presented demands for operational changes in administration to the president of the university and scheduled a supporting rally on campus. The demands included introduction of many new courses in black history, culture, languages, and art, and a significant increase in Negro enrollment in the university. All of these changes were to be accomplished within a few months.

The president of the university was extremely cooperative. He had already sent university personnel to local high schools to recruit actively among black students; he had requested and received funds for several full scholarships for Negroes; and he promised to ask department heads to set up as many of the desired courses as possible for the fall term. In spite of these innovations the student club criticized the administration for doing too little too slowly. Predictably, a sit-in demonstration occurred a few days later, in the president's office, and the student was quite literally carried off to jail with several other demonstrators.

On the way to jail, the leader of the group was quoted in the local newspaper as having said, "I always felt guilty about not having been arrested before." It was noted by observers that the unrest at this university seemed to stem more from "the awareness of national student rebellions than from any pressing needs at this university." We would add that they also stem from the need of these students to undergo a commitment act to "set" the new image of themselves as people of pride and power. Local officials seemed to be frustrating this need. All the students were given suspended jail sentences except for three off-campus "agitators" who were sentenced to ten days.

This created a new ferment, and demands for an appeal of their cases. The students declared that their off-campus members were part of the group and that if they went to jail, the rest of the group would go too. One might have predicted further unrest, escalating demands, and increased frustration for the administration, which accomplished more in a shorter time than would normally be expected of a ponderous academic system. Demands must be unrealistic in order that acts of commitment, such as demonstrations and jail sentences, can be experienced. Several months later, the young man who originally "had it made" emerged as the leader of the group committed to a militant stance. The latter required continuing pressure to meet escalating demands, and acts of protest—including the destruction of a minor piece of university property.

Support for the theory that participation in race riots may provide a commitment experience for black youth comes from a careful and statistically reliable study made after the Detroit and Newark riots of 1967 (224). It was made to test the deprivation and social disorganization theories. Caplan and Paige did not find these theories supported by their data. There was no difference between those ghetto residents who participated in the riots and those who did not, with respect to income, rate of unemployment, church attendance, family adjustment, or other measures of social maladjustment. Rioters tended to be slightly better educated than non-rioters. The important differences found by Caplan and Paige, however, had to do with those very attitudes which, according to our research, characterize committed participants in the Black Power Movement. Rioters preferred the use of the word "black" to "Negro" significantly more often than non-rioters. They were more insistent that blacks should study African history and culture. More rioters than non-rioters felt that the United States is not worth fighting for on foreign battlefields. More of the rioters resent the established order—not only the white power structure but also those affluent Negroes who have become part of it. The authors of the survey concluded that those who participate in riots "do so because their conception of their lives and their potential has changed."

We suggest that rioting may be an act which commits the individual to new attitudes and a new identity, a new image of himself. This may contribute to the pattern of riot activities. It has been widely observed that riots do not appear to recur in the same city, although they may shift from neighborhood to neighborhood within a city during a period of "disturbances." The important question is, do the same individuals participate in different riots, or do initiates "graduate" to other activities within the structure of the movement? Do such "graduates" lead others through the commitment experience (inciting to riot), engage in more calculated acts of "urban guerrilla warfare," and assume leadership in black patrol forces, youth associations, and community centers? It has been pointed out that "former rioters now involved with self-help programs have proved to be the best peacemakers during subsequent disorders" (257).

As we have noted, the function of rioting as an act of commitment to change is what Ward Goodenough has called "acts of eradication" —acts which often accompany personal identity change under conditions of rapid social change. Antisocial actions are, he suggests, "a tempting way to commit oneself to identity change; they are dramatic and effective." Whatever the consequences of such eradicatory acts, one cannot be the same person after one has committed them. Because identity change involves the replacement of certain features of the former self-image, it also requires eradication of some part of one's former self. We suggest that violent acts, therefore, symbolize a rejection of the existing social order, and actualize the personal change necessary for participation in a new order. One Negro mother, attempting to express what she thought was different about the youth today, said, "These youngsters are a different breed . . . unlike my generation. These children are willing to die—that's the difference.'

Obviously not all black young people are committed in this sense. But they are acquainted with the concept of violence as a commitment experience. Fanon's interpretation of violence emphasized its function in the positive psychological transformation of members of an oppressed group (242). It is an unpopular notion that rioting and other types of violence provide just such an opportunity, and that to be willing to die under such circumstances may produce the commitment necessary for an altered self-image and active participation in a movement. We suggest, however, that this is precisely what has been happening.

One of the most important changes in the self-image of black Americans is related to the male-female role reversal characteristic of the family life of lower class blacks. During the years of slavery, the forbidding of legal marriages between slaves and the sexual access to female slaves by white owners set a pattern of emasculation of the black male. Since the Civil War the employment of female Negroes as domestics, and the unequal job restrictions placed on Negro males, in many instances meant that black females had a greater earning capacity than black males. As one black woman wrote, "I wore the pants because he could not" (255). In addition, economic insecurity often forced Negro males to seek jobs in areas distant from their families. A matricentric family structure, with absentee or shifting fathers, thus became quite common. The radical change in self-image accompanying commitment to Black Power or "the revolution" involves not only replacing a sense of inferiority with pride, but also consciously attempting to restore the male role in Negro family life. Rapid change in psychological patterns formed during many generations is not a matter of gradual re-education. It requires a conversion experience. Violence is a tempting means with which to set the new role.

Another very interesting function of riot activities is the pressure they exert on non-rioters. Commitment in Black Power seems to be as contagious as commitment in Pentecostalism. In a city that had just witnessed its first riot, we talked with six young men about the effect on the black community in the riot area and in other sections of the city with black neighborhoods. None of these young men had been participants in the riot. Half of the group were against riots; the others were undecided or only moderately supportive. All agreed, however, that there had been one major outcome: "It forced us to ask ourselves, which side are we on?" This attitude was noticeable among adults as well. The commitment act of a few individuals forced many to the point of decision with regard to participation in the movement. A black psychologist from Watts reported that "the riots started all of us thinking. Symbolically they established manhood for blacks. It was a beginning for many of an acceptance of our blackness" (257). Similar evidence is presented by Blair Justice (260) in his study of attitude changes among blacks after riots.

We do not mean to imply that rioting is the only type of bridge-burning act or identity-altering experience for potential converts to Black Power. Nor do we suggest that fire bombing and looting are always commitment acts. We do suggest, however, that the function of riots as commitment experiences should be considered by members of the establishment in their attempts to counter and control the destruction. Chicago's Mayor Daley said in a television interview after the 1968 Chicago demonstrations that one of the main purposes of outside "agitators" was to "radicalize" a large group of young people. Ironically, the activities of the Chicago police were the major factors which enabled the "agitators" to accomplish their purpose.

Protest demonstrations and marches are often both an experience and an act by means of which some people, both black and white, become committed to Black Power. One such event in a midwestern city illustrates how several stages of the commitment process can be compressed into a period of few hours. Demonstrations for open housing were being sponsored by a militant group whose leader is a white Roman Catholic priest. For months daily marches for open housing were conducted. Sunday marches drew the largest groups of demonstrators from all over the country. Some whites, participating for the first time in this group's activities, came by buses from several other cities for one of the Sunday marches. One group of clergymen and active church laymen had had initial contact with participants in the movement through previously established relationships with individuals in a group of ex-freedom riders. These churchmen, whose commitment dated from the Selma marches, set up a group headquarters in Chicago in order to mobilize the churches for action. They supported the Catholic priest who was organizing this particular demonstration and who had recruited the neighboring metropolitan con-

tingent. The focus of needs through demonstration had already occurred. The needs of these particular ministers and laymen may be
broadly defined as part of a deep concern for the relevance of the
contemporary church to the social problems of today—and to Civil
Rights in particular. The demonstration effect of Selma and other similar activities was perceived as a successful first step which furthered
the goals of equality and freedom. Ministers, laymen, and a group of
white university students went by bus to the city in which the open
housing demonstrations were being conducted. They were accompanied by other whites who had participated in one of these marches
previously; some had been active only the week before.

Group interaction, already begun in face-to-face interchange
with ex-freedom riders, increased in intensity on the several hours'
bus ride. The songs of the Black Power Movement were sung: "We
shall overcome," "Sock-it-to-em, Rock-it-to-em, Black Power!" and
"Which side are you on?" These songs have a different beat from Pentecostal revival songs, but they fulfill the same function, inspiring the
kind of rhythmic foot-tapping, hand-clapping, swaying, and "letting
go" valued in both movements.

The three functions of group interaction identified previously—
cognitive restructuring, development of in-group ties, and formulation
of expectations concerning the commitment experience—were all
clearly present during this Black Power demonstration. On the buses,
ideology was discussed. New initiates and experienced converts considered whether or not integration of black Americans into existing
social structures is an outmoded and unworkable idea. They discussed
the need for pride in being black, and the need for the creation of the
black community as a power bloc in the American power structure.
The group dynamic that developed after long hours on the same bus,
learning and singing the same songs, sharing common hopes, and
heightening a sense of intimacy and separation from the world outside, tended to create and strengthen in-group ties. A foxhole camara-
derie developed as the dangers of the approaching demonstration became evident. University students on the buses exhibited mild hostility toward police who were present when the buses stopped for
lunch; the students began a loud conversation in the restaurant about
other whites who lacked the guts to join such a demonstration.

Initiates' expectations concerning the commitment experience were clarified when converts explained that they would be "hit with an experience like you've never had before." The group sang the praises of the Commandos—a patrol force of young black males who would protect the line of march. Initiates were prepared to accept the authority of these young men, who were described as figures of power. Respect for them was increased by the retelling of their conversion from street bums into a disciplined group of strong young heroes of the revolution.

It must be stressed that what is being outlined here is not a master plot hatched by brilliant manipulators who consciously utilized certain recognized steps in a commitment process. The development of this demonstration is described here in order to illustrate a process that we have identified through observation of the social dynamic of two different movements. Experienced movement leaders in both Black Power and Pentecostalism gain an empirical wisdom concerning movement dynamics and utilize them to some extent. But no one had ordered the Black Power converts on the buses to "sell" the Commandos as authority figures. They did so because they themselves regarded the Commandos in this manner and were sharing their conviction with newcomers.

When the buses arrived at the cathedral where the demonstration was being organized, the impressive sight of the Commandos in their black sweat shirts—with Black Power slogans on them—reinforced the expectations. Girls in similar sweat shirts and short cheerleader skirts completed the picture. The entire group of demonstrators, mostly black, was massing in the cathedral. Each demonstrator was asked to contribute to and become a member of the local NAACP youth league. This constituted an initial step in the process of decision, for those who refused were considered "just spectators"—a scornful evaluation.

Speeches by both black and white leaders in the cathedral clarified key points of ideology: Black Power is a black movement; the role of whites is only to aid. The speakers recapitulated racial injustices. They discussed open housing at length. There were more battle hymns, led by the group of young song leaders. The leader of the Commandos spoke, giving his "testimony" and spelling out the logistics of the march—women and children in the center, men along the outsides, flanked by the Commandos.

White participants and moderate blacks were given moral support by white moderate churchmen; their speeches provided the stamp of their approval as representatives of their respective denominations. An official statement of support for the purpose of the march by the Roman Catholic bishop of the area was reaffirmed.

As the crowd moved out into the courtyard, songs and speeches became more militant, and the theme of preparation for danger was re-emphasized. Jokes about local city officials, the police, and non-participating whites were shared and enjoyed enormously. The dynamic of polarity forced each individual closer to the point of decision. A final speech by Dick Gregory, a black entertainer who has become a leader in the movement, stressed the dedication of this crowd to the principles of non-violence. He also intimated that there were others in the city who believed in violence and that those espousing non-violence were unable to control this element. The success of this particular demonstration, then, became a sacred mission: not only to accomplish the stated goal of achieving open housing, but also to save the whole country from those who were advocating more violent means.

Then came the moment of decision. In Pentecostal revival meetings, this would have been the moment of the altar call. The crowd was asked, "Which side are you on? Are you with us or against us?" Outside the courtyard, in the street, hostile crowds, armored cars, and police with motorcycles were gathered. Potential danger was evident. Those who chose to go on the march were told to leave the courtyard, turn left, and line up as directed. Others were told to stay where they were or to keep to the right as they left the courtyard.

The march involved two levels of commitment. During the first part of the march, conservatives organized a counter-march to oppose open housing. Police managed to keep the two processions apart, but rumors of trouble flew along the lines of march. There were minor confrontations all along the parade route—with drivers of cars blocked in the traffic, with hostile onlookers who taunted white marchers, and with policemen who were coldly disdainful of the entire performance. As the marchers approached a drawbridge leading to a section of the city where opposition to open housing was greatest, special cars waited to take women with children and others who were tired back to the cathedral. At this second moment of decision, before the most dangerous part of the route, participants could drop out without losing face. Few took the option.

As demonstrators crossed the drawbridge (a conveniently symbolic barrier) angry crowds met them with Wallace-for-President posters, leaflets demanding the excommunication of the white Roman Catholics involved, curses, fist-shaking, and shouting. Commandos, serving as a human barrier between the crowds and the marchers, also chanted threats and made increasingly provocative gestures. Whites still in the march were now identified not only with a demand for justice but with open provocation, which angered other whites. Tension escalated as police donned gas masks. However, the demonstration did not become a riot.

When the marchers at last returned to the cathedral, they were exhausted; many had experienced a lasting change. On the return bus trip, one white protestant minister described the experience as one of "being in a daze. Now I know what it's like to be converted," he said. "For the first time, I've had a conversion experience."

His moment of transformation occurred upon arrival, when he walked into the cathedral and saw the white interior, the very white statue of the madonna, and the white and gold statues of the saints as background for a mass of black faces and the black Commandos and cheerleaders lined up across the altar steps. This subjective experience changed his attitudes and his sense of identity with respect to black Americans. The alteration of self-image was completed by the commitment act—joining a demonstration which overtly identified him with the movement and set him apart from non-participating whites.

A workable theory of movement dynamics and of the commitment process might help to clarify the types of change that underlie the student rebellions, white as well as black, on campuses across the nation. Like the black Americans, American students are acquiring a new self-image to which they must become converted and committed. Talk to any irate parent, and it is clear that the older generation clings to an image of the student as one who is preparing for life —one who is not yet a fully productive member of society, who has not yet proved himself. He therefore is not entitled to a position of social power or a voice in the administration of his institution. The parallel between the second-class citizenship of the black American and the status of the white student has been recognized and irreverently described by one college professor in an article entitled "The Student as Nigger" (311).

Adults like to pretend themselves and encourage their children to believe that a young person's study is comparable to his father's work. They talk about investment in the future and the importance of a higher education, but the image of the student as a non-productive dependent still persists. In a society where value-equals-success-equals-work-equals-money, this image is demeaning. In response, students are clearly creating commitment situations in order to experience bridge-burning acts. That these acts of rebellion are also identity-altering experiences is clear from a statement made by a white student involved in demonstrations at one university. Everyone—faculty, administration spokesmen, and students—admitted that the non-racial issue (four-letter words in a student publication) was only a catalyst. This is the student's own evaluation, written for a city newspaper, of the gains made by the rebellion:

> As irrelevant as it may seem, the battles we've won are mostly internal, in the hearts and minds of the students who, for the past week, have continually questioned our role in this society, our own personal relationships, and our own self concept. We have taken a stand which has called for sacrifice and understanding. We will never be the same again.

The valedictorian of the 1969 graduating class of the University of California at Berkeley stated the same ideas in almost the same words in a portion of the commencement exercise shown on national television. Challenging the adult hope that once out of college today's young people will change, "grow up," and fit the pattern, the Berkeley graduate insisted that the change had already occurred. She believed that those who have marched through police lines, experienced Mace and tear gas, planted grass in the park, or smoked it, stood with their black brothers and sensed the oppression of the ghetto, will never be like the alumni of a few years past. In her opinion, neither the graduating seniors nor the United States will ever be the same again.

In the case of both the Black Power Movement and the movement of student rebellion, acts of commitment are destructive of the old order. They function, however, to restructure black American and student self-images. Such acts help to create the notion of a people with power based on criteria different from those prevalent in the existing social structure. Both groups demand recognition and respect for themselves *in their present state;* they are not concerned about meeting existing social requirements for recognition and respect. Both demand power to control or to share in the control of institutions, even as they reject socially prescribed methods of gaining such power. In order to make these demands, and to bring about social changes still unenvisioned, both black Americans and white students must believe they already command respect and possess power. To the extent that they experience cognitive restructuring and a permanent change in self-image, through the process of commitment, they will behave *as if* they possessed social power—just as the Pentecostal behaves *as if* the all-powerful God answers every prayer, and as the Viet Cong behave *as if* under-equipped guerrillas can successfully oppose the United States armed forces. It is this "as if" behavior that causes the established order with its supposedly more realistic evaluation of the situation to misjudge movements completely. The power generated by commitment experience and bridge-burning acts can transform "unrealistic" goals into self-fulfilling prophecies.

This cross-cultural and cross-movement comparison of commitment clarifies a further point in the relationship between the commitment experience and the commitment act. It should be noted that a bridge-burning act may precede, follow, or occur simultaneously with the identity-altering experience. For many Pentecostals, the act and the experience are one. For others, the experience precedes the act. In some cases an experience which is not a bridge-burning act can be transformed into one by opposition. In certain non-Pentecostal congregations the experience of glossolalia may be considered nothing more than a different approach to the devotional life, until tongue speaking becomes "an issue" and church authorities declare it undesirable or dangerous. At this point, the glossolalic must either deny the validity of his experience or become committed after the act.

In some movements the bridge-burning act leads to, or itself becomes, an identity-altering experience. Participants in the student rebellions who "will never be the same again" are examples of this. The succession of ritual oaths taken by Mau Mau converts were bridge-burning acts which produced altered self-images.

It is undoubtedly true that the event through which commitment occurs is a phenomenological unit whether it occurs at one point in time or during a series of acts and experiences. We have separated the components of act and experience for the purposes of analysis; it should be remembered that they are complementary and mutually reinforcing halves of a whole.

Further study will be required to determine the function in movement dynamics of the different levels or depths of commitment on the part of different individuals in any movement. However, there have been studies linking depth of commitment to severity of initiation rites (4). Our field observations suggest that depth of commitment is also related to leadership roles. The proportion of hard core members to less deeply committed members which is optimum for movement growth should be studied. It is our impression that the less committed participants in a movement function in three important ways. First, they constitute a sort of buffer zone between the hard core and society at large, keeping levels of opposition high enough to require risk but low enough to avoid suppression. Second, they facilitate the recruitment of those who would be offended or repelled by the intensity or the doctrinal positions of the more committed hard core. We have seen less committed members of Pentecostal groups interacting patiently at low levels of intensity with potential converts over a period of weeks or months. Eventually, a typical potential convert is ready to graduate from "spiritual milk to spiritual meat." At this point he is introduced to a more dynamic and intensely committed individual for the *coup de grace*. A comparable role is played by some of the conservatives in the Black Power Movement. Black militants are coming to recognize the potential in "yoking" even the "Uncle Toms" (250). Third, less committed participants provide organizational stability. A higher percentage of hard core committed members would seem to produce more organizational fission. Less committed participants are more likely to compromise and to consolidate organizational gains.

In summary, commitment in a movement may be operationally

defined as a *psycho-social state which results from an identity-altering experience and a bridge-burning act. It is manifested as (a) primacy of concern with the belief system of the movement; (b) participation in the social organization of the movement; (c) some degree of charismatic capacity to influence others; (d) willingness to risk social, economic, or political sanctions exercised by opponents of the movement; and (e) some degree of behavioral change.*

Individuals may be prepared for a commitment experience and led to perform an act of commitment through a social process involving seven identifiable steps.

Personal commitment contributes to the spread of a movement by motivating face-to-face recruitment of others and by helping to create a segmented and proliferating organizational structure. The cognitive restructuring necessary for commitment in movements involving personal transformation and social change is evidence of the very close relationship between the factors of commitment and ideology in movement dynamics.

VI

Ideology

Much has been written about the ideology of certain movements in order to explain their appeal. There is no doubt that familiarity with the theology or the ideological formulations of a specific movement is essential to an understanding of it. There is also great value in the suggestion that the type of ideology of a movement should be studied with reference to the type of relative deprivation that facilitated its rise (1). There will be no attempt here, however, to describe systematically, to summarize, or otherwise explain the belief system of Pentecostalism, Black Power, or any other movement. We are not attempting a full explanation of either movement, but an analysis of the mechanisms by which they, as well as other movements, develop. In such an analysis of movement dynamics, there is more to be gained by identifying generic characteristics of movement ideologies—characteristics which may be found in the ideology of any movement—which are functional in terms of the growth of the movement, and which promote personal or social change. Reference to the belief systems of the movements we have studied will be for illustrative purposes only.

We would agree with Eric Hoffer's remark that "the effectiveness of a doctrine does not come from its meaning but from its certitude" (28). There are no better examples of this observation than the statements in which Pentecostal beliefs are couched. The same statements

159

can be heard in identical phraseology issuing from almost any pulpit in the land—Pentecostal or non-Pentecostal—on almost any Sunday. But where most pew-sitters nod approvingly, if indeed they hear at all, Pentecostals find their hearts beating faster; make mental notes of specific actions to be taken; and, if they are members of Catholic, Episcopalian, Methodist, or Presbyterian congregations, fight back the impulse to raise both arms and shout "Hallelujah! Amen!"

Outsiders usually describe this type of certitude as a form of dogmatism. There have been many studies of "authoritarianism," "dogmatism," or "closed systems thinking" (2, 42-46, 86, 119). These studies are largely attempts to describe a personality type character-ized by rigidity of thinking. Because committed movement partici-pants tend to display dogmatic certitude, they are sometimes—by extrapolation—assumed to be of a certain personality type. Field observation in the Pentecostal Movement leaves little doubt that par-ticipants were either brought up with or adopted at conversion what psychologist Milton Rokeach (44) would call "a closed cognitive organization of beliefs." Yet there is no evidence that Pentecostals as a group represent any particular personality type. We would suggest that investigating various personality types which may be associated with "closed system thinking" is not so important as studying the func-tion of such thinking in the spread and the effectiveness of a move-ment.

The function of "dogmatism"—or certitude in the process of per-sonal and social change—is not well understood. We suggest that a certain rigidity of belief structure is essential to motivate and sup-port a radical attitudinal or behavioral change. The luxuries of tolerance, relativism, eclecticism, and ambivalence are available to those who accept themselves and their society as given. Such attri-butes are even consistent with gradual and developmental personal or social change. But at points of radical change, when fundamental social innovation or personal transformation of any magnitude is required, there must be an ideological basis for decisive action. Movement participants must be able to select with confidence the right alternative, the adaptive course in terms of movement goals— or, as the Pentecostals would say, to perceive the will of God for them in any situation.

This conceptual certitude, we suggest, is a result of the commit ment process. We have called it the "cognitive closure" that climaxes the cognitive restructuring process. There is a sense of finality—of having got firm hold on a belief system or a conceptual framework that fully satisfies the human need for explanation and meaning. It is a recognition of an already existing reality, as it were. Pentecostals—in addition to those who, like Arthur Koestler, have experienced conversion to other movements—describe it as revelation. The belief system of the individual may be expanded, developed, elaborated, even changed to some degree subsequently, but there remains the certainty that on basic points, there will never again be any question. There can be cognitive restructuring and perhaps even some alteration in the self-image without the sense of closure. Commitment requires cognitive closure. As we are using the term, cognitive closure does not necessarily imply narrow-mindedness, or even closed-mindedness. Rather, it is a function of the decision-making process, one which must be dramatically irreversible even under conditions involving some risk. This point is of great importance in understanding the close interrelatedness of the commitment and ideology factors. It is also important in dealing constructively with what some people perceive as the "fanatical" or "irrational" quality in committed movement participants.

Closely related to the certitude, or "dogmatism," of movement ideology is a second characteristic: codification of beliefs into a common rhetoric—the well-known "party line." For an outsider, this is one of the most frustrating aspects of interacting with a committed member of any movement. Pentecostals seem to answer any question with a quotation, or at least a paraphrase of book-chapter-and-verse. Certain phrases like "God has no grandsons" have become cliches. Black Power participants also have certain stock phrases that pepper the conversation and seem to admit of no discussion: "Racism is your hang up," "Whitey is more interested in protecting property than human rights," "Respect is a right, not something you qualify for," and "You can't understand because you've never been oppressed." Black Power participants in any city can be heard repeating the same expressions. Movements, like some closely knit families, develop their own distinctive "languages."

Many people who agree wholeheartedly with the Pentecostal religious interpretation of experience, or with the Black Power militant's description of past injustices, wonder why these cannot be expressed in more original and individualistic terms. Continual use of Biblical quotations or of Black Power clichés irritates and bores some people. We suggest that the function of the "party line" in formulating movement ideology is twofold.

First, for the participant, the "party line" provides patterned answers to questions that will be raised by members of the established order who oppose the movement. Converts have ready, effective, and oft-tested answers to most objections. Curiously, these objections appear to be as patterned as the "party line" responses. Often one hears the white liberal or not-so-liberal say, "We respect your goals but we cannot condone your means." Or "Aren't you being just as segregationist as we were?" And many "Spirit-filled" Christians have been told: "We do not question your sincerity in seeking to yield yourself more fully to the Holy Spirit, but why confuse the issue by insisting on all this tongues business?" Scriptural responses are concise and provide the convert with assurance about the authority of Pentecostal beliefs.

Second, the codification of movement ideology into a "party line" facilitates its transmission to new converts and to those seeking the commitment experience. It provides, in short, the intellectual building blocks out of which cognitive restructuring can take place. The revelatory nature of the commitment experience requires the presence of conceptual models which spring into life and take on deep meaning. Pentecostal converts experience the Biblical statements they have heard all their lives as suddenly real—filled with a significance beyond rational comprehension. As we have noted, advanced Communist trainees report a similar experience when the "jargon" becomes meaningful and motivating.

Those opposed to a movement often make the mistake of assuming either that the spouting of the "party line" indicates lack of real understanding on the part of participants, or that by learning the movement ideology themselves, they can rationally convince "misguided" participants that they have been misled by demagogues. There are experts in the State Department and in the Central Intelligence Agency who specialize in studying Communist ideology, rhetoric, and style of confrontation. These men lecture to military, government, and Peace Corps personnel, preparing them to defend themselves and the ideology of the American Way against the Communist party line. Evidently they hope that people can be prevented from joining a movement by "seeing through" the ideology and by rational argument. Such an approach does not take into account the fact that the "party line" may be simply a functional codification of beliefs gained and accepted through a series of significant experiences. Such counter-spokesmen do not understand that the rhetoric provides confidence and assurance in the face of opposition; also, it serves as a simplified way of communicating a deep and ineffable experience. Against commitment, which is so closely related to ideological formulations, there is no rational argument. The latter, in fact, tends to take on a codification of its own, thus giving the ideologue further proof that his beliefs are right.

A third characteristic of movement ideology is that it includes a concept of personal power and control over one's own destiny or the destiny of the world. This sense of personal power may be combined with what appears to be a fatalistic or passive attitude toward control over events. Pentecostals, for example, take very seriously the Christian theory of an omnipotent God. They frequently use phrases such as "I am powerless without God," "God wants a yielded vessel," and "I am completely dependent upon God." A typical Pentecostal possesses the orientation of one who believes himself acted upon by a power external to the self. The ideology of Alcoholics Anonymous is similarly based upon a concept of the "power greater than one's self." The nature of this power is not clearly spelled out. It may be interpreted as the power of alcohol over the individual, as the power of the group to save him, or as the power of a Higher Being as each individual envisions him. This orientation is often assumed to be an indication of psychological weakness, of lack of ego strength, of lack of autonomy, of an inability to take the initiative. It is also, to an outsider, indistinguishable from the fatalism that results in lackluster acceptance of everything that happens as something willed by the gods, and the refusal to take any action at all. The same phrase, "I put myself in the hands of Allah," can be spoken by Turkish Muslims whose beliefs obstruct the process of modernization, or by a Malcolm X, whose intensity in precipitating change, both personal and social, was unsurpassed.

The difference between a despairing, do-nothing fatalism and the type of surrender to an outside power that is characteristic of Pentecostalism, Alcoholics Anonymous, the Black Muslims, and other religiously oriented movements is the commitment experience. The sense of personal power that characterizes movement ideologies comes from a personal experience by means of which the convert comes into a relationship with a source of power considered to be external to himself. This relationship confers power upon the convert at the same time that it relieves him of a restrictive sense of personal responsibility. If all is done in the service of God, or of Allah, then success and failure are all one, and the individual is free to take positive action in any direction he feels moved or directed.

In movements with no supernatural referent, power comes as a result of identification with the larger group. Personal surrender to the party, or identification with the group, brings both pride and the power conferred by the group. Some of the new sense of power among black Americans is based on an understanding of the self as a member of a larger, worldwide group of non-whites who constitute the majority of the human race and whose ideological (if not organizational) unity is emerging. The emphasis on the role of blacks in the building of this nation and on the heroes of slave rebellions and leaders of protest movements confers a sense of pride and power, and encourages black Americans to think of themselves as members of an unconquerable and powerful minority.

Movement ideologies also confer a sense of personal worth as well as personal power. There is something of the Doctrine of the Elect in every movement. The very nature of movements—their function in shaping personal and social change—inspires the assumption that destiny is on the side of the true believer, and that each believer has his own unique role to play as that destiny unfolds.

As we pointed out in chapters III and IV, this ideology of personal access to power is functionally interrelated with the factors of organizational structure of and recruitment to the movement. The processes of organizational fission, proliferation, and entrepreneurial exploitation of various social niches are all influenced by this sense of personal power, of divine guidance, of every man's right to have "his own bag." The power ideology typical of movements confers a sense of the charismatic power necessary to influence others. In this way, movement ideology is related to evangelical recruitment.

A fourth characteristic of movement ideology is what we have come to call its "split-level" nature. On one level of the ideology of any movement are those few basic concepts in which all participants find agreement. Other levels involve those infinite variations on the ideological themes that promote both ideological and organizational diversity.

That worldwide Communism does not enjoy complete ideological harmony is obvious. Even more obvious are the ideological differences among militant, moderate, and conservative wings of the Black Power Movement. They are so different, in fact, that some militants and some conservatives would deny each other's right to a place in the movement. Yet all stand on the concepts of black pride, black unity, and economic and political power for the black community.

The same sort of ideological divergence exists in the Pentecostal Movement. There are "Spirit-filled" Christians in Catholic or mainline protestant denominations, and even some in independent "interdenominational" churches, who hesitate to call themselves Pentecostal for fear of being identified with the "Holy Rollers." The compliment is heartily returned by some of the more separatist "Jesus Only" sects. Yet the most mutually critical antagonists will admit to the same Baptism of the Holy Spirit, the same tracing of glossolalia to the Day of Pentecost, and the same hope for a new order of things to come.

The basic and essential ingredients of each of these belief systems can be simply and forcefully condensed into credal statements or slogans to form the "upper story" of the "split-level" ideology—the Communists' "inevitable march of history," the Pentecostals' "Jesus is the answer," Black Power's "Black is beautiful." These and other statements form a basis for ideological unity within each movement which makes possible inter-cell leader exchange, sporadic mutual assistance, and the formation of temporary coalitions on action programs. Such statements also serve as the basis for a flow of financial and other material resources through non-bureaucratic channels; they contribute to an often surprising presentation of a united front in the face of opposition.

At the "lower level" of ideology an almost infinite variety of ideological emphases, interpretations, adaptations, and exegetical detours can be found in any movement. Attempts to stereotype more than Pentecostal theology's basic beliefs, therefore, can lead to a distorted perception of the movement. There are fundamentalist Pentecostals, liberal Pentecostals, liturgical Pentecostals, militantly anti-ritualistic Pentecostals, Pentecostals who smoke, and Pentecostals who will not even wear lipstick. All of these variations on the theme have ideological bases stoutly defended with at least three scriptural proofs.

In spite of the monolithic concept of worldwide Communism held by many Americans, there are Communists in Czechoslovakia, China, India, and North Vietnam who do not think of themselves as carbon copies of each other, or as puppets on Muscovite strings. The function of such ideological variation in the development of the segmented, reticulate, organizational structure of movements has been discussed. We have also noted that ideological variation facilitates recruitment from a wide variety of socio-economic, educational, cultural, and national backgrounds.

Both a cause and an effect of ideological variation typical of rapidly spreading movements is the intensity with which participants characteristically approach their beliefs. The humblest Pentecostal spends as much, if not more, time poring over verses in his Bible, looking them up in other translations, reading commentaries, and discussing them intently with others as any seminary student. Informal group discussions are largely concerned with the application of Biblical statements to very specific personal, family, community, or national problems. For participants in a movement, theology (a value system or a conceptual framework) is not just an inherited orientation. It is a matter of personal responsibility and daily concern. Self criticism in Communist cell groups serves something of the same function as the type of group discussions found in Pentecostalism and Black Power. Such discussions keep the individual continually alert to the practical implications of his beliefs as they affect his behavior, his decisions, and his attitudes toward others both inside and outside the movement. The developing ideology of Black Power is hammered out not only in informal bull sessions but also in active confrontation with those who oppose it. In this way the ideology becomes a very personal belief structure for each participant. Personal involvement in ideological formulation requires and also renews an individual's commitment to the movement.

Reporting in *Life* on the Students for a Democratic Society, Roger Vaughn noted that "while there are not many issues that hold

SDS together, those that do form the cement are basic and deep-running" (352). One of the cliches to which all participants subscribe is "participatory democracy." This phrase provides an ideological basis for movement unity. Definitions of it, however, are as numerous as those who define it. These definitions at the "lower level" of ideology are worked out in local groups, not only verbally but also by means of group decisions and activities of various sorts. Thus participants in the movement simultaneously deepen their own personal commitment and increase the diversity of the movement's organizational structure.

All ideologies or conceptual systems, including the vaguely defined values and ideals which characterize different nations or culture groups, are "split-level" in the sense that there are a few basic tenets shared by all, plus many variant, sometimes conflicting, values held by local or sub-cultural groups. Specific characteristics of movement ideology are the intensity with which the basic tenets permeate the consciousness of the individual participants, and the degree of personal involvement exhibited as participants develop and argue about particular emphases and variants.

A fifth characteristic of movement ideology is both a cause and a result of the fourth. It is a rejection of what we have called the ideal-real gap. All societies have a set of ideals for human behavior which are only approximated by the reality. Tolerance for this discrepancy is a mark of normalcy. Rejection of it is usually viewed as "fanaticism."

Psychologist Kenneth Kenniston (323), in a discussion of the hippie and the New Left movements among American college students, points out that the recognition of the gap between credal values and actual practices in any society is a powerful motor for social change. However, he also shows that in most societies where social change is slow and social institutions are relatively unchanging, there occurs what he calls the "institutionalization of hypocrisy." Children learn not only to respect the credal values of their society, but also to understand where inconsistency between these values and actual behavior is to be expected and, in fact, considered functional. Early inhabitants of the "Land of the Free" could own slaves without any sense of inconsistency by using this conceptual device. The ideal-real gap was institutionalized by means of Biblical arguments which held blacks to be sub-human. They were said to be created by God to serve whites; Africans and other "primitive" peoples were thought to possess no culture.

Institutionalization of the ideal-real gap is also supported by placing a value on the very tolerance of the gap. It is commonly considered a mark of maturity that one "doesn't go overboard on things," that one accepts the fact that "nobody's perfect." The "rational approach" to social problems is generally thought to include the realization that "change doesn't happen overnight" and that moderation in all things is a mark of decency.

During times of rapid social change, however, there is a breakdown in the institutionalization of hypocrisy. Values shift, and "new" values have not existed long enough for situational exceptions to their rules to be defined. As Kenniston puts it, "the universal gap between principle and practice appears in all its nakedness." Where tolerance of the ideal-real gap is in itself an ideal in most value systems, movement ideologies contain a strong and verbalized rejection of this gap. The fact that participants in movements do not always live up to their own ideals does not alter the importance of this characteristic of movement ideology. Whether or not there is a significant difference in "hypocrisy quotient" between movement participants and supporters of the established order has never been determined. There is some evidence from objective observers (some of them scientists) that participants in the Pentecostal Movement in various cultural settings do, indeed, come closer to closing the Christian ideal-real gap than their counterparts in conventional churches. Some describe Pentecostalism as a gap-closer in terms of desired social and moral behavior in this and other societies (154, 155, 177, 178). Others, even severe critics of the movement, consider Pentecostalism as a gap-closer in that it attempts to actualize Biblical ideals of spiritual experience, witnessing, and church participation (161, 168, 173, 191).

Observers of the leaders and hard core members of the Communist movement in its early stages in any area have generally found that ideals are taken seriously, that those who fail to live up to the ideals are severely criticized or punished, and that daily decisions and actions are subjected to the test of "fit" with movement ideology.

Members of an established order within which a movement is

spreading react to this characteristic of movement ideology in one of three ways. They credit participants with being "unquestionably sincere" but possibly misguided. Or they brand as a fanatic anyone who refuses to tolerate the ideal-real gap. Or they delight in any opportunity to point out failures of movement participants to live up to their stated ideals. Members of conventional churches often criticize "Spirit-filled" Pentecostals, calling their enthusiasm for witnessing a form of "un-Christian spiritual pride." White reactionaries are fond of noting any prejudice black Americans might display toward members of other minority groups. The foregoing are expectable reactions to that characteristic of movement ideology which rejects institutionalized hypocrisy and lays bare a long-existent ideal-real gap.

The sixth characteristic of movement ideology is ambiguity. At first glance this may seem to contradict what we reported earlier about conceptual rigidity and ideological codification. Obviously, movements differ in the degree to which they clarify and enunciate goals and means. Of the movement members we have studied, Pentecostals seem to be able to enunciate their ideology the most clearly, Black Power participants less so, and student rebels least. In part this is true because Pentecostal ideology contains widely acceptable Christian ideals. Similarly, blacks enunciate many goals which have been part of the American dream from the beginning. The New Left, on the other hand, is attempting to reformulate American ideals. To the extent that the ideology of a movement involves not only closing the ideal-real gap but also pressing beyond existing ideals, ideology becomes increasingly ambiguous. In fact it sometimes seems to be non-existent from the point of view of the opposition. For example, critics of student movements often ask for a statement of goals. When offered "participatory democracy," critics dismiss it as unclear." When a more specific goal is expressed, such as students' influence in matters of rating, hiring, and firing faculty members, such demands are written off as "unrealistic." Next, when movement participants protest with unacceptable methods, critics claim the stated goals are becoming "clouded" by irresponsible action. The same dynamic is obvious in the Black Power Movement. We have even observed it in interaction between "Spirit-filled" Christians and church establishments. A return to the vigor of the early church is an entirely acceptable goal even to critics of the Pentecostal Movement, but speaking in tongues—one of the means by which Pentecostals accomplish this—is seen as "confusing the issue" through irresponsible, divisive action. Pentecostal religious goals are then called into question.

We suggest three reasons for what appears to critics of a movement to be either lack of ideology or inability to enunciate it. First, movement participants deliberately put up ideological smoke screens. For example, blacks characteristically shift and escalate goals while members of the establishment offer to meet them—the "give them a hand and they'll take an arm" method. This confuses the establishment about the exact goals of the movement. Such shifting may be frustrating to the establishment but it is functional in terms of movement dynamics. It prevents the co-opting of the movement. If the existing social order could meet all the demands of movement participants, there would be no radical social change. Black Power participants want transformation of the system, not a place in the system as it exists. Therefore the movement cannot allow the system to implement movement objectives, even limited ones.

For similar reasons, Black Power advocates resist the incorporation of movement concepts, such as "soul," into the existing conceptual system. "Soul," "the force which energizes the black revolution," must be continually redefined in order to keep it from being degraded and "packaged" (232). Such resistance might be viewed as a mechanism which enables movement ideology to go beyond the closing of the ideal-real gap, and to redefine the ideal. The Black Power Movement has already moved beyond the original concept of integration to the concept of transforming the system through massive infusions of black "soul" force.

The second reason why the ideology of a movement is sometimes viewed as unclear by outsiders involves the relationship between ideology and the experience of commitment discussed in chapter V. Certain phrases, such as "participatory democracy" or "self determination" or "soul," or, in the case of Pentecostalism, "a real Christian," may sound vague to outsiders, or interpretable in a variety of ways. To a committed movement participant, however, these words have experiential connotations, are very clear in meaning, can be translated into specific goals, and entail certain behavioral consequences.

The third reason for ambiguity in movement ideology is the difference in attitudes about radical and developmental change. Members of the established order who want to keep social institutions essentially as they are and who understand the implications of the institutional changes proposed by Black Power and student movement spokesmen, must either brand their goals as unrealistic or pretend not to understand them. The same is true of church officials who understand the kinds of institutional transformation that would occur should the organizational design of first-century Christianity be recreated.

A seventh characteristic of movement ideologies is best expressed with terms developed in cybernetics. Magorob Maruyama, in an article on the "second cybernetics" (373), distinguished between morphostasis (structure stabilization) and morphogenesis (structure generation). Both are mutually causal feedback processes. The first is the deviation-counteracting process by which an organism achieves what physiologists know as homeostasis. Social scientists call it "stable equilibrium" in a society. Its function is to maintain the status quo and the stability of the organism (or of a society) within a normal range of physical or sociological limits. Deviation, in other words, is kept within acceptable and externally determined limits. Deviation-counteracting or "negative feedback" processes ensure the health of a mature organism. This is a morphostasis.

Morphogenesis, on the other hand, is a term describing the process of growth from conception to maturity. It is the process of ontogenesis, of unidirectional growth, or evolution. It involves deviation amplification, rather than counteraction, and results in what physicists sometimes call "spin off." A small initial deviation from the norm, with positive rather than negative feedback, develops into a large deviation well outside of the limits defined as "normal" or desirable for maintenance of the system. According to Maruyama, deviation amplification may be a concept by which the mechanisms of biological growth may be better understood. It is a concept consistent with the Darwinian theory of adaptation and natural selection. A small deviation, or mutation, with survival value because of adaptiveness to a changing environment may, in time, produce a deviation so large that the end result is viewed as an organism of a different species.

There is a useful analogy between these two different cybernetic processes (deviation-amplification and deviation-counteracting) and the function of ideology in a social movement as compared to that in an established order. Members of an established social system allow the negative feedback of "reality" to balance the motivating force of ideals and values; in this way they maintain a sort of homeostatic conceptual orientation. The "fanatic," however, has a way of filtering out the negative feedback so that all events, stimuli, and experiences are interpreted as positive affirmations of his ideological position. This is possible because of a characteristic of movement ideology which involves reinterpretation. What might appear to an outsider to be a failure is reinterpreted by the participant either as a sign of future success, or as a temporary test of devotion and courage.

A committed Pentecostal, for instance, knows that Christ lives in and through him, and that the Holy Spirit guides his decisions and leads him into those situations in which he can best serve the purpose of God. If a decision leads to apparent failure, or a turning away from the originally envisioned purpose, this simply indicates that God was using certain means to lead him on to other, more significant lines of action. A job offer that takes a Pentecostal halfway across the country at his own expense and then evaporates into thin air produces only anticipation for the even better and more wonderful type of service that God has in store for him. The original job offer is viewed as God's way of moving him into position for the real task. Serendipity is the watchword, and the unexpected is commonplace.

Organizational failures, or, in the case of political movements, tactical setbacks, are merely the belt-tightening tests of commitment, the "fire that burns away the dross."

Immediately after the Baptism experience a newly "Spirit-filled" Pentecostal is almost invariably assailed with doubts concerning the validity of his experiences. He is prepared for this, and is told that these doubts indicate the increased activity of demonic forces as the believer comes into ever closer union with Christ. What supposedly more "realistic" and "rational" Christians might regard as debilitating doubt, which could even disprove the experience, becomes, for a committed movement participant, clearer evidence of the opposing evil, increased assurance that he is on the right track and an unmistakable sign of eventual victory. The same interpret tion is given to organizational factors. What the conventional Christian might point to as numerical weakness, the committed Pentecostal sees as proof of the relatively greater spiritual strength of God's few anointed ones. On those occasions when prayer for healing appears to have gone unanswered, the faith of the committed Pentecostal is sustained by reinterpretation of the meaning of the problem or by emphasis on the success of past healings and the expectation of future ones.

This capacity for reinterpretation and the resulting "positive feedback" that movement participants get even from apparent failure enhance that unmeasurable quality known as "morale." Consideration of "morale" introduces a factor in the equation which members of the established order consistently underestimate. Failure to understand this aspect of movement ideology can produce unpleasant surprises for those who attempt to deal with movement participants according to a more "rational and objective" evaluation of a situation.

By objective and rational measures, the Red Chinese were destroyed by Chiang Kai-shek when they began the "long march" in the 1930s.

By objective and rational standards, increased bombing in North Vietnam should have "increased the cost of war" and demoralized the citizenry so thoroughly that popular support for the Viet Cong should have crumbled and Hanoi long ago accepted peace on American terms.

By objective and rational considerations, more powerful anti-riot weaponry, better trained police and National Guard units, freer use of tear gas, Mace, and other means of enforcing law and order should have stopped campus "unrest."

Since the established order evaluates situations and plans future actions on the basis of "realistic" perception of homeostatic negative feedback, it characteristically misjudges the ability of a movement to persist despite setbacks and to be strengthened by the very measures that have been designed to defeat it.

The cognitive deviation-amplification mechanism characteristic of committed movement participants includes an ideological filter. Some Asian Communists can see only imperialists, colonialists, capitalists, or counter-revolutionaries on the other side of the peace table. For some Black Power militants any white face represents the oppres-

sive white power structure, institutional if not personal racism, o:
even the Devil himself. Failure to understand this filter brings many
a well-meaning white liberal to bewildered frustration. Stepped-up
employment opportunities, integrated schools, the presence of more
black models on television commercials, and the appointment of ad
ditional black members to citizens' councils are all development
which should be hailed as progressive by any member of the black
community. Instead, militant voices warn their brothers of the white
man's duplicity, of "tokenism," of his attempts to "buy the black ma:
off." It is as if the Black Power ideological filter reinterprets wha
should be success as failure. Confusion and anger are evident in the
rejoinders of those who ask, "What do these people *want* anyway
They've been given so *much* already!"

An eighth characteristic of movement ideology is related to th
deviation-amplification principle of accepting only positive feedbac
and reinterpreting failure (or negative feedback) either as success c
as a more powerful rationale for the existence of the movement. Thi
is a dichotomous world view that provides a clear definition of th
opposition.

The in group, out-group self-image of participants in movemen
has long been noted. All movements include a dichotomous categor
zation of people and a method of placing any individual in one cam
or the other. The Pentecostal world view emphasizes the Biblica
dichotomy between God and Satan, Christ and anti-Christ, heave
and hell. The relevant question for categorization is "Have you ac
cepted Christ as your savior?" Black Power ideology, in its most sim
plistic form, utilizes skin color—the same criterion that white Wes
erners have employed since explorers first discovered the vast numb
of different groups peopling the face of the earth. Subtler criter
have developed by which individuals are classified according to the
acceptance or rejection of the existing American power structure,
the system, or the establishment. By these criteria some whites a:
members of the Black Power in-group, and some Negroes are mem
bers of the out-group.

The essential ideological difference between a movement partic
pant and a non-participant is the difference between one who is cor
mitted to radical personal or social change and one who holds to

radualist concept of developmental change. This dichotomy is quite
lear to committed participants.

Pentecostals take seriously Christ's double warning: "He that is
ot against us is for us" and "He that is not with me is against me"
Luke 9:50 and 11:23). There is little gray in the black and white
orld of movement ideology. This does not necessarily involve antag-
nism toward non-participants. Pentecostals may have real under-
anding of and deep compassion for the non-participant, but when
e chips are down, participants regard everyone as falling to one side
r the other of the ideological razor's edge. Committed Pentecostals
ill explain that there are people who "almost make it"—earnest
hristians who believe in the Biblical command to be "born again," to
e filled with the Holy Spirit, and to go forth with the power to con-
rt and to heal. But the almost-believer will inevitably make a verbal
ip and the Pentecostal will know that he has not caught the point.
lmost-believers will state that conversion can be a gradual thing,
at a Christian is automatically filled with the Holy Spirit when bap-
zed as an infant, that faith healing is no longer necessary now that
od has provided the miracles of modern medicine, or that demon
ssession is simply a medieval way of explaining psychiatric prob-
ms. Almost-believers regard speaking with tongues as a necessary
ay to start the church in an era when people needed and expected
igns," and add that it is no longer necessary for sophisticated modern
hristians. The real tip-off is their suggestion that the Pentecostal ex-
rience may be right "for some people" but that it is not the only way.

The sympathetic member of the Christian establishment often
nnot really grasp the difference between his religious position and
e Pentecostal's. He interprets the differences in terms of degree or
emphasis. The Pentecostal, in turn, knows that they stand on either
le of an ideological glass wall.

The committed Black Power participant feels the same thing
en he hears white liberals saying, "I respect your goals and agree
th them wholeheartedly, but I cannot go along with your methods."
ack Power ideology includes not only the long-range goals of equal
portunity, equal rights and self-respect for black Americans; it also
cludes the argument that if the means to these ends were actually
ailable in the American political, economic, and social structure as

it now exists, the goals would long ago have been reached. The belie
that such means do not, in fact, exist, and therefore must be created
by radical social innovation, constitutes an ideological glass wall be
tween the Black Power militant and the earnest white liberal or the
conservative black Civil Rights worker.

The "Free Huey" movement which developed following the ar
rest of Black Panther leader Huey Newton in 1967 provides an ex
treme example of the prevalence of this ideological glass wall. Mili
tant blacks and radical whites took the position that white America is
the mother country, while black America is an exploited colony
They regarded Newton as a revolutionary attempting to free his
people from oppression: his actions were considered to be those of
soldier at war, not those of a suspected criminal, subject to civil law
The real issue, in their opinion, had nothing to do with whether or no
he had killed a policeman. As *Ramparts* editor Gene Marine observed
"To the liberal or conservative white American . . . the simple ide
that Huey Newton ought to be freed no matter what happened o
October 28 is mind-bending" (272, p. 106).

Participants in movements know the glass wall is there, and nor
participants characteristically do not. Participants, therefore, have
certain freedom from the necessity of explaining themselves. Nor
participants who have no intention of joining the movement, but wh
want to understand it, often find this freedom irritating. A Blac
Power militant will "tell it like it is" and a Pentecostal will "witnes
for the Lord" so long as there is a possibility that the non-participar
will change his stance. But after a certain point, the Black Power mil
tant will say "I only talk to brothers who will listen." At a certain poi
a Pentecostal stops "casting his pearls before swine." This pu
members of the established order at a disadvantage. They want
understand the movement *without changing their own position*
Participants know this is impossible, and do not care whether no
participants "understand" or not. To "understand" movement ideolog
is to make the conceptual switch from the deviation-counteracti
mental process, in which only gradual or developmental change
possible, to the deviation-amplification process, which brings abo
fundamental or radical changes in orientation. The switch is accor
plished through the commitment process—the cognitive restructuri
and cognitive closure described in chapter V. Between a committe

movement participant and an uncommitted but sympathetic member of the established order, there will always be a conceptual glass wall. This is an important factor in what is called the process of polarization.

The functions of movement ideology in relation to other factors of intra-movement dynamics have been noted. Movement ideology provides the cognitive building blocks for the potential convert, with which a revelatory commitment experience may be created; commitment in turn motivates the personalization and developmental variation of "split-level" ideology. Ideological codifications provide a framework of meaningful communication between movement participants. They give the committed recruiter effective formulations with which to reinterpret prospective converts' needs, discontents, and desires. The "split-level" nature of movement ideology provides a basis for both organizational fission and fusion. Various ideological emphases are related to organizational splits and proliferation, yet such variations enable the organization to recruit across class and cultural boundaries. The basic ideological tenets provide strong linkages between disparate cells and the kind of loose conceptual unity common to acephalous movements.

Ideology also functions in the interaction between movement participants and members of the established order. It has already been noted that ideological ambiguity exacerbates opposition. In fact, the differences between a movement ideology and the conceptual system of a typical stable society enable movement participants to use what we have come to call revolutionary judo—techniques with which movement participants can keep the authorities constantly off base, sometimes by calculated effort, more often by virtue of the very nature of the movement ideology. Revolutionary judo enables military revolutionaries to accomplish more with fewer people and resources. Revolutionary judo involves, first, exploiting the ideal-real gap; second, shifting the rules on which interaction takes place; and third, forcing the opposition to over-react.

Constant emphasis on the ideal-real gap inherent in movement ideology is very likely to increase the previously tolerable guilt level among the more sensitive members of a society. Christians who attend church out of purely social needs, who are not particularly interested in the Bible, and who take their religion with a grain of salt, can remain impervious to Pentecostal ideology. It is the serious Christian

who feels he should read more of the Bible, who is vaguely aware o
its "impossible ethic," and who has come to expect some sort of mean
ingful experience to occur within his religious institution, who can b
touched by Pentecostal witnessing.

Black militancy produces only contempt among those white
who truly believe in white superiority and who have never take
the ideals of equality and self-determination seriously. It is the whit
liberal who believes in the "self-evident" truths whose confidence ca
be shattered by clear statements of Black Power ideology, even thoug
the means may seem repulsive. Once a sufficient number of the estab
lished order respond with guilt to the revelation of institutionalize
hypocrisy, opposition to the movement is undermined by indecisior
self-doubt, and ambivalence. It is in this manner that movements be
come the mechanism for social change—by exploitation of the idea
real gap, the built-in motive power for social change in any society

A second way in which movement ideology facilitates revolu
tionary judo is that it permits movement adherents to operate on
different set of rules from those which bind members of the estab
lished order.

A Lutheran pastor who had become deeply committed to Chris
through the Pentecostal experience of the Baptism of the Holy Spir
and speaking with tongues, and who had been very successful in lead
ing others into the same experience, came under fire directed by off
cials within his synod. His church had split over the issue of speaking
with tongues, and the synod officials threatened to foreclose the mor
gage and remove the pastor on the grounds that he was offending
certain Christians, that church membership had decreased, and tha
the remaining members would not be able to meet the church's finan
cial obligations. The pastor fearlessly faced his "oppressors" and wa
quite honest about the fact that he refused to "play it their way." Ac
cording to his rules, the effectiveness of a pastor was demonstrated b
how many souls he had led to confrontations with Jesus, not how man
dues-paying members he had in his church. Furthermore, he re
minded the officials, in Jesus' rule book there is nothing wrong witl
offending Pharisees. He then proceeded with his work, leading sou
to Christ by Pentecostal means. This left the synod officials in the irr
tating position of reacting to his initiative rather than of directing th
destiny of the church. When they finally did foreclose the churc

mortgage, many previously uninvolved persons considered their action unjust. This strengthened the pastor's personal position and increased his effectiveness as a recruiter to the movement. He no longer needed the status provided by affiliation with the synod.

"Spirit-filled" Catholics at one large meeting called by church officials made similar use of revolutionary judo. Ostensibly, Catholic participants in the movement were meeting with non-participants to discuss the entire Pentecostal phenomenon and to come to some sort of meeting of minds concerning its value in the life of the church. Parliamentary procedure, rational discussion, and decision by majority vote, however, were not the ground rules by which the Spirit apparently chose to act. There were outbursts of praise in tongues during plenary sessions of the conference, to the great disgust of more conservative, non-participating Catholics. To charges of disorderly and undisciplined conduct, movement participants could respond with a we-told-you-so shrug. By their standards, institutionalized religion had once more proved its incapacity to respond to the moving of the Spirit.

Leaders of student rebellions, whether racial or non-racial issues are involved, have discovered that movement ideology leads them to the psychological advantage of rule-changing. One student leader on a large university campus took his group's demands to the appropriate officials, with whom he found some areas of agreement, on goals if not on means. Little action followed this meeting, however. He and his colleagues next seized the initiative on a very formal occasion, when the president of the university was addressing an illustrious audience of community leaders. The radicals barged into the hall wearing beads, sandals, and sideburns. Brushing aside those who attempted to halt their progress, the leader announced the group's demands to the president across the heads of the assembled audience. A university official, in an attempt to quiet the disturbance, mollified the student leader by saying that he respected his ideas, but that his ideas would receive more sympathetic attention if he were to go home, cut his hair, put on a tie, and take his demands up through the proper "channels." Part of the students' ideology, of course, holds that one deals with persons, not with roles. The haircut and dress styles are an outward symbol of their rejection of a role-valuing society. The leader therefore replied that if his ideas were respected, why should they not be taken directly to the president, since the president was the only one in the chain of command who had the power to make the decision called for. The surprise tactics plus the unanswerable logic caught the officials off guard. The student leader ended up on the platform talking with the president, without having waited in countless outer offices, and without having changed his hair style or attire. Again, the established order, with all the power of authority and physical force at its command, found itself on the defensive because it was in the position of responding to a group which operated on a completely different set of premises and rules.

Guerrilla warfare is, of course, the most obvious example of a set of rule-changing techniques characteristic of revolutionary movements. Against a committed guerrilla band, a regular army using conventional tactics is at a great disadvantage, even if it is superior in numbers and weaponry.

Spiritual revolutionaries are fond of a Biblical parable which proves a stumbling block to many church-goers. A householder, whom Jesus selected to describe the nature of the Kingdom of Heaven, went out one morning to hire some laborers for his vineyard. He hired more at noon, and still others just an hour before "closing time." When he paid all the laborers the same amount he had promised the first group, those who had worked all day responded with proper indignation. The householder, who may be compared with revolutionaries having more temporal goals, had behaved according to a set of rules based on an entirely different conception of justice and material rewards than that of the laborers. The final sentence of this uncompromising story is a most succinct statement of rule-changing judo: "So the last shall be first, and the first last" (Matthew 20:16).

A third variety of revolutionary judo is the ability to force the opposition to over-react. An example of this is the use of verbal "taunts and obscenities" characteristic of young demonstrators, both black and white. Wise parents, teachers, and even children value the perspective and the maturity of those able to reply to verbal abuse with a "sticks and stones" detachment. This capacity for detachment in police and National Guard units during demonstrations can be sorely tried by verbal expressions that push freedom of speech to the limit. Revolutionary judo consists of using language and gestures that raise the emotions of the authorities until they behave as childishly, as sav agely, or as irrationally as the demonstrators themselves. Then, because the authorities are the ones who are armed, they are in the untenable position of having attacked "defenseless children" or "oppressed and unarmed minorities."

The Chicago police were subjected to just such taunts during the 1968 Democratic Convention demonstrations. Their "cool" had also been seriously tested by previous threats, published in underground newspapers, concerning the type of activities the revolutionaries were planning—nails spread on the expressways, a mobile radio jammer to disrupt police communications, girls who would slip LSD into delegates' drinks, cars painted as taxis and used to take delegates far away from the city. Conventional force was obviously useless against such homemade tactics. Mayor Daley and his forces nevertheless responded with Maginot Line technology: barbed wire, armored vehicles, anti-riot weapons, and massive manpower. Police intelligence was also flooded by assassination threats and an "unnerving rumor" that demonstrators planned to murder a female McCarthy supporter and blame the act on the police. According to Mayor Daley's official report (306), none of these threats were carried out. The revolutionary judo consisted of luring the authorities to prepare for over-reaction. Whether or not their "brutal attacks" were justified becomes a confused issue. No matter how it might be officially resolved, the confidence of the public in the police, and consequently the self-image of the police as mature and responsible citizens, was seriously undermined. The legitimate use of force requires a precise definition of right and wrong, in any given situation. When revolutionaries can exploit latent public guilt (about racism or about undeclared war in Vietnam) and, simultaneously, lure authorities into over-reaction and subsequent misuse of conventional force, another battle in a most unconventional war has been won.

Characteristics of movement ideology, then, which distinguish it from the world view and system of values generally accepted by the society at large are:

— dogmatism and certitude on one hand and adaptive ambiguity on the other;
— codification of beliefs into a common rhetoric or "party line";
— belief in the personal access to a source of power;

— a combination of basic unifying beliefs with the development of variants through intense personal involvement and constant application of ideology to specific situations;
— the rejection of the ideal-real gap;
— a conceptual filter which permits only positive reinforcement and reinterprets negative feedback;
— a dichotomous world view which is used to define the opposition; and
— a rationale for techniques of revolutionary judo with which guilt concerning the ideal-real gap is exploited, rules for interaction are shifted, and the opposition is forced to over-react to threats posed by participants.

VII

Opposition

The fact that a kite flies against the wind is certainly not a new discovery, but it does have great significance for the understanding of movement dynamics. If, as we have suggested, movements are mechanisms for social change, then conflict with the established order is inevitable. It is important to remember that this very conflict is one of the reasons for the successful spread of the movement.

Obviously, by its very nature, opposition can facilitate the spread of a movement. Without opposition from the established order, there would be no risk, no bridge-burning, and hence no commitment required for participation. We have already described how opposition to the tongues movement from officials of conventional churches increases the bridge-burning aspect of the commitment experience. This in turn increases the willingness of the committed Pentecostal to take risks in other areas of life—to "step out in faith" and "stand on the promises of God." All this affects the participant's social and economic behavior, and produces some of the social effects of Pentecostalism that have been noted in non-Western societies.

There is increasing evidence that commitment to the student movements or to Black Power is greatly enhanced by the opposition of police and other authorities to demonstrators and rioters. Leaders of these revolts recognize this, seek out, welcome, and plan for such opposition. Revolutionary judo tactics designed to draw heavy-handed police action often produce the confrontations which "radicalize" new participants. Young people who witnessed the demonstrations at Columbia University and in Chicago during the Democratic Convention of 1968 report that the actions of the police destroyed their faith in gradualism, non-violence, and conventional methods of working out solutions through "lawful means." An older participant in the march on the Pentagon in October of 1967 described a similar disillusionment. He reports that even among adults the experience "made believers of sympathizers, activists of the passive." Those who went to protest returned prepared to resist. One participant was quoted as having said: "I understand how the Viet Cong holds out now. When those bastards started beating us with those sticks, and we were just *sitting* there, I knew they wouldn't make me give in. They could arrest me and chase me away, but not make me quit. Not now" (320).

This kind of mutual escalation of opposition and commitment is tragically unrecognized by most people. It is, however, a hard fact of movement dynamics and a powerful weapon in the hands of those who understand it.

Opposition of whatever nature from the established order is of course external to the movement, and should not be included as one of the internal factors of movement dynamics. However, our observations indicate that the fifth operationally significant factor in the internal dynamics of a movement is *perceived* opposition. This might seem to be splitting hairs except for the fact that we have noted cases where more opposition is perceived by participants than seems to exist objectively. The strength and growth of the movement are affected more directly by the perceived than by the real opposition. In this context it is important to remember that two characteristics of movement ideology are a dichotomous view of society or the universe and a clear definition of the "enemy." There are other cases where the real nature of the opposition as experienced by participants is not perceived by outsiders.

There are Pentecostal churches—particularly the long-established sects containing second- and third-generation Pentecostals—which have been accepted by both Catholics and Protestants as separate denominations, and tolerated if not admired. It is in these sectors of the movement that one hears nostalgic accounts of the opposition in earlier days. Haitian Pentecostals still talk of the early 1940s, when the overt practice of their faith was outlawed by the government. One member of a well-established Pentecostal sect in Port-au-Prince lamented that "the old fire is gone." "We are no longer fighting against oppression by the Catholics," he explained. "It is not like the good old days of my youth when we struggled and some, like my mother, were martyred."

The passing of the "good old days," when opposition forced Pentecostals to "stand up and be counted," is mourned in many American sects, too. Some sect leaders accept this and note with sadness that the more dramatic outpourings of the Spirit accompanied by miraculous healings, prophecies uttered in tongues, visions, and revelations have also dwindled as the opposition declined. Others respond by pretending that the opposition still exists. This is undoubtedly characteristic of some Pentecostal sects that have inspired sociologists to attribute a "psychology of persecution" to them (121). What has not been so widely noted is that this "unrealistic" notion of opposition can be very functional in terms of maintaining movement strength. Even in some Neo-Pentecostal groups where opposition is very real and the outpourings of the Spirit are correspondingly dramatic, certain leaders are conscious of the relationship, and wary of becoming inoffensively routinized.

It is easy to observe a type of "persecution psychology" in most movements, but the implication that this is pathologic is inaccurate and misleading, if one wants to deal successfully with the phenomenon. Opposition, as understood by a movement participant, is relative to his personal position in the existing social structures and to his own particular set of values. We have often noted that the risks accepted by a Neo-Pentecostal who becomes a tongue speaker seem minimal when compared to the risks run by the Black Power militant, who faces imprisonment, possible brutality, and other hardships. The Neo-Pentecostal faces only ridicule, or pity for a "temporary derangement," or—at worst—exclusion from his church. Some persons feel that this difference in objectively perceived degree of risk makes comparison between the two movements invalid. If opposition is a factor in movement growth, then one might argue that those movements involving greater risks should grow faster. The dynamic that motivates movement growth, however, does not depend directly on the amount of "real" opposition or the type of risk, but on participants' subjective perception of these influences.

The typical convert to Pentecostalism is a serious Christian who loves his non-Pentecostal church, has worked on boards and committees or taught Sunday school, and has looked to the church as a place of spiritual refreshment. With conversion to the movement, his own spiritual growth reaches a climax: a personal confrontation with Christ in the Pentecostal experience. Persons to whom church involvement has never been of deep concern cannot understand the pain the convert feels at being rejected by his church because his religious faith is considered "immature" and even "unspiritual," his attempt to witness for Christ "un-Christian," and his enthusiasm disruptive of church unity. In analyzing the type of opposition perceived by participants in any movement, the degree of risk must be evaluated in terms of the orientations and value systems of the participants themselves.

A similar situation exists for Haitian Pentecostals, for whom the threat of retaliation by evil voodoo spirits is very real. Haitian Pentecostals must put their faith in Jesus Christ to heal them and to protect them from the misfortunes, diseases, and death that can be brought upon them by the curses of a voodoo priest. This requires a leap of faith with important implications for degree of commitment. That Haitian participants do not become ill or die does not reduce their awareness of the risks involved. Rather it constitutes a powerful demonstration of Christ's power and affects recruitment rates.

There are movements in which opposition as perceived by participants is invisible to members of the established order or to social scientists studying the movement. Nathan Gerrard, in his study of a serpent handler's cult (21), found that responses to certain questions on the Minnesota Multi-Phasic Inventory could be used to classify the individual quite differently, depending on the sociological context of the respondent. Affirmative answers to questions about being plotted against, or feelings that "people are out to get me," are usually taken to indicate paranoia. They may indeed indicate paranoiac tendencies in a white middle class suburbanite, but for a serpent handler in the West Virginia mountains who has been shot at for his belief and may risk further dangers, an affirmative answer is realistic.

The same problem exists with psychological testing of black ghetto youth. Attitudes which may be used to explain the militant wing of Black Power in terms of deviants, misfits, or psychopaths may in fact be the realistic responses of individuals who have been persistently mistreated by those in authority. So long as large numbers of the established order refuse to acknowledge the actualities of police persecution, as attested by the *Kerner Report* and other reports, such persons cannot properly evaluate the function of this form of opposition as a factor in the spread of the Black Power Movement. Many well-meaning whites who feel themselves to be unprejudiced cannot understand the range or the subtlety of the daily pressures which black Americans call institutional racism. These whites, pointing to great strides in Civil Rights legislation, are unable to understand the insistence of black demands for "Freedom now!" Such individuals are also incapable of assessing the strength of the Black Power Movement or of dealing with it successfully.

By contrast, an opposite problem faces those whites who try to meet black demands without understanding the function of perceived opposition in the dynamics of the movement. There are Black Power participants, particularly the more militant ones, who appear to be willing to risk their very lives. As the tide of public opinion in any city turns, however, the most militant members of the black community are likely to be courted by anxious whites or by members of the local Urban Coalition. Indeed, some Black Power militants in the cities we have studied have found themselves occasionally in the position of having to drum up some opposition. They must assume wiretapping where it does not exist, or spread rumors about genocide, or provoke anger with uncouth behavior and four-letter words, in order to maintain the pressure of opposition. This dynamic confuses both well-meaning police authorities and cooperative administrative personnel. They cannot understand the persistence of a sense of persecution when they do not see that it is realistic. Nevertheless, this "unrealistic" perception of opposition may be very useful in promoting movement growth, since it is an alternative to provoking major conflicts when real opposition declines.

A study which seeks to increase the understanding of any movement must analyze the types of opposition that different groups within that movement are actually experiencing. Not all serpent handlers get shot at. Not all black Americans get roughed up by police. Not all Pentecostals are ejected from their churches of origin. Instead, they may be experiencing a more subtle form of opposition, or they may be reacting to a symbolic perception of it. Both types—real opposition, and its differential perception by various groups in the movement structure—must be recognized. Similarly, it should be noted that decreased opposition from the established order may be answered by unrealistic demands or extremist behavior on the part of those movement participants who understand the practical importance of opposition. They fear diminished opposition as a threat to the vigor of the movement. They also fear being lulled into accepting reforms rather than radical changes. When evaluating opposition to any movement, or attempting to interact with participants, all of these possibilities must be kept in mind.

In assessing the function of opposition in movement dynamics, the line between "real" and "perceived" opposition becomes very fine indeed, and it behooves the observer to take care that he does not assume reality to be coterminous with his perception of it.

Certain generalizations can be made about the optimum conditions of opposition for the growth of a movement. We have found that the spread of Pentecostalism—and probably the spread of other movements as well—can be inhibited by following either of two extreme policies: (a) local authorities pose no opposition whatsoever; or (b) such officials manage to apply effective measures of social control.

As we have already noted, lack of opposition reduces the risk of participation, obviating the need for deep commitment, thus robbing the movement of its strength. This is most clearly seen in those sectors of Pentecostalism where the routinization process has reduced the differences between a Pentecostal congregation and a conventional fundamentalist church. Some Pentecostals even talk about how new converts to the movement are "coming out of" these routinized Pentecostal sects. One of the problems facing any movement which has been successful in overthrowing and replacing an established order is the maintenance of personal commitment. Mao Tse-tung's efforts to re-create the revolutionary spirit among second-generation Communist Chinese youth is a case in point. Maintaining a revolutionary stance often requires artificially provoked conflict situations.

The alternative to lack of opposition is effective suppression. This can be accomplished in either of two ways. First, by the effective application of force. Second, by utilizing enough actual social control of interpersonal relationships at the grass roots level to make recruitment impossible.

Leaders of an established order, when faced with a movement, usually assume that it can be controlled with law enforcement techniques. The application of church law, however, has not stopped the spread of the Pentecostal Movement within American denominations; nor has law enforcement been notably successful in preventing urban riots or campus rebellions.

Anthropologist E. Adamson Hoebel has defined law as "social norms," infractions of which are regularly met by legitimized force (367:28). Hoebel's interpretation of law is based on his study of a wide range of primitive as well as complex modern societies. He includes both written and unwritten codes in his concept of social control. His theory is extremely relevant to our attempt to understand the operational relationship between a movement and the established order within which it has risen and whose authority it threatens. The term "social norms" refers not only to codified and written law but to that body of custom which we classify as the "moral" or "proper" thing to do. By Hoebel's definition, such mores are not law unless infraction results in the threat or application of legitimized force—that is, action by an individual or group possessing the socially recognized privilege of acting with force. This may be a police force or a less official body similarly legitimized by popular consent.

Many unwritten codes in the southern United States concerning approved behavior for Negroes were and still are enforced, if not by police, then by informal means—groups of individuals which punish infractions of unwritten laws by uncoded means. Lynching, burning of homes, and various forms of personal injury are not technically legitimate. Such methods of code enforcement have been legitimized, however, in the sense that Hoebel uses the term, by majority consensus. Groups or individuals using these means are recognized by the local majority, and by those who could stop them, as having the privilege so to act. When consensus as to this privilege changes, the "legitimacy" of the action is called into question.

When sufficient numbers of citizens in any society begin to question the validity of certain laws, written or unwritten, or to reject them, consensus is lessened, and the entire structure of mutual expectations weakens. Police then lose the consensual or moral legitimacy on which their use of physical force is based. Loss of morale on the part of law enforcement personnel follows upon this. In two urban centers in which we studied local Black Power organizations, such loss of morale was expressed by several National Guardsmen who had been called to service during riots. One said he would "rather have been called up for active duty abroad." Another was quoted in the local newspaper: "It is a terrible feeling to take up arms and realize you may have to confront other Americans. You don't want to do it. You just can't help thinking this is not the answer." Law enforcement under these conditions cannot be called effective suppression of the movement. Such enforcement affords, in fact, optimal conditions of opposition for movement growth.

The undermining of consensus and the challenging of conventional law enforcement may be paralleled by the rise of new codes, new sets of rules. These rules are enforced by new agents considered legitimate by movement participants but not by members of the established order. The trials and executions of captured South Vietnamese officials by the Viet Cong were considered acts of terrorism by the South Vietnamese and the United States governments. The Viet Cong, however, considered the acts to be just punishments for enemies of the people who had violated the new norms.

The rise of black patrols in ghetto areas of many United States cities is an attempt to take over social control under the new rubric of self-determination. Riots may also be considered a form of relatively spontaneous "enforcement" of new codes unrecognized by the established order—unwritten laws requiring ghetto store owners and landlords to stop exploiting the poor with high prices and high rents. A recent study suggests that looting during urban riots is based on a different concept of property rights from that held by members of the established order. The study suggested that looting is one method of forcing the society as a whole to re-examine and redefine property rights (238).

Informal social sanctions within the black community are exerting increasing pressures against "Toms" and "traitors," blacks thought to be selling out their less fortunate brethren by refusing to take a stand against "the man."

More premeditated violence is already being used against specific targets to enforce rules endorsed by movement participants. Sabotage of heavy machinery belonging to a white construction firm on a job in the ghetto area in one city was viewed by many (both black and white) as simply a violation of law, a criminal act. To those who committed the act, it was a way of enforcing the hiring of a Negro construction firm to do the work in the black community, after less violent and "lawful" methods had failed. The new "law" was that black firms should get a bigger share of contracts let for work in black areas. Whether or not an act is violation of or enforcement of a law depends on one's view of what the law is. In this case the illegitimate "law enforcement" was successful. White businessmen involved accepted the new norm while insisting that they had not been "pressured." Boycotts have become an even more frequently used and effective means of enforcing a new rule accepted by some participants in the Black Power Movement but not by the society at large: stores in black communities should either be owned by blacks or employ black workers. A similar rule also enforced by boycotts is that store owners in ghetto areas should not charge higher prices than do other stores outside the ghetto.

When a movement has reached the point where significant numbers of participants have redefined the laws and "taken the law into their own hands," the only kind of effective crackdown on the part of the established order is the maximum—forcible restraint of all participants (18). Such extreme force requires a clear and ready capacity to do the following: (a) massacre or imprison large groups—a concentration camp approach; (b) employ counter-terror and reprisal (for example, the policy followed by the Nazis when they executed ten civilians for every one of their own soldiers shot by a partisan); (c) employ an extensive and pervasive secret police and information system; (d) control all sources of public information including the press, radio, television, publications, and films. The Soviet Union proved willing to exert such maximum force in Hungary, and could therefore threaten similar measures in Czechoslovakia. Such tactics are not a realistic approach to the suppression of revolutionary movements in the United States. To rely upon massive force would be to abandon humanitarian ideals, alienate a significant portion of the loyal majority, and bring about the condemnation of world opinion.

George Odiorne, management consultant to large corporations, comes to a similar conclusion. He urges businessmen to recognize that riot control is not the answer to riots, and suggests they turn their energies to more innovative ways to respond to the problem (376).

The use of limited force, as we have pointed out, merely provides the type of opposition on which a movement flourishes. Because of the tactics of revolutionary judo employed by movement participants, those attempting to use limited force and conventional law enforcement measures are lured into over-responding; innocent or ambivalent bystanders are injured, and the manipulative leaders often go free. Increasing numbers of non-participants thus become disillusioned with the established order and can be more easily recruited.

Furthermore, limited conventional force is ineffective in coping with the tactics characteristically employed by movement participants. The list of activities which New Left militants threatened to carry out in Chicago during the 1968 Democratic Convention included those mentioned in the last chapter as well as the following:

— infiltrating hotel and restaurant kitchens to drug or poison the food;
— commandeering a gas station;
— dynamiting natural gas lines;
— lobbing mortar shells at the amphitheatre;
— putting gas into the amphitheatre air conditioning system;
— hijacking a gas tanker truck, putting it into gear and aiming it at a hotel, police station, or theatre;
— storming the amphitheatre;
— forging credentials to get saboteurs into the amphitheatre;
— cutting the power and telephone lines;
— sabotaging police and military vehicles by putting sugar in the gas tanks; and
— jamming electronic control power centers in hotels to stop elevators between floors.

It is possible that Mayor Daley, some of the police, and some sectors of the general public believed that these acts of terrorism could have been stopped by the type of action the police and guardsmen did take: the police forming lines, charging demonstrators attempting an illegal march, cracking heads, spraying tear gas. A moment's reflection upon this list of threats is discomforting in the extreme. The march on the amphitheatre, attacks on the candidates, even the sabotaging of police vehicles, were subject to control by the police and the National Guard phalanx. But the other activities could have been carried out in spite of conventional police riot control tactics. In fact, the concentration of police against the overt crowd made the city more vulnerable to small bands or individuals, had they actually planned and executed their proposed acts of urban guerrilla warfare. Conventional force is, in short, a defective response to revolutionary judo. For people who feel they have a just cause, who have had some form of commitment experience, and who are participating in a vitalizing movement, force short of the obliterating maximum only fans the fires of resistance and expands the scope and membership of the movement.

The spread of a movement can be inhibited if recruitment of new members can be stopped. Because recruitment to a movement occurs through face-to-face contact at the level of daily interaction of family members, close friends, and neighbors, there must be effective control by agents of the established order at this lowest level of social structure.

In Colombia, so long as the Catholic Church and the Colombian government were so closely identified as to constitute a single authority, Pentecostalism did not spread. Popular consensus gave the local priest effective influence over the most personal relationships. A man's job, his marriage plans, and his freedom to interact socially with his friends could all be effectively controlled by local politico-religious authorities. Family structures were sufficiently tied in with religious organization to make possible effective consensual control over individuals. Where these conditions have liberalized, however, Pentecostalism has taken root and spread rapidly.

There are still counties in Mexico where the local Catholic official maintains strict vigilance over the daily activities of his parishioners. Any show of interest in a protestant church results in an immediate visit by the local priest, who has a variety of legitimized "threats" at his command (177). Stonings of Pentecostals are still remembered by older villagers. This sort of control works well so long as every known rebel can be punished without compunction. But the liberalization of Catholicism robs officialdom of its guiltless control. Tolerance and humanitarian ideals conflict with and weaken rigid discipline. The sporadic stonings then become fuel for the fires of the movement. When enough converts have been made, even economic and social sanctions lose their incapacitating effect, because converts can band together in mutual aid and support. Threats then only serve to optimize commitment.

Optimum opposition, then, lies just short of annihilation or incarceration of members, just short of effective control of recruiting relationships; but it must still be pervasive enough to provide the bridge-burning risks which give meaning to commitment. We are tempted to view existing American government attempts at "counter-insurgency," both at home and abroad, as the kind of opposition which contributes to the growth of the revolutionary movements it seeks to suppress.

There is another approach to opposing a movement that is equally ineffective. As Mircea Eliade has pointed out, movements are not only related to socio-political circumstances, they are "creations of the human spirit," and "the task of the analyst is to bring out their autonomous value" (72). Most students of movements ignore this and concern themselves largely with the generating conditions which gave rise to the movement. When it becomes evident that the movement cannot be suppressed by force, action to remove the generating conditions is planned on the assumption that the movement will then disappear. Even movement participants can be caught in this linear cause-and-effect trap. Pentecostals, answering the sincere questions of non-participating church officials, will often talk at length about the reasons for the movement—the "deadness" of the established churches, their emphasis on organization rather than experience, their failure to communicate the immanence of the Holy Spirit, their "liberalizing" of the scriptures, their lifeless routines of worship. Yet Pentecostals know that even if all such churches came alive, led their members to the Baptism of the Holy Spirit, and accepted the charismatic gifts, these innovations would only be the prelude to the radical changes they believe are coming at the close of the present age. Such innovations might hasten this event, but they could not substitute for it.

Similarly, Black Power leaders speak endlessly of the problems of housing, employment, educational opportunity, and police brutality. Yet this is only part of it. Leaders of the march for open housing described earlier were asked what they would do when they reached this goal. "March for better jobs," they answered. And if they got better jobs? "March for something else." One black Detroit pastor, acting as a panelist with other community leaders, spent the discussion time "getting to the roots of the problem"—jobs, housing and other current issues. Yet at the end he said, "It will not make any sense for white people to think they can buy their way out of this mess with more jobs, better housing, and better schools. It's gone way beyond that now." What is the real goal, then? There are many answers, but their general drift can be summed up as follows: "Whitey's system is what has got us where we are. Once the brothers get together, we'll have the power to change that system." This is a very different goal from that of asking for the removal of the conditions that give rise to the movement. It goes beyond social reform to radical social change.

Conditions of social disorganization, deprivation, or oppression (or, in the case of Pentecostalism, the failure of the church to be alive and "relevant") are the soil in which the seeds of a movement can be nourished. But when the plant begins to grow, it can be plucked up and transplanted to social soil where the generating conditions do not exist. According to our observations, when the five factors of movement dynamics are all present and interacting, the movement becomes independent of its generating conditions. When evangelistic face-to-face recruiting by truly committed individuals begins to create a network of organizational cells united by a shared ideology, the movement lifts off the launching pad of causal conditions and becomes an autonomous social entity.

Once a movement has passed the "lift off" point and achieved functional autonomy, efforts to suppress it generally produce disruption to the established order. Movement activity increases, even if it is forced underground. Reactionary panic leads to even less realistic attempts at suppression. In this atmosphere, the most irresponsible elements—the real deviants and psychopaths who hover on the fringes of any movement—are more likely to attract a following. More moderate members of the movement will permit or even encourage their activities, if the alternative is increased oppression.

Although it is undoubtedly true that social change is inevitable and that movements are major mechanisms of such change, there is nothing inevitable about the particular form and direction of any specific movement. Nor is it an eternal fixture on the social scene. A movement is a social institution designed for implementing change. Therefore it is destined, even if successful, to transcend and outmode itself in time. The degree of destruction of the established order and the form of the social changes brought about in the process depend on the type of oppositional interaction between participants in the movement and members of the established order.

One of the least adaptive responses to a movement on the part of members of the established order is to assume that there can be a return to a previous status quo, that a little "pacification"—the control of certain generating conditions plus more emphasis on "law and order"—will somehow bring things back to "normal." Unless a movement already past the point of lift off is recognized as a mechanism *for* as well as a result *of* rapid social change, opposition from the established order can always be turned to the advantage of the movement. It is only by looking *beyond* the movement to the radical social changes it foreshadows that members of the established order can hope to help direct these changes or participate in directing them, rather than default to movement participants.

It has been impossible to discuss any of the five key factors significant in the spread of a movement without repeated reference to other factors and to their interrelatedness. Opposition provides the risk necessary for genuine commitment. The commitment of a true believer invariably offends and calls forth opposition from members of the established order. Personal commitment is one of the causes of organizational segmentation, while organizational diversity provides charismatic elbowroom for further commitment. Commitment increases the ability to recruit, and recruitment initiates the process by which commitment occurs. Recruitment is also facilitated by the diversity of ideological emphases and organizational cell-structures. The fission and proliferation of organizational cells, in turn, increase the "surface area" of the organism as it comes into contact with the larger society, which enhances recruitment potential.

The nature of the commitment experience and the cognitive restructuring involved make it impossible to separate the factor of commitment from that of ideology, except for purely analytical purposes.

Movement ideology also contains the conceptual basis for individual organizational initiative, for carrying the message to "the ends of the earth," or to all oppressed men everywhere, as well as for courageous behavior in the face of opposition.

We have separated these factors in order to understand the mechanisms of a movement. We must now emphasize their functional interrelatedness and their phenomenological unity. Participation in the Pentecostal Movement is an experiential whole. Converts do not see themselves going mechanically through a recognizable series of steps in a commitment process. Organizational activity is not considered separate from recruiting or "witnessing," from opposing the forces of evil, from discussing ideology, or from being committed. Pentecostals will explain that Pentecostalism is not a movement or a belief or even a single experience. It is a *way of life* with Christ. Black Americans say that Black Power is not an organization or a codified ideology—it is a *mood.* They are right. There is a quality of experience in any movement which cannot be imparted by rational means but must be communicated through existential means. But for analytical purposes, we have in this book divided the seamless fabric of reality into portions for separate study. It must be made clear that they cannot remain separate and unrelated, and in actuality constitute a unified whole.

VIII

New Perspectives

)ur research into the internal dynamics of movements has led us to he following conclusions:

1. A social, political, or religious movement is characterized by a) segmented organizational units linked together into a reticulate network by various personal, organizational, and ideological ties; b) face-to-face recruitment along lines of pre-existing significant social relationships of positive affect; (c) personal commitment on the part of most, if not all, participants resulting from an identity-altering experience, a bridge-burning act or both; (d) an ideology which provides the basis for overall unity as well as segmentary diversity, which exploits the motive power of an ideal-real gap, and which constitutes a comprehensive conceptual framework by means of which events are interpreted and the opposition defined; (e) the perception of opposition from the established order within which the movement is spreading.

2. When all five of these key factors are present and interacting, the movement becomes an autonomous social institution and can grow independently of the original generating conditions.

3. Opposition from the established order, short of total annihilation, after the movement has passed the point of "lift off" serves only to provide optimal conditions for its growth.

For those concerned with escalating threats from Black Power and other "dissident" groups in America and with the prospects of "backlash" and polarization, these conclusions may seem to offer very little that is useful in planning constructive action. Such an analysis can give the impression that men are but helpless puppets being driven by, or at least watching, a process over which there is no control. Scientific findings *per se* do not constitute a blueprint for action. They are arrived at and presented with a certain detachment and with some degree of objectivity. In the role of scientific investigator, one refuses to answer the Pentecostal challenge, "He who is not with me is against me," or the Black Power participant's "Which side are you on, brother?" The mere elucidation of a social process is a contribution to knowledge. However, most people want more from scientific analysis. There is a temptation to block out the problem, or to minimize it, if no solution is forthcoming.

The collection, processing, and dissemination of information leads to recommendations for policy making. At this point there is a role shift from observation and analysis to formulation of goals as guidelines for practical action. This involves a value judgment, a willingness to accept one course of action as desirable and to reject another as undesirable—to judge responses as adaptive or maladaptive. Such judgments, in turn, require a wider perspective on evolutionary social and cultural change against which to measure the specific changes wrought by a particular movement.

Revolution is often posed against evolution as if the two were polar opposites. Most people tend to view evolution as good and revolution as bad. Evolution is viewed as a gradual unfolding, or natural development, while revolution connotes radical change by means of rebellion and overthrow. We suggest that revolution may be part of evolution, that evolutionary change is both developmental and radical.

Biologist Theodosius Dobzhansky (357) uses the term evolution to refer to the processes of genetic variation, mutation, and adaptation through natural selection. This is slow and gradual evolutionary change. But he also points out that the evolutionary development of the universe occurs in different dimensions, or on different levels of existence: the inorganic, the organic, and the human. The emergence of a new dimension is, according to Dobzhansky, "a critical event in evolutionary history"—a "point of evolutionary transcendence. Chemical evolution transcended itself when it produced life. Biolog

al evolution transcended itself when it gave rise to man—or what we
vould call the psycho-social level of organization. These are periods
f radical and relatively rapid evolutionary change. Evolutionary
hange, then, is both developmental and radical. It may occur gradu-
lly through adaptation, or more abruptly through a step-change. It
; not inconsistent to assume that both types of changes occur within
ach of the three broad levels of organization or "dimensions of
xistence" to which Dobzhansky refers.

Anthropologists have been wary of accepting the concept of
ultural evolution as a framework for theoretical formulations. Early
volutionists in the field of anthropology held an oversimplified and
thnocentric view which led them to place any known culture on an
volutionary continuum with the culture of Victorian England as the
bvious culmination. Subsequent reactions to this naïve view led later
:hools of anthropologists into the quicksands of relativism in which
ll cultures were viewed as functional equals. Traits or institutions
vere studied only in the context of other traits and institutions within
iat same culture. It was considered very bad form to imply a "higher"
r "lower" position on an evolutionary scale. Evolutionary principles,
) thoroughly accepted in other scientific disciplines, still constitute
sort of "biological analogy" in the minds of many anthropologists.

There has been a remarkable lack of argument, however, over
iologist Julian Huxley's view of cultural evolution as *sub specie
olutionis* (370). Huxley rejects the idea of a simple biological anal-
zy, maintaining that the same basic principles operate on the in-
ganic, the organic, and the human or psycho-social levels of organi-
tion. Furthermore, he views cultural evolution as a continuation, in
new direction, of the evolutionary process, both superimposed on
id superseding biological evolution.

Some evolutionary anthropologists link the emergence of radi-
lly new types of political, social, and religious institutions to the
ajor shifts in technological methods of harnessing the energy re-
urces of the physical environment. Using this yardstick, cultural
olution can be divided into four stages or phases. Societies in the
ost primitive stages harness only manpower and employ simple tools
order to hunt and gather food. The largest possible political units
e the tribe, the village, or the confederacy of tribes and villages. Do-
estication of plants and animals greatly increased the amount of

energy harnessed and controlled. Within a few thousand years th
great civilizations of Mesopotamia, Egypt, and the Mediterranea
appeared. Cities, nations, advanced tribal states, even empires, b
came possible. With the harnessing of the energy in fossil fuels an
the emergence of the machine age, modern political structures an
complex industrial societies replaced the feudal systems of the la
agricultural age. The advent of the nuclear age should produce
radical a change in existing political, social, economic, and religio
institutions as occurred after the agricultural and fuel "revolution
(382, 388, 389).

Of great importance to the evolutionary perspective is the e
ponential rate of change in socio-cultural evolution. The period du
ing which all human societies had a relatively simple hunting ar
gathering culture began when man appeared on earth nearly tw
million years ago and lasted for one million, nine hundred and nine
thousand years. Only in the last twelve thousand years have the
been agricultural societies, and complex industrial societies are le
than two hundred years old. Anthropologists Irven De Vore ar
Richard Lee note that cultural man has been on earth for some tv
million years and that for ninety-nine percent of this time he lived
a hunter-gatherer. They suggest that unless man can create soc
institutions which can effectively manage "the exceedingly compl
and unstable ecological conditions he has created for himself . . . int
planetary archeologists of the future will classify our planet as one
which a very long and stable period of small-scale hunting and ga
ering was followed by an apparently instantaneous efflorescence
technology and society leading rapidly to extinction" (356).

Taking a somewhat more optimistic view, we can set oursel
and the social and religious movements we have been studying agai
this background of socio-cultural evolution and recognize the rap
changes of recent years as part of an evolutionary step-change of r
ical nature. We can expect the emergence not simply of reformed l
of radically changed political, economic, social, and religious insti
tions. Movements in general may be expected to be one mechani
through which such changes will be brought about. The question th
becomes, what role do the specific movements that concern us p
in this type of change?

The first question to ask of any movement is, are the five ba

actors present and interacting? The second concerns its relationship
to the particular society in which it has risen: is it an isolated phenomenon or does it seem to be one strand in a multilinear change?
The third question is, what is its relevance beyond that society?

We believe the black revolt in America is linked with the student
rebellions, the New Left, the Yippies, the hippies, and the peace
movement. We certainly do not consider these groups as part of any
"master plot" but as separate grass roots movements which will tend
to coalesce into a single socio-political revolution. As our analysis of
movement organization indicates, revolutionary social changes can
be brought about without central organization. We are already beginning to trace linkages between these movements through (a) individuals who are active is more than one, and through (b) the diffu-
sion of tactical models. Although there is as yet no common ideology
—in fact there is great resistance among many Black Power participants to this idea—a few key concepts overlap. Black Power adherents and the rebellious students all question the institution of private
property; and they join with the peace movement to question the legitimacy of the power of the "military-industrial complex." Our recent
research into what some call the "New Conservation" and we term
Participatory Ecology, a movement in embryo," leads us to predict
that a cause capable of uniting all these movements might be the
quest for solutions to what De Vore and Lee call "exceedingly complex
and unstable ecological conditions" (356).

In a similar fashion, Pentecostalism can be viewed as one of a
number of thrusts that are breaking through the traditional patterns
of modern churches. The same conditions in organized Christianity
which gave rise to the Pentecostal Movement have also inspired isolated groups of Christians, both inside and outside the Pentecostal
Movement, to introduce additional religious innovations—to turn to
the "underground church," the "secular church," the "inner city
church," the "church of the streets." These innovations often reject traditional litury, organization, and even buildings. Their appearance coincides with a multitude of new theological conceptualiza-
tions. None of these theological or organizational "mutations" are
widely accepted. Some will prove more adaptive than others in meeting new social conditions, thus forming the basis for new religious
structures. Perhaps the unique contribution of the Pentecostal Move-

ment in this religious revolution has been the revitalization of the pan
human capacity for supra-rational, ecstatic experience. Historically
coterminous with human culture, this capacity would appear to be
one of the most effective means of experiencing those non-human
forces that act upon man—no matter how such forces are described
by any given culture. Anthropologist Melville Herskovits, a student of
cultural variation in human religious experience, observes that "of all
the means by which the individual achieves oneness with the supernatural, none is more striking, more convincing to those who believe
and apparently more satisfying, than possession" (87). Although
most Pentecostals see no link between their movement and others
within the framework of the institutionalized church, some not only
understand the link but are also active in both kinds of groups. Furthermore, a few socially active Pentecostals are deeply involved in
inner city problems which link them with certain participants in the
Black Power Movement and which prompt them to cooperate with
local Black Power groups.

In the past, major technological advances in the type of energy
harnessed by man have been followed by radical religious as well as
socio-political changes. It is possible to identify both Pentecostalism
and Black Power, as well as other contemporary movements, as part
of a cultural revolution that is broader in scope than a mere social
revolution within one society.

It is often argued that it is presumptuous to use the term "revolution" for the activities of dissident American minorities. Unlike the
revolutionary colonial peoples such as the American colonists or
modern African societies, blacks in this country are thought to be too
small a minority ever to seize power. Hippies, Yippies, and New Left-
ists (it is assumed) will "grow up and settle down"; in any event
they constitute a very small minority even of their own generation.
According to this view, continued violence on the part of minorities
will "backfire" and an outraged majority will finally put them down.

The danger of this argument is that it does not take into account
the type of social change that can be caused by a dedicated minority
willing to call out the repressive force of the majority. Sociologist
Saul Bernstein, in a study of alienated ghetto youth (218), warns of
the very real danger of the development of a group of "career revolutionaries." Youths now deaf to Civil Rights leaders are responding

o more belligerent exhortations. Experience and training with mili-
ant groups, however, prepare such young people for no role in this
society except as members of local bands of Che Guevaras. Those
participants in the student rebellions, the off-campus SDS groups, and
he New Left, who are in their late twenties and early thirties and
who make their living in protest groups, are clearly a nucleus of career
revolutionaries. By and large these are educated and able men. Many
are also committed and imaginative. Their leadership of the alienated young and not-so-young over the years may never directly overthrow the established order, but it can create sufficient disturbance,
harassment, and disruption to make police state tactics mandatory.

Urban guerrilla warfare on a small but persistent scale, with
utilities, public communication lines, and transport systems as prime
targets, can plunge an urban society into chaos. That such possibilities
are already being considered is demonstrated by an article by a black
sociologist and "elder statesman" of the campus wars: "When a few
years back the lights went out in the New York area leaving a city
helpless and stranded in darkness . . . authorities sought vainly for an
explanation, some going so far as to suggest that God did it. Undoubtedly, some colored watchman pulled that switch. *Or so he could have*"
250, author's italics). Equally chilling suggestions are published
constantly by the so-called underground press and are available at
local newsstands for anyone to read. Most of the writers are dismissed
by the Federal Bureau of Investigation, whose agents read these
publications carefully, as "Communist dupes" (341). Little effort is
made by either government officials or the general public to distinguish between protesters who want to create an American Communist State, and protestors who want to faciliate the emergence of
entirely new political and economic forms unlike either Russian Communism or American capitalistic democracy. If protesters become
sufficiently disillusioned to take concerted action, and if disillusionment becomes sufficiently widespread to provide a moral base for
such action, threatened plans may cease to be idle chatter.

Careful observation of past confrontations between the Black
Power and youth movements of the establishment indicate that once
a movement has achieved "lift off," the only type of crackdown which
can stop it decisively is complete and crushing force. Limited and
controlled force, no matter how repressive, serves only to stimulate

movement growth. Maximum extreme force requires a clear and
ready capacity for overkill; such force would make a mockery of
American ideals of freedom, of past struggles for human rights, of our
vision of one world with self-determination for all nations. These
ideals are embedded too deeply in our national and individual con
sciences to be surrendered even for the purpose of maintaining "law
and order." Many regular soldiers and guardsmen, as well as many
policemen, may be expected to refuse to participate in extreme acts o
repression. Mutiny in the army is not unthinkable under such condi
tions. One of the more noticeable indications of this trend occurred
when over a hundred regular soldiers at Fort Hood refused to go on
duty in Chicago, where they might have been used against demon
strators during the Democratic National Convention in 1968. Since
that time, incidents of dissidence in the army have been frequently
reported in the press, and were recently the subject of Congressiona
debate.

If the maximum force is used, numerous non-demonstrating ci
vilians—liberal, moderate and even conservative—would also protes
vigorously. Police and army commanders would then find it necessar
to develop "special units" of persons who, because of their views an
their training, could be trusted to take and carry out any order. Whe
law enforcement is based on a broad popular consensus, relativel
small staffs are required to maintain order. As consensus is weakene
by popular shifts in values or by questioning of existing policies, th
number of police and other law enforcement personnel must be pro
portionately higher. As the ratio of policemen per capita increases, i
dividual freedoms must be curtailed. This tends toward the creatio
of a police state. If that should happen, American society would the
have been transformed, but in a manner deplored by the vast majorit
of Americans, as well as by the protesters themselves. Existing soci
institutions can be destroyed, not by revolutionaries, but by membei
of the established order who are forced into extreme counter-insu
gency measures. In short, a small, dedicated minority can cause
nation to commit moral and institutional suicide.

Those who understand the potential of these movements, wh
are willing to view them in the perspective of evolutionary soci
cultural change, yet who cannot accept the approach to change take
by participants, find themselves in a classic double-bind. Failure

act constitutes tacit acceptance of present trends. Yet opposition to the movements, no matter how justified or on what grounds, simply strengthens movement adherents and propels them in the direction they are already going. Even enlightened members of the established order are apt to feel "damned if they do act and damned if they don't." A feeling of helplessness pervades members of those groups who are beginning to glimpse the magnitude of the changes that must be made, but who are finding no answers to the questions "What can I *do?*" "Where do we start?" Even the most verbal blacks, who have much to say about what white society as a whole should *stop* doing, become very vague when asked about practical positive steps concerned white individuals might take. More and more people are beginning to suspect that fundamental social change cannot be made by means of existing institutions. Columnist Sydney J. Harris puts it this way: "All organizations pretend to themselves that they are deeply interested in 'innovation,' but what they really want are new changes that can be handled the same old ways by the same old people with the same old attitudes" (366).

In the religious sphere, increasing numbers of church-goers are concerned about the lack of vitality in their churches. They are trying all manner of programs to make their existing institutions come alive, to "become relevant" to today's problems. Like the Pentecostals, they read the accounts of the era when the early church was bursting with religious zeal, when lives were being changed, and when, in spite of persecution, the church was growing by leaps and bounds. Yet their contemporary efforts to revitalize, either from the top of the religious bureaucracy down or from the bottom of the local church up, have resulted in remarkably little lasting change in the overall picture. Either administratively instituted changes are not effectively implemented by the rank and file, or the grass roots changes in local churches die out, while their members revert to old patterns, with shifts in leadership. Without the enthusiasms of a true movement, the inertia of tradition is too strong.

There is still a feeling among many black Americans as well as among student rebels that if the establishment really wanted to change, it could. But there is a growing awareness among some of the more visionary members of society that even those who acknowledge the existence of white racism do not know how to eliminate it. Others

earnestly seek to abolish poverty, to "give" dignity and pride to the
poor, the oppressed, and the aged; but they are unable to accomplish
such goals. Throughout the country individuals and groups are generating ideas about how to solve problems of education, jobs, housing
and community relations. But it appears that changes are being successfully implemented only if they are on a small enough scale so that
a group of dedicated people in one department or organization can
actually initiate and carry them out. Large-scale programs, given
top priority, tend to bog down in bureaucratic delays. Or worse, a
typical program may be accomplished by a massive effort of a particularly well-oiled bureaucratic machine, only to have it discovered
that the resulting changes did not accomplish the original objectives.

One analysis of the long-range failure of an erstwhile "model
city" is enlightening. According to Allan Talbot, a political scientist
who was active in the planning and administration of the city, those
brilliant thoughts now crossing the minds and drawing boards of
countless mayors, councilmen, city managers, or Urban Coalition
have been tried in New Haven, Connecticut, since 1955. They were
not only tried, but were also successful. A coordinated urban renewal
anti-poverty, and rehabilitation plan was conceived and expertly
carried out by the mayor and an able staff over a ten-year period. New
Haven was considered a pace-setter among American cities. How
ever, summer riots in 1967 and continued tension since that time have
convinced the planners that the solutions so brilliantly conceived and
efficiently implemented were largely irrelevant to the basic problem
(288). This situation, we suggest, is a good example of the pressure
that can be exerted by a movement which has passed the "lift off"
point. Even "successful" attempts to reform the generating condition
—by providing housing, school programs, jobs, job training, and
health care—failed to protect the city from the same violence that
erupted in cities which had shown little foresight and less planning

Hindsight, of course, is a great comfort. Many can look at New
Haven's story and assume that if only this or that had been done
differently, it would have worked. But Talbot and others are beginning to feel that the greatest lesson to be learned from the experience
of the last ten years is "the inability of the cities to deal with all of the
problems that fall within their boundaries"—the powerlessness of the
power structure to transform itself.

Planning boards at city, county, state and federal levels are being created across the country in the hope that bigger boards, broader representation, and more comprehensive planning will produce solutions to serious urban problems. The same political and economic system which unwittingly generated the problems in the first place is going into high gear to solve them. A logical prediction would be that the problems will be reproduced on a massive scale in new forms.

Both movement participants and members of the established order who are attempting to cope with the revolutionary surge recognize a linear cause-and-effect relationship between certain conditions produced by the system and the resulting movements of protest and revolutionary social change. However, movement participants seek ways to resolve or remedy the generating conditions—solutions which can lead to revolutionary change—while members of the established order seek solutions as a means of avoiding revolutionary social change. We have observed Urban Coalitions and other planning boards engaged in the usual quest for causes. They operate with the clear assumption that if causes of the unrest can be identified, they can be eliminated by appropriate action. Even the *Kerner Commission Report* expresses this assumption, identifying the cause (white racism) behind the causes (inadequate housing, poverty, educational inequality, police brutality). The same assumption underlies attempts by those university administrations that seek to "get at the roots of the problems" of student unrest. To find the roots and eliminate them will allow a return to "normalcy."

The obvious implication of this cause-and-effect approach is that movements of revolutionary change are bad and must be eliminated, as though they were social maladies like measles or malaria. This approach is impractical because it appears that the system that produced the conditions is unable to eliminate them and remain unchanged. It is maladaptive in a conceptual sense because it puts members of the established order in the position of opposing change—reacting negatively, out of guilt and fear, rather than positively, to the challenge of social evolution.

For example, just a few years ago, university faculty members and administrators criticized students for being "gray flannel suit types" —for being apathetic, concerned only with getting a "gentleman's C," and interested only in occupying niches in the corporate structure.

Now that certain sectors of the student body have come alive and are protesting both corporatism and the kind of education that perpetuates it, administrators seek to determine the causes of student vitality so that such causes can be eliminated. A similar fate has befallen those citizens who used to be called apathetic ghetto Negroes.

This is not to suggest that those conditions which give rise to a movement do not require changing. Certainly they do. Rather, it is to suggest that the existence of a movement be accepted both as an indicator of needed change and as a potential mechanism for actually bringing about that change.

One of the criticisms most commonly leveled at the Black Power Movement and at the student or youth movements is concerned with their lack of projected programs. "All they do is try to destroy the system," the argument goes. "They don't have anything to put in its place." Thoughtful participants in these movements are acutely aware of this shortcoming. Black Power literature is long on the history of injustice, long on the importance of the black man's contributions to American culture, but very short on details of the social structures that should replace the existing defective ones. Earnest soul searching on this score occupies the private discussions of many spokesmen of the movement, but is understandably withheld from their public pronouncements. Leaders in the New Left are similarly occupied with such questions as: "Is this an evolutionary or a revolutionary period? A cultural revolution or a political one? With Russia and America both repressive societies, must there be a political model before one acts, or will the political forms evolve from one's actions?" (341).

In attempting to evaluate these movements, it is well to remember that most revolutions began as protests. Energy is largely directed toward overthrowing or challenging political and social institutions believed to be inadequate. Motivation for conflict is generally negative—demands for changes in the existing system, not specific blueprints for social institutions of the future. Positive goals are only vaguely defined in terms of large-scale ideals. The American Revolution was fought and won before the constitution was drawn up. "Taxation without representation" was the battle cry, not a description of the political forms which would remedy the situation. In the past, the first step in any radical social change has been to "throw off the yoke of oppression." The creation of new structures has had to await the rise to power of those who desire radical change. Unless the revolutionaries intend to model their utopia on other existing political and economic structures, the shape of things to come is indistinct until the revolution is accomplished. That shape, however, is foreshadowed by a variety of innovative attempts to tackle old problems.

The common cry of the welfare worker and of the educated middle class Negro has been criticism of the mores relating to black ghetto family structure in the "culture of poverty"—mother-centered families, absentee fathers, high divorce rates, prostitution, and serial sexual alliances. It is clear that the Black Power Movement is contributing to a new image of the male role and of family structure in black society. Black males are beginning to take the initiative both in the family and in community leadership, even if their action takes the form of social protest. What social workers and integrated blacks have been trying unsuccessfully to accomplish for years by persuasion and moralistic preachment is beginning to occur by means of the mechanism of conversion and commitment and the altered self-image offered by participation in a movement.

A far more successful attack on the problems of prostitution and drugs has been mounted by the puritanical ethics of Black Muslims and by the pressure of black coalition leaders in many cities than was ever effected by Christian sermons in Negro churches or by well-meaning white service organizations. The energy thus released in the black community is being directed at programs designed to alleviate other problems.

One of the facts that must be faced by members of the established order is that they cannot solve problems *for* ghetto blacks. No matter how inefficient ghetto blacks may seem to efficiency-minded whites, white initiative and direction can only repeat the formation of generating conditions. Through the mechanism of a movement, ghetto blacks can begin to do what the established order has not done and cannot do. A movement taps a source of human energy which is unavailable to those using conventional means.

Another reason for the failure of the existing power structure's attempts to attack and remove generating conditions is that such attacks are invariably planned to eliminate the "trouble"—the movement itself. What in fact happens is that such programs set in motion

a process of serial social changes which actually increase the power of
the movement, and contribute to trends in the direction of social innovation, not in the direction of return to the status quo.

In many cities one of the first solutions adopted to meet the problem of youthful agitators was the establishment of community centers.
Both blacks and whites worked together to build such centers in order
to get the young people off the street and to reduce interracial hostility. Initially the programs did just this, and both moderate blacks
and their liberal white supporters were greatly encouraged. Then
came stage two in the change process. The centers, which were in
fact headquarters for youthful blacks, became focal points and
training grounds for even more militant behavior. Activists gathered
in the centers began making escalating demands on the white community. In addition, following a very common pattern, the increased
militancy of black youths tended to "radicalize" black adults who
worked with them. As a result there were many disillusioned whites.

The same process can be observed in the attempt to create a
system of internal law in the inner city. The Blackstone Rangers in
Chicago and black patrol forces in other cities succeeded in harnessing
the previously destructive energies of young blacks; these patrol
groups were credited with keeping the peace in certain crisis situations. However, many of these organizations have assumed a very
militant stance, and are themselves becoming mechanisms which generate the sorts of crises they formerly sought to control. So long as
members of the established order consider such programs a means of
pacifying or of removing the causes of the movement, they will be dis-
appointed. What advocates of "restoration of law and order" fail to understand is that in the first flush of success, before a new program
reaches stage two, social innovation has already taken place. Experience in black self-determination has been accumulating. If the goal
is a return to the status quo, all of these attempts must be judged
failures. If the goal is social evolution, the "wasted effort" must be
viewed as the social equivalent to biological processes of variation
and mutation—a notoriously wasteful and inefficient procedure.

The most recent thrust of social planners, at the time of this
writing, is to encourage black capitalism in the ghettos. The initial
phases of such programs inspire hope in the hearts of white capitalists
and are written up enthusiastically in national magazines. There are

already indications that lack of training and entrepreneurial know-how produces a high percentage of business failures. Furthermore, those enterprises which do succeed tend to generate competition and conflict that is destructive of black community integration. Where such programs are administered from a distance by federal agencies, these failures result in disillusionment with and abandonment of the program. A similar fate has befallen programs of the Office of Economic Opportunity around the country. Where black economic organizations are directed and supported locally, interested individuals or groups can stay with their organizations, and see them through the period of disillusionment. Or, new supporters can be recruited as the original ones fall away; the newer enthusiasts replan and reorganize according to the specific problems facing the enterprise. The result of such a discontinuous process of success and failure is an increased ability to make flexible and imaginative responses that are not necessarily patterned after white capitalism. Thus, businesses are emerging that are better suited to the needs and capabilities of the black individuals and communities involved. Black leaders are already advancing the view that black socialism or black cooperatives are more functional types of economic organization than black capitalism.

Long-range economic changes may also emerge from the small-scale economic activities of some participants in the white youth movements. Rejecting what members of the established order consider necessary evils—rigid scheduling of time, depersonalization of work, escalating material demands, non-democratic corporate structures—the young people have refused to train for "successful" participation in the existing order. In order to support themselves without violating their own standards, they have chosen to limit their consumption so that it is consistent with their concept of work. This has involved a redefinition of man's "basic needs" and a redefinition of the purpose of work. One such group views the loss of the artisan in an industrial society as a social ill, and is making a conscious attempt to re-create this approach to productivity. Insisting on the principle of satisfaction and creative pleasure in work, some have trained themselves in such skills as stonecutting, carpentry, and cabinet work. They work irregular schedules, earning only what is necessary to meet their minimal needs. Sufficient numbers of the establishment, as well as members of their own youth community, desire their services and tolerate their unconventional attitudes toward time and efficiency. In effect the "drop-out" response to the existing social order is economically feasible, even for those with children. Other groups with a similar orientation toward work have found that the community of alienated youth is sufficiently large to provide a market for a variety of goods and services, and make a living providing them.

The recently publicized communes of young whites that are springing up all over the country are another example of social innovation. These groups, often supporting themselves by means of subsistence agriculture, stress cooperation rather than competition and reject the traditional American bases for division of labor. Marriage patterns, child rearing practices, and methods of group decision making are also innovative. These "drop-outs" from the existing order are not just those who have failed within it or who have never tried. Some have participated very successfully in the competitive American system, and bring a variety of skills to the experiment. It is possible that such a group might constitute a better "survival group" in the event of large-scale disaster than any that exists in conventional society.

Such small-scale changes in the economic behavior of a few minority groups here and there quite clearly have not affected the existing economic order in any significant way. Yet it is out of such seemingly insignificant innovations that large-scale social changes originate and take shape. The cottage industries of the late Middle Ages are now viewed as the precursors of the factories of the early industrial age and as factors in the attendant social upheavals. But the first families who began to weave extra lengths of cloth for sale to itinerant buyers would not have seemed to be making much of a "dent" in the feudal agricultural economy of the day. Equally important to the overt activities of those who initiate social change are the attitudes and values on which changed behavior is based. The profit motive, now so widely accepted as to be considered by some as an integral part of human nature, was once a revolutionary attitude. It is not difficult to imagine the kind of criticism that would have been leveled at those sixteenth-century profit-advocating innovators by their neighbors, their extended kin groups, and probably the local landowners. The first entrepreneurs in a tribal or agricultural peasant society today, after exposure to Western methods, are subjected to the same opposition. However, these individuals are not innovators in the sense that we have been using the term. Rather, they model both their values and their behavior on social institutions that already exist in another society. Those who envision economic and social changes in the United States modeled upon social institutions that exist within Communist countries are in the same position. Social innovation, in the sense we are using it, involves the development of social institutions and values for which there are no existing counterparts, or which combine elements of different existing structures to produce a "mutant."

Such a mutation in value systems is occurring among those black writers seeking to enunciate the meaning of "soul." They are trying to codify something that has emerged from the unique experience of blacks in America over the years. They consider "soul" as part of a new value system which is needed by all Americans, white and black, in order to arrest the growing sense of impersonality, anomie, mechanization, fragmentation of relationships, and powerlessness in the face of modern technology. They are interested in a new life style, a "relaxed and non-competitive approach to being, a complex acceptance of the contradictions of life, a buoyant sadness, a passionate spontaneity and a gay sorrow" (215, p. 89). Such writers are also concerned with the deep wellsprings of vitalizing energy from which white society has cut itself off. If allowed to flow into society from its source in the black community, these spokesmen are saying, such energy can transform the whole. The revolutionary concept of this emerging value system is the idea that the problem involves much more than allowing blacks to enter into a social structure created by whites. Visionary blacks are suggesting not that whites are being asked to give up a share of something, but rather that whites accept the contribution of blacks as essential to their own well being. They insist that by incorporating in white culture the values derived from the black experience, whites will acquire a sense of empathy with the "humiliated" peoples of the world whom they now presume to lead. In this way, the new values will be expressed concretely in terms of national foreign policy. Such a major shift in value orientation would tend to transform other social institutions as well.

Although scientific positivists have dreamed of such developments, radically new economic, political, social, or religious institutions have not sprung full-blown from the foreheads of technocrats and qualified social planners. Such institutions have developed from multilinear origins in grass roots activities. The necessity of coping with daily life under rapidly changing environmental, technological, or social conditions is the mother of social innovation. The more adaptive of the small innovations diffuse and crystallize until an *ex post facto* recognition of the new social structure is possible.

A social innovation can be defined as adaptive or maladaptive only with respect to the selective pressures operating upon it. Selective pressures that operate upon the social "mutants" being created by participants in various movements are to be found in the interactions between the movement and the established order. Some of the selective pressures which determine the viability of small innovations made by Pentecostal, Black Power, or youth movement participants are (a) the degree of commitment of the participants and their willingness to take risks and make sacrifices for the new way of behaving; (b) the availability of financial support from sources both inside and outside the movement; and (c) the response—negative or positive—of members of the established order to the ongoing activities of the group.

Those who are neither committed to a movement nor definitely opposed to it, who have escaped the so-called polarization, occupy what might be called the interface between the movement and the established order. As one student of the dynamics of social change has suggested, accelerated change occurs at the interfaces of the human world—just as geological shifts occur along fault lines. It is not the mere aggregation or acquisition of disparate ideas from which the great advances of mankind have come, but from a "certain type of mental activity which is set up by the opposition of different idea systems" (364).

Those who find themselves along the interface between a movement and the established order must: first, understand the nature of the movement and the five basic factors crucial to its growth; second, allow movement participants, demagogues, and preachers to identify the areas of social, economic, political or religious life that require change; third, accept the necessity for fundamental rather than developmental change and be able to tell the difference; fourth, either in relation to or independently of the movement, embark on the Vision Quest for the shape of things to come.

Movements are like tracer elements coursing through a social system, illuminating its deficiencies and weaknesses. They serve to identify the points at which radical social change must, and will, take place. Members of the established order who genuinely want to create a social system free of those particular flaws can use the same mechanism for mobilizing energy as the protesters use to reveal those flaws—the dynamics of a movement.

It is important to understand the mechanisms by which movements rise, spread, and change the social order because this knowledge reduces fear, which debilitates, paralyzes, and provokes maladaptive responses. Such understanding also makes possible the intentional utilization of the vitalizing energy produced by the process. Conscious participation in the process of social evolution should not be equated with control of it. Nor should it be equated with large-scale planning and top-down administration of logically selected courses of action by those in positions of power. Conscious participation in the processes of social evolution involves:

— personal commitment on the part of individuals who believe they have the power to initiate changes within their own sphere of influence;
— enthusiastic persuasion of friends, relatives, and neighbors to join in the small-scale effort;
— articulation of beliefs and ideals appropriate to this particular period in national and world history and to this particular stage of technological development;
— flexible, non-bureaucratic cell-group organizations which can be created, altered, or dissolved at the desire of participants; and
— expectation of and willingness to face opposition from those dedicated to the maintenance of the status quo in spite of its present deficiencies, weaknesses, and flaws. Opposition may come in the form of physical force, or various types of pressure exerted through institutional channels. Or it may come in the form of ridicule from those who are still secure in the notion that power is based only on position within and ability to manipulate the existing power structure.

The most obvious fact about social, religious, or political movements is the amount of power that can be mobilized *outside* the power structure of a society, and the surprising pressure this power can exert upon that structure.

The most effective response to a movement is another movement, for in times of rapid social change, survival lies not in stability but in flexibility, not in devotion to the past but in commitment to the future.

Appendix: Techniques of Data Collection

We began our research into Pentecostalism and the dynamics of movements during the summer of 1965. Techniques of data collection included informal interviews, tape recorded structured interviews, attendance at services in a wide range of Pentecostal churches and groups in urban and rural North America, a computerized questionnaire, intensive participant observation in selected groups, library and mass media research, and short field trips to Haiti, Mexico, Colombia and Jamaica. We filmed (16mm cinema and 35mm still) and recorded on tape pertinent aspects of the Pentecostal Movement, especially in Haiti, Colombia and Mexico. Sequences from this as well as from our footage on Black Power are shown in our film *People, Power, Change* (17).

We studied the Pentecostal Movement in the United States intensively in one large metropolitan area. In addition, we surveyed the movement briefly in two other urban centers and in a rural midwestern community. Fieldwork in the metropolitan area of major concern included observation of thirty groups by team members who visited each group on at least two occasions and in some instances more frequently. Such periods of observation characteristically incorporated informal interview and discussion. Fourteen of the groups thus studied were churches affiliated with an established Pentecostal sect, nine were independent bodies (five with memberships of fifty to three hundred and four with memberships of forty or fewer), and seven were informal groups which met regularly in homes or church parlors and were composed largely of "hidden" members. Single visits and interviews with leaders or lay members of other churches raised the number of groups contacted to more than fifty. Research in the rural area included the observation of three Pentecostal groups. One of these, a church affiliated with an established Pentecostal sect, had about thirty members. The other two were independent, and each had fewer than fifteen participants.

Library research, conducted simultaneously, included the examination of Pentecostal literature, tracts, exegetical books and articles, and documentary accounts of the history of the movement. It also included examination of magazine articles, newspaper clippings, books written by non-Pentecostal observers, and reports of investigations made by officials of non-Pentecostal denominations into the spread of the movement into their denominations. Communication was maintained with four other scientific investigators in other cities who were studying different aspects of the movement.

Our purpose in collecting case histories was to build a file from which we could gain phenomenological insight into the experiences of individuals as they were drawn into and became committed participants in the movement. The histories were collected by means of interviews—usually one to three hours in length—which were relatively unstructured and in which interviewer-respondent rapport was encouraged and cultivated. We were less interested in quantifiable data than in the spontaneous expressions of the concerns which led the individual to desire the Baptism of the Holy Spirit, the emotional-psychological effects of the glossolalic experience itself, and the subjectively perceived meaning of participation in the movement. The interviews were taped and transcribed. Full cooperation with our investigation and previous rapport with at least one member of our team were obviously necessary for us to secure the kind of subjective expressions we sought. There was no attempt, therefore, to make a statistically representative selection of individuals. However, we did succeed in interviewing both men and women, ministers, lay leaders and ordinary members, and individuals from a range of socio-economic and educational backgrounds. We also made certain that some interviews came from each of the four types of groups we had identified.

Our purpose in employing a printed questionnaire was quite different. With this instrument we hoped to collect quantifiable data for the purpose of testing some of the hypotheses emerging from our observations. The eight-page questionnaire was designed for self-administration. It elicited sociometric data and information concerning religious beliefs and training, manner of recruitment to the Pentecostal Movement, type of glossolalic experience, perceived rewards of participation in the movement, orientation to national political issues, and participation in non-religious community activities.

Selection of individuals by random sampling was out of the question for two reasons. First, it was not possible to define the statistical universe. Well-known Pentecostal sect churches are easily located but independent Pentecostal groups are not listed in church or any other type of directory. Even after four years, word-of-mouth contacts keep turning up groups previously unknown to us. Furthermore, groups continually come into existence, merge, split and are dissolved. Of course the "hidden" tongue speakers in non-Pentecostal churches are by nature and by choice hopelessly uncountable. The second reason why a statistically random sample proved impossible was the differential willingness of individuals or group leaders to cooperate. Although warmth and openness were characteristic of most of our contacts within the movement, we did encounter some opposition to the questionnaire. This can be attributed only partially to the distrust of scientific investigation and intellectualism which is supposed to be characteristic of sect members of the lower socio-economic and educational levels. Some of the least cooperative individuals were the better educated members of "hidden" groups. They had painfully discovered, with Paul, that spiritual gifts are folly to those who seek wisdom by rational means. Many were also very sensitive about being identified with the "Holy Roller" stereotype. One group expressed the fear that our information would lead to some sort of persecution. These persons were lower middle class Neo-Pentecostals who had been subjected to ridicule and in some cases ostracization from their non-Pentecostal churches. Their "persecution psychology" might be considered partially realistic.

The questionnaires were distributed among the members of

twelve churches which had leaders who were willing to cooperate. In seven cases the distribution was initiated by a member of our research team who made a presentation, usually at the Sunday morning service, explaining the purpose of our study. The explanation included the usual statements about the limitations of scientific inquiry into religious experience and the non-evaluative approach. We stated our interest in Pentecostalism as a movement and our emphasis on *how* it was spreading rather than *why*—a question that is readily answered by any "Spirit-filled" Christian with one or two well-chosen verses of scripture. The questionnaires were handed out to all who were present at the service. Because our pre-testing had indicated the need for forty minutes to an hour for thoughtful answering of our questions, respondents were asked to fill them out at their convenience.

In five of the churches which cooperated, the minister accepted a certain number of questionnaires, usually ten to twenty-five, for distribution to individuals of his choice. Five leaders of informal prayer and study groups took several for distribution within their own or other home groups. In the case of the "hiddens," one non-Pentecostal tongue-speaking minister and four laymen of different non-Pentecostal denominations gave questionnaires to other "Spirit-filled" Christians known to them. All respondents were given the option of mailing their questionnaires directly to the research project headquarters or of returning them through their minister or leader. Of approximately six hundred questionnaires distributed, two hundred and thirty-nine were returned in time to be included in the analysis. Of these, sixty-one came from established Pentecostal sect churches, ninety-two came from independent churches with memberships of fifty to three hundred, forty-four came from independent churches with memberships of fewer than forty and forty-two came from tongue speakers "hidden" in non-Pentecostal churches.

The resulting sample cannot safely be considered representative of the Pentecostal community as a whole. Those respondents chosen by their ministers would tend to skew the sample toward the most dedicated and involved participants. The nature of the questionnaire itself would tend to rule out very low literacy levels, and the explanation of our purpose would select for those members who can tolerate the culturally prescribed value of scientific inquiry. For these reasons we have utilized the questionnaire for internal comparisons only. It is both valid and informative to divide a non-random sample on the basis of one variable and to test for significant differences between categories based on other variables. This was done by means of a multivariate analysis of variance, with certain variables such as age, sex, socio-economic status, and frequency of glossolalic experience selected as independent variables and tested for effect on dependent variables such as degree of participation in the movement, behavioral changes reported, self-image vis-à-vis the larger society, and relationship with the recruiter. Several analyses were run using the X^2 test for k independent samples. Correlations between variables or effects of independent upon dependent variables were accepted as significant if the probability of the null hypothesis being true was .05 or less.

The third method of data collection was participant observation, conducted during a period of from several months to a year in each of seven Pentecostal groups. This provided information on Pentecostalism both as a movement and as an experience. The opportunity for extended relationships with a few informants gave us an insight into the phenomenon of conversion and commitment and opportunities to observe recruiting methods, organizational structure, and inter-group ties. We were also able to assess the ideological differences between groups and to study the degree and kind of opposition which the movement inspires in non-Pentecostal institutions.

In selecting the seven groups described in chapter II, we again relied on fortuitous circumstances of rapport with certain leaders, but we were careful to choose groups representing the major variations we had already observed.

To this list of methods of data collection should be added the brief but informative trips we took in order to survey Pentecostal groups in other cultural settings. Comparative data were collected by Luther Gerlach during two periods of field studies in Port-au-Prince, Haiti, and environs, and two periods in Bogotá, Colombia, and nearby rural towns; by James Olila during two visits in Mexico City and Otomi Indian villages; and by Virginia Hine during one visit to Montego Bay, Jamaica. We saw in these cross-cultural surveys an opportunity to add useful perspective to our work and to test our propositions about the five movement factors. For example, the manner in which Haitian converts to Pentecostalism exorcise the voodoo spirits, receive the Baptism of the Holy Spirit, and burn their voodoo ritual objects gave us important comparative data about the nature and function of the commitment process. Comparing two Otomi Indian communities in Mexico, one Pentecostal, the other "folk" Catholic, illustrated the influence of Pentecostal religious change on social and economic behavior. The study of conflict and competition among different lay evangelical groups visiting Jamaica and Colombia gave us an important insight into the function of factionalism and schism. Analysis of the expansion of the Pentecostal network in all of these areas illuminated both the general nature of movement recruitment and organization, and specific adaptations to varying social-cultural contexts.

One methodological principle should be mentioned which was important in every research area we visited. An alternative to relying on cooperative informants, which has been tried by some investigators into religious movements, is to pose as a potential convert in order to gain admittance to the community. It was one of our methodological ground rules that our team members would be honest about our purpose in the investigation and about their own religious attitudes if questioned. Personal responses to the movement, different among team members, were never misrepresented to our informants. We have found this approach personally satisfying as well as scientifically sound. Margaret Mead, at the 1966 annual meeting of the American Anthropological Association, pointed out the importance of the fact that a modern anthropologist's informants may one day read his monographs. His or any other anthropologist's future welcome in that community may depend not only on an honest reporting of the data, but also on a scientific interpretation and theoretical formulation of the data that does not distort the phenomenologically perceived reality. Anthropologists and other social scientists characteristically impose upon their data certain personal and scientific conceptions about the nature and purpose, cause and effect of behavior and belief. We recognize the utility of such functional analysis, and have ourselves employed it. But we also would heed Paul Bohannan's advice that anthropologists should recognize the difference between "folk" and anthropological explanations of phenomena, and should consider both approaches when developing models and theory (8, especially chap. 1).

We have found it scientifically therapeutic to remember that many of our informants will read our publications. We have encouraged this possibility by means of a mimeographed report circulated to the Pentecostal community after the questionnaire data had been collected and a preliminary analysis made. In addition to this report, we submitted other relevant manuscripts—including a draft of a scholarly paper on the movement—to those informants sufficiently interested to read and comment on them. We also presented oral reports and several lectures on our research and findings to a number of interested Pentecostal and public groups. As background to these presentations, we usually explained the premises underlying our approach to the subject.

Pentecostals frequently explained to us the limitations inherent in attempting to explain the supernatural by means of the ideas and techniques of naturalistic science. We realize that our scientific interpretation of the religious and other movement phenomena we have studied is, indeed, likely to "miss the point" experienced by the participant. We further point out that any objective analysis which clearly contradicts the subjective experience is also missing the point, even scientifically, and is of little use in understanding or successfully dealing with the phenomena in question.

As we progressed in our research on Pentecostalism, we compared our findings about it with available information concerning such movements as early Islam, Mahdism in the Sudan, early Christianity, Communism in Asia, Mau Mau in Kenya, the T'ai P'ing movement in China, and various American Indian politico-religious movements, including those which have focused on the use of peyote. Discussions with anthropologists who have studied in Oceania led us to a consideration of the Cargo Cult as a movement.

In the summer of 1967 we widened the scope of our study to include field and literature research into the Black Power Movement. A major concern of this research was to examine Black Power in terms of the five-factor model we had developed in our Pentecostal study. We studied the movement intensively in one large metropolitan area in the North and surveyed aspects of it more briefly in two other urban centers, one also in the North and one in the Southeast. Techniques of data collection varied somewhat from those we used on the study of Pentecostalism. We did not employ a formal, computerized questionnaire, and we reduced the use of formal interviews to elicit case histories.

Because of the sentiments existing in the black community

against "more of the same" social science research, we felt that we could best obtain the data we desired through more informal interviews, both structured and unstructured, and through observation, both as participants and as observers, of a wide variety of Black Power groups and their activities. We found this approach quite useful. Again, we were more interested in gaining phenomenological understanding of patterns in Black Power and of the beliefs and behaviors of its participants than in securing quantifiable data. Many such participants in the groups studied were very helpful, and we established good relationships with a number of them. We were also able to film and tape record important aspects of the movement, including a major open housing march and activities at a black community center.

Field work in the northern metropolitan area of major concern included the study of ten different Black Power groups ranging along the spectrum of types described in chapter II. This study depended on direct observation, interview, and discussion, and daily examination of radio, television, and newspaper reports of relevance. As with the Pentecostal research, selection of groups depended upon establishment of rapport with key participants and also upon the extent to which groups appeared to represent different types of Black Power associations.

By means of interviews, news stories, and discussions with knowledgeable blacks and whites we were also able to learn at secondhand about many other Black Power groups, including a large coalition encompassing much of the black community in the area, and a number of *ad hoc* and short-lived groups formed to respond to specific situations.

Field work in the southeastern city included observation of a group of militant university students, two groups organized to articulate and present black community demands to the city in the days immediately following a riot of moderate scope, and a youth group organized to present the black American viewpoint on an educational television program. We learned from primary and secondary sources about a number of additional developing Black Power groups of varying mission, composition, and duration.

Research in the other northern city examined was concerned primarily with the study of a major and lengthy campaign of marching and confrontation to secure open housing and other objectives for black residents. By means of participant observation, interview, and survey of the mass media we collected data about the campaign, its participating and supporting groups and individuals, both black and white, and the response of the established order.

In conjunction with the study we also examined some of the significant ways in which whites have responded to the Black Power Movement by participating in various collective efforts. By means of participant observation, interview, and media survey we studied a number of white groups of positive and negative response located in the three areas of our Black Power research. In particular, we have been able to observe—sometimes as active participants—such positive response efforts as Urban Coalition task forces and various associations based on churches and educational institutions. We have not conducted much research on citizens' groups organized in opposition to Black Power.

To add necessary perspective and depth to our study in the major northern city we also conducted useful interviews and participated in significant discussions relevant to Black Power and establishment response with appropriate leaders and members in religion, education, business, government, and politics.

We must admit that our sympathies while conducting this research have lain with the Black Power Movement and with that establishment response which seeks to move ahead with the movement rather than attempt to suppress it. But, following the principles which we employed during the Pentecostal study, we attempted to make clear to everyone that our interest with the Black Power Movement and establishment response was based on our roles as anthropologists and researchers, not as participants. We have tried to see and experience the movement and response from the broadest perspective; we have sought to communicate our findings objectively to all concerned. We have put forth in varied public forums most if not all of the ideas, facts, and suggestions noted in this book. The public has had occasion to respond to our approach and we have profited greatly by such response. Through the crucible of such interchange, we have tested, rejected, modified, and retained many of our important ideas.

A major component of our research has been the survey and study of a broad range of literature, as well as programs on radio and television. There is a growing scholarly literature on the Black Power Movement and the establishment response, much of it written by blacks, and we have examined a large amount of it. More popular magazines and newspapers have also provided us with a significant quantity of information. Included in such sources are not only the main-line publications of both black and white America, but also the magazines and papers which reflect more militant and special positions concerning the movement, supporting it or opposing it. Since the spring of 1968 we have been collecting, coding, and filing such information, with the aim of forming the basis of a comprehensive media data system pertaining to contemporary movements and to establishment response.

Bibliography

A. The Anthropology, Sociology, and Psychology of Movements

1 Aberle, David. 1965. "A note on relative deprivation theory as applied to millenarian and other cult movements." In *Reader in Comparative Religion,* edited by W. A. Lessa and E. Z. Vogt. New York: Harper and Row.

2 Adorno, Theodor W.; Frenkel-Brunswick, Else; Levinson, D.; and Sanford, R. M. 1950. *The Authoritarian Personality.* New York: Harper.

3 Allport, Gordon W. 1954. *The Nature of Prejudice.* New York: Doubleday.

4 Aronson, Elliot, and Mills, Judson. 1959. "The effect of severity of initiation on liking for a group." *Journal of Abnormal and Social Psychology* 59 (2): 177-81.

5 Barber, Bernard. 1941. "Acculturation and messianic movements." *American Sociological Review* 6 (5): 137-45.

6 Bettelheim, Bruno, and Janowitz, Morris. 1949. "Ethnic tolerance: a function of social and personal control." *American Journal of Sociology* 55 (2): 137-45.

7 Bohannan, Paul. 1954. "The migration and expansion of the Tiv." *Africa* 24 (1): 2-16.

8 ———. 1963. *Social Anthropology.* New York: Holt, Rinehart & Winston.

9 Brehm, Jack W., and Cohen, A. R. 1967. *Explorations in Cognitive Dissonance.* New York: Wiley and Sons.

10 Cantril, Hadley. 1940. *The Invasion from Mars*. Princeton: Princeton University Press.

11 ———. 1941. *The Psychology of Social Movements*. London: Chapman and Hall.

12 Cantril, Hadley, and Katz, Daniel. 1939. "The problem of objectivity in the social sciences." In *The Psychology of Industrial Conflict*, edited by George Hartmann and T. Newcomb. New York: Dryden.

13 Clemhout, Simone. 1964. "Typology of nativistic movements." *Man* (January-February), Number 7.

14 Cohn, Norman. 1957. *The Pursuit of the Millennium*. London: Secker and Warburg.

15 Devereux, George. 1957. "Normal and abnormal: the key problem of psychiatric anthropology." *Some Uses of Anthropology*. Washington: Anthropological Society.

16 Festinger, Leon. 1957. *A Theory of Cognitive Dissonance*. Evanston: Row, Peterson.

17 Gerlach, Luther P. 1968. "People, power, change: A study of movements of revolutionary change." 16mm sound-color film; photographed in Minneapolis, Milwaukee, Colombia and Haiti; produced in association with the University of Minnesota Audio-Visual Service.

18 ———. 1969. "Which way America?" *McCormick Quarterly* 22 (2): 99-110.

19 Gerlach, Luther P., and Hine, Virginia H. 1968. "Five factors crucial to the growth and spread of a modern religious movement." *Journal for the Scientific Study of Religion* 7 (1): 23-40.

20 ———. 1969. "The social organization of a movement of revolutionary change: case study, Black Power." In *Afro-American Anthropology*, edited by Norman Whitten, Jr. New York: Free Press.

21 Gerrard, Nathan L. and Louise B. 1966. "Scrabble Creek folk: mental health." Mimeographed. Charleston, West Virginia: Morris Harvey College.

22 Glock, Charles Y. 1964. "The role of deprivation in the origin and evolution of religious groups." In *Religion and Social Conflict*, edited by R. Lee and M. W. Marty. New York: Oxford University Press.

23 Goldschmidt, Walter R. 1944. "Class denominationalism in rural California churches." *American Journal of Sociology* 49 (4): 348-55.

24 Goodwin, Richard N. "Our stake in a big awakening." *Life*, 11 October 1967, pp. 66-83.

25 Heberle, Rudolph. 1940. "Observations on the sociology of social movements." *American Sociological Review* 14 (3): 346-57.

26 Hine, Virginia H. 1967. "Deprivation and disorganization theories

of social movements." Mimeographed. Minneapolis: University of Minnesota.

27 ———. 1968. "Personal transformation and social change: The role of commitment in a modern religious movement." Master's thesis, University of Minnesota.

28 Hoffer, Eric. 1965. *The True Believer*. New York: Harper and Row.

29 ———. 1963. *The Ordeal of Change*. New York: Harper and Row.

30 Janis, Irving L. 1954. "Personality correlates of susceptibility to persuasion." *Journal of Personality* 22 (4): 504-18.

31 Johnson, Chalmers. 1966. *Revolutionary Change*. Boston: Little, Brown & Co.

32 Komorita, S. S., and Bernstein, Ira. 1964. "Attitude intensity and dissonant cognition." *Journal of Abnormal and Social Psychology* 69 (3): 323-29.

33 Kopytoff, Igor. 1964. "Classifications of religious movements: analytical and synthetic." *Proceedings of the 1964 Annual Spring Meeting of the American Ethnological Society*. Seattle: University of Washington Press.

34 Lanternari, Vittorio. 1963. *The Religions of the Oppressed*. Translated by Lisa Sergio. New York: Knopf.

35 Linton, Ralph. 1943. "Nativistic movements." *American Anthropologist* 45: 230-40.

36 Lipset, Seymour Martin. 1963. *Political Man*. London: Mercury.

37 Mannheim, Karl. 1936. *Ideology and Utopia*. Translated by L. Wirth and E. Shils. New York: Harcourt, Brace & Co.

38 Meadows, Paul. 1943. "An analysis of social movements." *Sociology and Social Research* 27: 223-28.

39 Muelder, Walter. 1945. "From sect to church." *Christendom* (Autumn): 450-62.

40 Niebuhr, H. Richard. 1951. "Christ against culture." In *Christ and Culture*. New York: Harper and Row.

41 ———. 1954. "The churches of the disinherited." *The Social Sources of Denominationalism*. New York: Holt and Rinehart.

42 Rokeach, Milton. 1954. "The nature and meaning of dogmatism." *Psychological Review* 61 (3): 194-204.

43 ———. 1956. "Political and religious dogmatism: an alternative to the authoritarian personality." *Psychological Monographs* 70 (18).

44 ———. 1960. *The Open and Closed Mind*. New York: Basic Books.

45 ———. 1961. "Authority, authoritarianism, and conformity." In *Conformity and Deviation*, edited by I. A. Berg and B. M. Bass. New York: Harper and Row.

46 Rokeach, Milton, and Kerlinger, Fred. 1966. "The factorial nature of the F and D scales." *Journal of Personality and Social Psychology* 4 (4): 391-99.

47 Sargant, William. 1949. "Some cultural group abreactive techniques and their relation to modern treatments." *Royal Society of Medicine Proceedings* 43 (January-June): 367-74.

48 ———. 1951. "The mechanism of conversion." *British Medical Journal* 2: 311-16.

49 ———. 1957. *Battle for the Mind.* New York: Doubleday.

50 Suinn, Richard M. 1965. "Anxiety and cognitive dissonance." *Journal of General Psychology* 73 (1): 113-16.

51 Talmon, Yonina. 1962. "Pursuit of the millennium: the relation between religious and social change." *Archives Européennes de Sociologie* 3 (1): 125-48.

52 Toch, Hans. 1965. *The Social Psychology of Social Movements.* Indianapolis: Bobbs-Merrill.

53 Wallace, Anthony F. C. 1956. "Revitalization movements." *American Anthropologist* 58: 264-81.

54 Worsley, Peter, 1957. *The Trumpet Shall Sound.* London: MacGibbon and Kee.

B. The Anthropology, Sociology, and Psychology of Religion

55 Allemann, Sarah A. 1963. "The structure and content of belief systems." Ph.D. dissertation, Purdue University.

56 Allen, Edmund E., and Hites, Robert W. 1961. "Factors in religious attitudes of older adolescents." *Journal of Social Psychology* 55 (2): 265-73.

57 Allen, Russell, and Spilka, Bernard. 1967. "Committed and consensual religion: a specification of religion-prejudice relationships." *Journal for the Scientific Study of Religion* 6: 191-206.

58 Becker, Ernest. 1962. "Relevance to psychiatry of recent research in anthropology." *American Journal of Psychotherapy* 16 (4): 600-17.

59 Bellah, Robert N. 1964. "Religious evolution." *American Sociological Review* 29 (3): 358-74.

60 Belo, Jane. 1960. *Trance in Bali.* New York: Columbia University Press.

61 Beres, David. 1965. "Psychoanalytic notes on the history of morality." *American Psychoanalytic Association Journal* 13 (1): 3-37.

62 Boisen, Anton J. 1936. *The Exploration of the Inner World: A Study

Bibliography

of Mental Disorder and Religious Experience. New York[...]
Row.

63 ———. 1955. *Religion in Crisis and Custom.* New York: [...]
Row.

64 Borhek, J. T. 1965. "Role orientations and organizational s[...]ity."
Human Organization 24 (4): 332-38.

65 Bourguignon, Erika. 1965. "The self, the behavioral environment, and
the theory of spirit possession." In *Content and Meaning in Cultural
Anthropology,* edited by Melford E. Spiro. New York: Free Press.

66 Bourguignon, Erika, and Pettay, Lorianna. 1964. "Spirit possession,
trance and cross-cultural research." *Proceedings of the American Ethnological Society* (Spring): 38-49.

67 Cattell, Raymond B. 1938. *Psychology and the Religious Quest.* New
York: Nelson and Sons.

68 Clark, Walter H. 1962. "A religious approach to the concept of the
self." *Annals of the New York Academy of Sciences* 96: 831-42.

69 Cutten, George B. 1927. *Speaking With Tongues.* New Haven: Yale
University Press.

70 Durkheim, Emile. 1961. *The Elementary Forms of the Religious Life.*
Translated by J. W. Swain. New York: Collier.

71 Eister, Allan. 1967. "Toward a radical critique of church sect typolo-
gizing." *Journal for the Scientific Study of Religion* 6: 85-90.

72 Eliade, Mircea. 1961. "History of religions and a new humanism."
History of Religions 1 (1): 1-8.

73 ———. 1961. "Recent works on shamanism." *History of Religions* 1
(1): 152-86.

74 Ennis, Phillip H. 1957. "Ecstasy and everyday life." *Journal for the
Scientific Study of Religion* 6: 40-48.

75 Firth, Raymond. 1959. "Problem and assumption in anthropological
study of religion." *Journal of the Royal Anthropological Institute* 89:
129-48.

76 Fisher, Seymour. 1964. "Acquiescence and religiosity." *Psychological
Reports* 15 (3): 784.

77 Frank, Jerome D. 1957. "Some aspects of cohesiveness and conflict in
psychiatric outpatient groups." *Johns Hopkins Hospital Bulletin* 101:
224-31.

78 ———. 1957. "Some determinants, manifestations, and effects of cohesiveness in therapy groups." *International Journal of Group Psychotherapy* 7: 53-63.

79 ———. 1961. *Persuasion and Healing: A Comparative Study of Psychotherapy.* Baltimore: Johns Hopkins Press.

Bibliography

80 Gerlach, Luther P. 1965. "The spirit possession complex of the Digo of Kenya, East Africa." Presented at the December meeting of the American Anthropological Association, Denver.

81 Gerth, H. H., and Mills, C. Wright, editors and translators. 1946. *From Max Weber: Essays in Sociology*. New York: Oxford University Press

82 Gill, Merton M., and Brenman, Margaret. 1959. *Hypnosis and Related States*. New York: International University Press.

83 Goodenough, Erwin R. 1965. *The Psychology of Religious Experiences*. New York: Basic Books.

84 Hall, Mary H. 1968. "A conversation with Michael Polanyi." *Psychology Today* 1 (12): 20-25, 66-67.

85 Hamer, John and Irene. 1966. "Spirit possession and its socio-psychological implications among the Sidamo of southeast Ethiopia." *Ethnology* 5 (4): 392-408.

86 Harvey, O. J.; Hunt, D. E.; and Schroder, H. M. 1961. *Conceptual Systems and Personality Organizations*. New York: Wiley and Sons

87 Herskovits, Melville. 1948. *Man and His Works*. New York: Knopf.

88 Hine, Virginia H. 1969. "Pentecostal glossolalia: toward a functional interpretation." *Journal for the Scientific Study of Religion* 8 (2).

89 James, William. 1902. *The Varieties of Religious Experience*. London Longmans, Green & Co.

90 Jung, Carl. 1958. "Psychology and Religion: West and East." *Collected Works* 11. New York: Pantheon.

91 Kiev, Ari. 1962. "Psychotherapy in Haitian Voodoo." *American Journal of Psychotherapy* 16 (3): 469-76.

92 ———. 1964. "The study of folk psychiatry." In *Magic, Faith, and Healing: Studies in Primitive Psychiatry Today*. New York: Free Press of Glencoe.

93 King, Morton. 1967. "Measuring the religious variable: nine proposed dimensions." *Journal for the Scientific Study of Religion* 6: 173-9

94 Lanternari, Vittorio. 1962. "Messianism: Its historical origin and morphology." *History of Religions* 2 (1): 52-72.

95 Lapsley, James N., and Simpson, John M. 1964. "Speaking in tongues: token of group acceptance and divine approval." *Pastoral Psychology* (May): 48-55.

96 ———. 1964. "Speaking in tongues: infantile babble or song of the self?" *Pastoral Psychology* (September): 16-24.

97 Laski, Marghanita. 1961. *Ecstasy: A Study of Some Religious and Secular Experiences*. Bloomington: Indiana University Press.

98 Lee, Robert. 1964. "Religion and social conflict." In *Religion and S*

cial Conflict, edited by R. Lee and M. Marty. New York: Oxford University Press.

99 Lenski, Gerhard. 1961. *The Religious Factor*. New York: Doubleday.

100 Lessa, William A., and Vogt, Evan Z. 1965. *Reader in Comparative Religion*. 2d ed. New York: Harper and Row.

101 Lowe, Warner L. 1955. "Religious beliefs and religious delusions." *American Journal of Psychotherapy* 9 (1): 54-61.

102 Lowie, Robert H. 1924. *Primitive Religion*. New York: Boni and Liveright.

103 ———. 1963. "Religion in human life." *American Anthropologist* 65 (3): 532-42.

104 Malhotra, J. D. 1963. "Yoga and mental hygiene." *American Journal of Psychotherapy* 17 (3): 436-42.

105 Mandelbaum, David G. 1966. "Transcendental and pragmatic aspects of religion." *American Anthropologist* 68 (5): 1174-91.

106 Maslow, Abraham H. 1954. *Motivation and Personality*. New York: Harper and Row.

107 ———. 1962. *Toward a Psychology of Being*. New York: Van Nostrand.

108 ———. 1964. *Religions, Values, and Peak Experiences*. Columbus: Ohio State University Press.

109 ———. 1966. *The Psychology of Science*. New York: Harper and Row.

110 ———. 1968. "A theory of metamotivation: the biological rooting of the value life." *Psychology Today* 2 (2): 38-39, 58-61.

111 Meares, Ainslee. 1963. "Theories of hypnosis." In *Hypnosis in Modern Medicine*, edited by Jerome Schneck. Springfield, Ill.: Thomas.

112 Metraux, Alfred. 1959. *Voodoo in Haiti*. New York: Oxford University Press.

113 Mischel, Walter and Frances. 1958. "Psychological aspects of spirit possession." *American Anthropologist* 60 (2): 249-60.

114 Moore, Joseph G. 1965. "Religious syncretism in Jamaica." *Practical Anthropology* (March-April): 63-70.

115 Nadel, S. F. 1946. "A study of shamanism in the Nuba mountains." *Journal of the Royal Anthropological Institute* 76: 25-37.

116 ———. 1952. "Witchcraft in four African societies." *American Anthropologist* 54: 18-29.

117 Odea, Thomas. 1954. "The sociology of religion." *American Catholic Sociological Review* 15 (1).

118 ———. 1960. "Anomie and the quest of community: the formation

of sects among the Puerto Ricans of New York." *American Catholic Sociological Review* 21 (1): 18-36.

119 Pattison, E. Mansell. 1965. "The effects of a religious culture's values on personality psychodynamics." Presented at the December meeting of the American Association for the Advancement of Science, New York.

120 ———. 1965. "On the failure to forgive or be forgiven." *American Journal of Psychotherapy* 19 (1): 106-15.

121 Pope, Liston. 1942. *Millhands and Preachers.* New Haven: Yale University Press.

122 Salisbury, W. Seward. 1964. *Religion in American Culture: A Sociological Interpretation.* Homewood: Dorsey Press.

123 Salzman, Leon. 1953. "The psychology of religious and ideological conversion." *Psychiatry* 16 (2): 177-87.

124 Schneider, Louis. 1964. *Religion, Culture and Society.* New York: Wiley and Sons.

125 Shor, Ronald. 1959. "Hypnosis and the concept of the generalized reality-orientation." *American Journal of Psychotherapy* 13 (3): 582-602.

126 Silverman, Julian. 1967. "Shamans and acute schizophrenia." *American Anthropologist* 69: 21-31.

127 Spiro, Melford E. 1952. "Ghosts, Ifaluk, and teleological functionalism." *American Anthropologist* 54 (4): 497-503.

128 ———. 1964. "Religion and the irrational." *Proceedings of the American Ethnological Society* (Spring): 102-15.

129 ———. 1966. "Religion: problems of definition and explanation." *Anthropological Approaches to the Study of Religion*, edited by M. Benton. New York: Praeger.

130 Spiro, Melford E., and D'Andrade, Roy G. 1958. "A cross-cultural study of some supernatural beliefs." *American Anthropologist* 60 (3): 456-66.

131 Stanley, Gordon. 1964. "Personality and attitude correlates of religious conversion." *Journal for the Scientific Study of Religion* 4: 60-63.

132 Troeltsch, Ernst. 1951. "Sect-type and church-type contrasted." *The Social Teaching of the Christian Churches.* Translated by Olive Wyon. London: Allen and Unwin.

133 Underhill, Evelyn. 1911. *Mysticism: A Study in the Nature and Development of Man's Spiritual Consciousness.* New York: E. P. Dutton & Co.

134 Van Gennep, Arnold. 1908. *The Rites of Passage.* Translated by Mo

ika B. Vizedom and Gabrielle L. Caffee. Reprint. Chicago: University of Chicago Press, 1960.

135 Wach, Joachim. 1951. *Types of Religious Experience*. Chicago: University of Chicago Press.

136 Wallace, Anthony F. C. 1956. "Mazeway resynthesis: a biocultural theory of religious inspiration." *New York Academy of Sciences Transactions* 18: 626-38.

137 ———. 1957. "Mazeway disintegration: the individual's perception of socio-cultural disorganization." *Human Organization* 16 (2): 23-27.

138 ———. 1959. "Cultural determinants of response to hallucinatory experience." *Archives General Psychiatry, American Medical Association* 1 (July-December): 58-69.

139 ———. 1961. *Culture and Personality*. New York: Random House.

140 ———. 1966. *Religion: An Anthropological View*. New York: Random House.

141 Weber, Max. 1947. *Theory of Social and Economic Organization*. Translated by A. M. Henderson and Talcott Parsons. Edited by Talcott Parsons. New York: Oxford University Press.

142 ———. 1963. *The Sociology of Religion*. Translated by Ephraim Fischoff. Boston: Beacon Press.

143 Whisson, Michael G. 1964. "Some aspects of functional disorders among the Kenya Luo." *Magic, Faith and Healing*. Edited by Ari Kiev. New York: Glencoe.

144 White, Victor. 1961. *God and the Unconscious*. Cleveland: World Publishing Company.

145 Wittkower, E. D. 1964. "Spirit possession in Haitian Vodun ceremonies." *Acta Psychotherapeutica* 12: 30-72.

146 Yinger, J. Milton. 1957. *Religion, Society and the Individual*. New York: Macmillan.

C. The Pentecostal Movement

147 Alland, Alexander. 1961. "Possession in a revivalistic Negro church." *Journal for the Scientific Study of Religion* 1 (2): 204-13.

148 American Lutheran Church. 1965. "Report of the Field Study Committee on Speaking in Tongues." Mimeographed. Minneapolis, Minnesota: Commission on Evangelism.

149 Block-Hoell, Nils. 1964. *The Pentecostal Movement*. Oslo: Universitetforlaget.

150 Boisen, Anton T. 1939. "Economic distress and religious experience: a study of the holy rollers." *Psychiatry* 2 (2): 185-94.

151 Briggs, Jean L. 1963. "The role of the Holy Spirit in acculturation: a study of Pentecostalism." Mimeographed. Cambridge: Harvard University.

152 Brown, Daniel G., and Lowe, Warner L. 1951. "Religious beliefs and personality characteristics of college students." *Journal of Social Psychology* 33 (February): 103-29.

153 Brumback, Carl. 1961. *Suddenly From Heaven: A History of the Assemblies of God.* Springfield, Missouri: Gospel Publishing House.

154 Calley, Malcolm. 1965. *God's People: West Indian Pentecostal Sects in England.* London: Oxford University Press.

155 Damboriena, P. 1966. "Pentecostal fury." *Catholic World* 202 (January): 201.

156 Elinson, Howard. 1965. "The implications of Pentecostal religion for intellectualism, politics, and the race relations." *American Journal of Sociology* 70: 403-15.

157 Erasmus, Charles J. 1961. *Man Takes Control.* Minneapolis: University of Minnesota Press.

158 Farrell, Frank. "Outburst of tongues: the new penetration." *Christianity Today,* 13 September 1963, pp. 3-7.

159 Gustatis, Rasa. 1967. "The Pentecostals." *Jubilee* 15 (1): 8-15.

160 Harper, Gordon P. 1963. "The children of Hippolito: a study of Brazilian Pentecostalism." Mimeographed. Cambridge: Harvard University.

161 Hoekema, Anthony A. 1966. *What About Tongue Speaking?* Grand Rapids: Eerdmans.

162 Hollenweger, Walter J. 1966. "The Pentecostal movement and the World Council of Churches." *The Ecumenical Review* 18 (3): 310-20.

163 ———. 1969. *Enthusiastiches Christentum.* Zurich: Zwingli, Flamberg Verlag.

164 Holsteen, Melvin. 1968. "Controlled resistance to change in a Pentecostal church." Master's thesis, University of Minnesota.

165 Holt, John B. 1950. "Holiness religion: cultural shock and social reorganization." *American Sociological Review* 5 (5): 740-47.

166 Jaquith, James R. 1967. "Toward a typology of formal communicative behaviors: glossolalia." *Anthropological Linguistics* 9 (8): 1-8.

167 Johnson, Benton. 1961. "Do holiness sects socialize in dominant values?" *Social Forces* 39: 309-16.

168 Kelsey, Morton T. 1964. *Tongue Speaking.* New York: Doubleday.

169 Kendrick, Claude. 1966. "The Pentecostal movement: hopes and hazards." *Christian Century* 80 (19): 608-10.

170 Loewen, Jacob A.; Buckwalter, Albert; and Katz, James. 1965. "Sha

manism, illness and power in Toba church life." *Practical Anthropology* (November-December): 250-80.

171 Martin, Ira Jay. 1960. *Glossolalia in the Apostolic Church.* Berea, Kentucky: Berea College Press.

172 May, L. Carlyle. 1956. "A survey of glossolalia and related phenomena in non-Christian religions." *American Anthropologist* 58 (1): 75-96.

173 McDonnell, Kilian, O.S.B. 1967. "The ecumenical significance of the Pentecostal movement." *Worship* 40: 608-29.

174 ———. "The ideology of conversion." Presented at the Central States Meeting, American Anthropological Society, April 1967, Chicago.

175 ———. 1968. "Pentecostals and drug addiction." *America* 118 (30 March): 402-06.

176 ———. 1968. "Holy Spirit and Pentecostalism." *Commonweal* (8 November): 198-204.

177 McGavran, Donald. 1963. *Church Growth in Mexico.* Grand Rapids: Eerdmans.

178 Mintz, Sidney W. 1960. *Worker in the Cane.* New Haven: Yale University Press.

179 Nichol, John T. 1966. *Pentecostalism.* New York: Harper and Row.

180 Nouwen, Henri J. M. 1967. "The Pentecostal movement: three perspectives." *Scholastic* 109 (22 April): 15-17.

181 O'Connor, Edward, C.S.C. 1967. "A Catholic Pentecostal movement." *Ave Maria* 105 (22): 6-10.

182 Olila, James. 1966. "The Pentecostal concept of power." Mimeographed. Minneapolis: University of Minnesota.

183 ———. 1968. "The social organization of the Pentecostal movement." Master's thesis, University of Minnesota.

184 Palmer, Gary. 1966. "Trance and dissociation: a cross-cultural study in psycho-physiology." Master's thesis, University of Minnesota.

185 ———. 1967. "Trance." Paper read at Central States Anthropological Society Annual Meeting, April 1967, Chicago.

186 Pattison, E. Mansell. "Speaking in tongues and about tongues." *Christian Standard,* 15 February 1964.

187 Pike, James A. Pastoral Letter issued 2 May 1963 to churches in the Diocese of California, Protestant Episcopal Church. Mimeographed. San Francisco.

188 Plog, Stanley. 1964. "UCLA conducts research on glossolalia." *Trinity* 3 (1): 38-39.

189 ———. 1965. "Summary of group questionnaires on the Blessed Trinity Society meetings, Los Angeles Christian Advances, and St. Luke's church, Seattle." Mimeographed. Los Angeles: UCLA Medical Center.

190 Protestant Episcopal Church. 1963. "Preliminary Report of the study
     commission on glossolalia, Diocese of California." Mimeographed. San
     Francisco.

191 Read, William. 1965. *New Patterns of Church Growth in Brazil.* Grand
     Rapids: Eerdmans.

192 Rooth, Richard. 1967. "Social structure in a Pentecostal church."
     Master's thesis, University of Minnesota.

193 Sadler, A. W. 1964. "Glossolalia and possession: an appeal to the
     Episcopal commission." *Journal for the Scientific Study of Religion*
     4: 84-90.

194 Samarin, William J. 1968. "The linguisticality of glossolalia." *Hartford*
     Quarterly 8 (4): 49-75.

195 ———. 1968. "Forms and functions of nonsense language." *Linguis-*
     tics, in press.

196 ———. 1968. "Glossolalia as learned behavior." Paper read at annual
     conference Society for the Scientific Study of Religion, Montreal, Oc-
     tober 1968.

197 Sherrill, John. 1964. *They Speak With Other Tongues.* New York:
     McGraw-Hill.

198 Simpson, George E. 1956. "Jamaican revivalist cults." *Social and*
     Economic Studies 5 (4): 321-442.

199 Sorem, Anthony. 1969. "Some secular implications of the Pentecostal
     denomination." Master's thesis, University of Minnesota.

200 Tschuy, Theo. 1960. "Shock troops in Chile." *Christian Century* 77:
     1118-19.

201 Vivier, Lincoln Morse Van Eetveldt. 1960. "Glossolalia." Ph.D. disser-
     tation, University Witwaterstrand, South Africa. (Microfilm copies at
     University of Chicago, Union Theological Seminary.)

202 Webster, Douglas. 1964. *Pentecostalism and Speaking With Tongues.*
     London: Highway Press.

203 Whalen, William J. 1967. "The Pentecostals." *U. S. Catholic* 32 (10):
     12-16.

204 Wilkerson, David. 1964. *The Cross and the Switchblade.* New York:
     Pyramid.

205 Willems, Emilio. 1964. "Protestantism and culture change in Brazil
     and Chile." In *Religion, Revolution and Reform,* edited by W. V.
     D'Antonio and F. B. Pide. New York: Praeger.

206 ———. 1966. "Religious mass movements and social change in
     Brazil." In *New Perspectives on Brazil,* edited by E. Baklanoff. Nash-
     ville: Vanderbilt University Press.

207 ———. 1967. "Validation of authority in Pentecostal sects of Chile

and Brazil." *Journal for the Scientific Study of Religion* 6: 253-59.

208 Wilson, Bryan R. 1959. "Role conflicts and status contradictions of the Pentecostal minister." *American Journal of Sociology* 64 (5): 494-504.

209 ———. 1961. *Sects and Society*. Berkeley: University of California Press.

210 Wood, William W. 1965. *Culture and Personality Aspects of the Pentecostal Holiness Religion*. Paris: Mouton.

211 Zwack, Daniel D. 1968. "Building African community." *Maryknoll* (April): 16-20.

D. The Black Power Movement

212 American Friends Service Committee. 1967. *In Place of War: An Inquiry into Non-Violent National Defense*. New York: Grossman.

213 Apter, David. 1965. *The Politics of Modernization*. Chicago: University of Chicago Press.

214 Barbour, Floyd B. 1968. *The Black Power Revolt*. Boston: Porter-Sargent.

215 Bennett, Lerone, Jr. 1964. *The Negro Mood*. Chicago: Johnson Publishing Co.

216 ———. 1965. *Confrontation: Black and White*. Chicago: Johnson Publishing Co.

217 Bernard, Jessie. 1966. *Marriage and Family Among Negroes*. Englewood Cliffs, New Jersey: Prentice-Hall.

218 Bernstein, Saul. 1967. *Alternatives to Violence: Alienated Youth and Riots, Race and Poverty*. New York: Association Press.

219 Bontemps, Arna, and Conroy, Jack. 1966. *Anyplace But Here*. New York: Hill and Wang.

220 Brink, William, and Harris, Louis. 1966. *Black and White*. New York: Simon and Schuster.

221 Broderick, Francis L., and Meier, August. 1965. *Negro Protest Thought in the Twentieth Century*. Indianapolis: Bobbs-Merrill.

222 Buckmaster, Henrietta. 1967. *Let My People Go: Story of the Underground Railroad and the Growth of the Abolition Movement*. Boston: Beacon Press.

223 Cameron, William Bruce. 1966. *Modern Social Movements*. New York: Random House.

224 Caplan, Nathan S., and Paige, Jeffrey M. 1968. "A study of ghetto rioters." *Scientific American* 219 (2): 15-21.

225 Carmichael, Stokely, and Hamilton, Charles. 1967. *Black Power: The*

Politics of Liberation in America. New York: Random House, Vintage Books.

226 Cartey, Wilfred. 1968. "Earth flow in Zionism and negritude." *Negro Digest* (August): 54-61.

227 Clark, Kenneth B. 1955. *Prejudice and Your Child*. Boston: Beacon Press.

228 ———. 1965. *Dark Ghetto: Dilemmas of Social Power*. New York: Harper and Row.

229 Cleage, Albert. 1969. *The Black Messiah*. New York: Sheed and Ward.

230 Conot, Robert. 1968. *Rivers of Blood, Years of Darkness*. New York: Morrow.

231 Coles, Robert. 1964. *Children of Crisis: A Study of Courage and Fear*. Boston: Little, Brown & Co.

232 Cook, Mercer, and Henderson, Stephen. 1969. *The Militant Black Writer in Africa and the United States*. Madison: University of Wisconsin Press.

233 Cruse, Harold. 1967. *The Crisis of the Negro Intellectual*. New York: Morrows.

234 Debray, Regis. 1967. *Revolution in the Revolution*. New York: Grove Press.

235 DeCoy, Robert H. 1967. *The Nigger Bible*. Los Angeles: Holloway House.

236 Drake, St. Clair, and Clayton, Horace R. 1961. *Black Metropolis: A Study of Negro Life in a Northern City*. New York: Harper and Row.

237 DuBois, W. E. Burghardt. 1904. *Souls of Black Folk: Essays and Sketches*. Chicago: A. C. McCourg & Co.

238 Dynes, Russell, and Quarantelli, E. L. 1968. "What looting in civil disturbances really means." *Trans-Action* 5 (6): 9-14.

239 Ekirch, Arthur, Jr., ed. 1964. *Voices in Dissent*. New York: Citadel Press.

240 Essien-Udom, Essien Udosem. 1962. *Black Nationalism: A Search for an Identity in America*. Chicago: University of Chicago Press.

241 Etzioni, Amitai. 1964. *Winning Without War*. New York: Doubleday.

242 Fanon, Frantz. 1966. *The Wretched of the Earth*. Translated by Constance Farrington. New York: Grove Press.

243 Franklin, John Hope. 1956. *The Militant South*. Boston: Beacon Press.

244 Frazier, E. Franklin. 1967. *Negro Youth at the Crossways*. New York: Schocken.

245 Ginzberg, Eli. 1965. *The Negro Potential*. New York: Columbia University Press.

246 ———. 1967. *The Middle-Class Negro in the White Man's World.* New York: Columbia University Press.

247 Glasgow, Robert W. 1968. "The urban crisis." *Psychology Today* 2 (3): 18-21.

248 Handlin, Oscar. 1964. *Firebell in the Night: The Crisis in Civil Rights.* Boston: Beacon Press.

249 Haralambos, Michael. 1969. "Soul music and the blues: their meaning and relevance in northern United States black ghettos." In *Afro-American Anthropology,* edited by Norman Whitten, Jr. New York: Free Press.

250 Hare, Nathan. 1968. "New role for Uncle Toms." *Negro Digest* (August): 14-19.

251 Hayden, Tom. 1967. *Rebellion in Newark.* New York: Random House.

252 Higginson, Thomas W. 1870. *Army Life in a Black Regiment.* Boston: Fields, Osgood & Co.

253 Hobsbawm, Eric J. 1959. *Primitive Rebels.* New York: Praeger.

254 Hoetink, H. 1967. *The Two Variants in Caribbean Race Relations: a Contribution to the Sociology of Segmented Societies.* Translated by Eva M. Hooykaas. London: Oxford University Press.

255 Holland, Mignon. 1968. "A black woman's soliloquy: in the face of fire I will not turn back." *Negro Digest* (August): 20-23.

256 Jackson, Bruce, ed. 1967. *The Negro and His Folklore in the 18th Century Periodicals.* San Antonio: University of Texas Press.

257 Johnson, Thomas A. "Negro self-rule linked to prevailing ghetto calm." *Miami News,* 21 October 1968: 10-A.

258 Jones, LeRoi. 1966. *Home.* New York: Morrow and Company.

259 ———. 1967. *Blues People.* New York: Morrow and Company.

260 Justice, Blair. n.d. "Effects of racial violence on attitudes in the Negro community." *Law Enforcement Science and Technology.* Washington: Thompson Book Co.

261 Keil, Charles. 1966. *Urban Blues.* Chicago: University of Chicago Press.

262 King, Martin Luther. 1967. *Where Do We Go From Here?* New York: Harper and Row.

263 Leonard, George B. 1968. *The Future Now.* New York: Delacorte Press.

264 Leyburn, James G. 1966. *The Haitian People.* New Haven: Yale University Press.

265 Lincoln, C. Eric. 1963. *The Black Muslims in America.* Boston: Beacon Press.

266 ———. 1968. *The Sounds of the Struggle.* New York: Morrow.

267 Lomax, Louis. 1963. *The Negro Revolt.* New York: Signet.

268 ———. 1967. *Thailand: The War That Is, The War That Will Be.* New York: Vintage.

269 ———. 1968. *To Kill a Black Man.* Los Angeles: Holloway House.

270 Lynch, Hollis R. 1967. *Edward Wilmot Blyden: Pan-Negro Patriot. 1893-1912.* London: Oxford University Press.

271 Malcolm X. 1964. *The Autobiography of Malcolm X.* New York: Grove Press.

272 Marine, Gene. 1969. *The Black Panthers.* New York: New American Library.

273 Meisel, James H. 1966. *Counter-Revolution: How Revolutions Die.* New York: Atherton Press.

274 Mills, C. Wright. 1956. *The Power Elite.* New York: Oxford University Press.

275 Momboisse, Raymond M. 1967. *Riots, Revolts, and Insurrections.* Springfield, Illinois: Thomas.

276 Murphy, Raymond J., and Elinson, Howard, eds. 1966. *Problems and Prospects of the Negro Movement.* Belmont: Wadsworth.

277 Myrdal, Gunnar. 1944. *An American Dilemma.* New York: Harper & Brothers.

278 ———. 1964. *The Negro Social Structure.* New York: McGraw-Hill.

279 Postgate, Raymond. 1962. *Revolution from 1789 to 1906.* New York: Harper and Row.

280 Raab, Earl, ed. 1962. *American Race Relations Today.* New York: Doubleday.

281 Ranger, Terence D. 1967. *Revolt in Southern Rhodesia 1896-1897.* Evanston: Northwestern University Press.

282 Rudwick, Elliott M. 1968. *W. E. B. DuBois: Propagandist of the Negro Protest.* New York: Atheneum.

283 Shaplem, Robert. 1966. *The Lost Revolution.* New York: Harper and Row.

284 Silberman, Charles E. 1964. *Crisis in Black and White.* New York: Vintage.

285 Speigel, Hans B. C., ed. 1968. *Citizen Participation in Urban Development.* Washington: National Training Laboratories Institute.

286 Styron, William. 1967. *Confessions of Nat Turner.* New York: Random House.

287 Sydnor, Charles S. 1952. *American Revolutionaries in the Making.* New York: Free Press.

288 Talbot, Allan. 1968. "The lessons of New Haven, the erstwhile model city." *Psychology Today* 2 (3): 22-27.

289 Thompson, Daniel C. 1963. *The Negro Leadership Class*. Englewood Cliffs: Prentice-Hall.

290 Tolbert, Richard C. 1968. "Needed: a compatible ideology." *Negro Digest* (August): 4-12.

291 U. S. National Advisory Commission on Civil Disorders. 1968. *Report*. Introduction by Tom Wicker. New York: Dutton.

292 Washington, Booker T. 1900. *Up From Slavery: An Autobiography*. New York: Doubleday.

293 Woodward, C. Vann. 1955. *The Strange Career of Jim Crow*. New York: Oxford University Press.

294 Yinger, J. Milton. 1965. *A Minority Group in American Society*. New York: McGraw-Hill.

295 Zinn, Howard. 1964. *SNCC: The New Abolitionists*. Boston: Beacon Press.

E. Other Movements

296 Aberle, David F. 1966. "The Peyote religion among the Navaho." *Wenner-Gren Foundation for Anthropological Research, No. 42*. New York: Viking Fund Publications.

297 Assemblies of God. 1965. "Overseas Statistics." Mimeographed. Springfield, Missouri.

298 Barber, Bernard. 1941. "A socio-cultural interpretation of the Peyote Cult." *American Anthropologist* 43 (4): 673-75.

299 Barnett, Donald L., and Njama, Karari. 1966. *Mau Mau From Within*. London: Monthly Review Press.

300 Belshaw, Cyril S. 1950. "The significance of modern cults in Melanesian development." *Australian Outlook* 4: 116-25.

301 Brodie, Fawn. 1945. *No Man Knows My History*. New York: Knopf.

302 Carr, Edward H. 1950. *Studies in Revolution: Saint-Simon, Marx, Proudhon, Herzen, Lassale, Plekhanov, Lenin, Stalin*. New York: Grossett and Dunlap.

303 Chou Tse-tsung. 1960. *The May Fourth Movement: Intellectual Revolution in Modern China*. Cambridge: Harvard University Press.

304 Cohen, Mitchell, and Hale, Dennis. 1962. *The New Student Left*. Boston: Beacon Press.

305 Collins, June. 1950. "The Indian Shaker church: a study of continuity and change in religion." *Southwestern Journal of Anthropology* 6 (4): 399-411.

306 Daley, Richard J. 1968. *Crisis in Chicago: 1968, Mayor Richard J.*

Daley's Official Report—The Untold Story of the Convention Riots. New York: Bee-Line Books.

307 Draper, Hal. 1965. *Berkeley: The New Student Revolt.* New York: Grove Press.

308 Eister, Allan. 1950. *Drawing Room Conversion.* Durham: Duke University Press.

309 Engels, Friedrich. 1967. *The German Revolution: The Peasant War in Germany.* Edited by Leonard Krieger. Chicago: University of Chicago Press.

310 Fall, Bernard, ed. 1967. *Ho Chi Minh on Revolution: Selected Writings, 1920-1966.* New York: Praeger.

311 Farber, Jerry. "The student as nigger." *Los Angeles Free Press,* 3 March 1967.

312 Festinger, Leon; Rieken, Henry W.; and Schachter, Stanley. 1956. *When Prophecy Fails.* Minneapolis: University of Minnesota Press.

313 Gibb, Hamilton. 1940. *Mohammedanism: An Historical Survey.* London: Oxford University Press.

314 Gluckman, Max. 1963. *Order and Rebellion in Tribal Africa.* Glencoe: Free Press.

315 Guillaume, Alfred. 1956. *Islam.* New York: Barnes and Noble.

316 Hitler, Adolf. 1941. *Mein Kampf.* Editorial Sponsors: John Chamberlain, Sydney B. Fay, John Gunther, Carlton J. H. Hayes, Graham Hutton, Alvin Johnson, William L. Langer, Walter Millis, Raoul de Roussy de Sales, and George N. Shuster. New York: Reynal and Hitchcock.

317 Hitti, Philip K. 1949. *The Arabs.* Chicago: Henry Regnery.

318 Hogg, Donald. 1960. "The Convince Cult in Jamaica." *Papers in Caribbean Anthropology.* Edited by Sidney W. Mintz. Yale University Publications in Anthropology No. 58.

319 Hurt, Wesley R. 1960. "Factors in the persistence of Peyote in the Northern Plains." *Plains Anthropologist* 5 (9): 16-27.

320 Jackson, Bruce. "The Battle of the Pentagon." *Atlantic Monthly,* January 1968, pp. 35-42.

321 Jameson, J. Franklin. 1956. *The American Revolution Considered as a Social Movement.* Boston: Beacon Press.

322 Kasdan, Leonard, and Murphy, Robert F. 1959. "The structure of parallel cousin marriage." *American Anthropologist* 61: 17-29.

323 Kenniston, Kenneth. 1968. "Youth, change, and violence." *American Scholar* 37 (2): 227-45.

324 Koestler, Arthur. 1950. "The initiates." In *The God That Failed,* edited by Richard Crossman. New York: Harper.

325 Kraus, Wolfgang H. 1967. "Thoughts on political ideology." *George Washington University Magazine* 3 (4): 15-18.

326 Lawrence, Peter. 1964. *Road Bilong Cargo: A Study of the Cargo Movement in the Southern Madang District of New Guinea.* Victoria: Melbourne University Press.

327 Leakey, Louis B. 1954. *Defeating the Mau Mau.* London: Methuen.

328 Leary, Timothy, and Clark, Walter H. 1963. "Religious implications of consciousness expanding drugs." *Religious Education* 58: 251-55.

329 Lee, Robert. 1967. *Stranger in the Land.* London: Lutterworth.

330 Lewis, Oscar. 1964. "Seventh Day Adventists in a Mexican village." In *Process and Pattern in Culture*, edited by R. A. Manners. Chicago: Aldine.

331 Lifton, Robert J. 1956. "Thought reform of Western civilians in Chinese communist prisons." *Psychiatry* 19: 173-95.

332 Lofland, John. 1966. *Doomsday Cult.* Englewood Cliffs, New Jersey: Prentice-Hall.

333 Mead, Margaret. 1956. *New Lives for Old.* New York: Morrow.

334 Messing, Simon D. 1958. "Group therapy and social status in the Zar cult of Ethiopia." *American Anthropologist* 60 (6): 1120-26.

335 Michelet, Jules. 1847-1853. *History of the French Revolution.* Translated by Charles Cook. Edited by Gordon Wright. Chicago: University of Chicago Press, 1967.

336 Middleton, John, and Tait, David, eds. 1958. *Tribes Without Rulers.* London: Routledge and Kegan Paul.

337 Myrdal, Jan. 1965. *Report from a Chinese Village.* Translated by M. Michael. New York: New American Library.

338 Nordhoff, Charles. 1875. *The Communistic Societies of the United States.* Reprint. New York: Schocken Books, 1965.

339 Payne, Robert. 1966. *Mao Tse-Tung.* New York: Pyramid.

340 Rockefeller, John D. III. 1969. "When you're over thirty like me." *Episcopalian* 134 (1).

341 Romm, Ethel. 1968. "Blueprint for revolution." *New York* 1 (28): 20-29.

342 Schein, Edgar H. 1956. "The Chinese indoctrination program for prisoners of war." *Psychiatry* 19: 149-71.

343 ———. 1961. *Coercive Persuasion.* New York: Norton and Company.

344 Schwartz, Theodore. 1962. "The Paliau Movement in the Admiralty Islands—1946-1954." *American Museum of Natural History* 49 (2).

345 Sherrod, Robert. "Notes on a monstrous war." *Life*, 27 January 1967, pp. 21-29.

346 Simpson, George. 1955. "The Ras Tafari movement in Jamaica: a

study of race and class conflict." *Social Forces* 34 (December): 167-70.

347 Singer, Milton. 1962. "The Radha-Krishna Bhajans of Madras City." *History of Religions* 2 (2): 183-226.

348 Slotkin, J. S. 1965. "The Peyote Way." In *Reader in Comparative Religion*, edited by W. A. Lessa and E. Z. Vogt. New York: Harper and Row.

349 Stewart, Omer C. 1941. "Southern Ute Peyote cult." *American Anthropologist* 43 (2): 303-08.

350 ———. 1944. "Washo-Northern Paiute Peyotism." *University of California Publications in American Anthropology and Ethnology* 40 (3): 63-141.

351 Tang Tsou. 1963. *America's Failure in China.* Chicago: University of Chicago Press.

352 Vaughn, Roger. "Confrontation and disruption." *Life*, 18 October 1968, pp. 76-96.

353 Walker, Richard L. 1956. *China Under Communism.* London: Allen and Unwin.

354 Werblowsky, R. J. Zwi. 1961. "Mystical and magical contemplation: the Kabbalists in 16th century Safed." *History of Religions* 1 (1): 9-36.

F. General

355 Coon, Carleton S. 1958. *Caravan: The Story of the Middle East.* 2d ed., rev. New York: Henry Holt.

356 De Vore, Irven, and Lee, Richard B. 1969. *Man the Hunter.* Chicago: Aldine.

357 Dobzhansky, Theodosius. 1967. *The Biology of Ultimate Concern.* New York: New American Library.

358 Eiseley, Loren C. 1946. *The Immense Journey.* New York: Random House.

359 ———. 1960. *The Firmament of Time.* New York: Atheneum.

360 ———. 1966. "Science and the unexpected universe." *American Scholar* 35 (3): 415-29.

361 Emmet, Dorothy. 1958. *Function, Purpose, and Powers.* London: Macmillan.

362 Evans-Pritchard, E. E. 1940. *The Nuer.* Oxford: Clarendon Press.

363 ———. 1956. *Nuer Religion.* Oxford: Clarendon Press.

364 Fabun, Don. 1967. *The Dynamics of Change.* Englewood Cliffs: Prentice-Hall.

365 Goodenough, Ward H. 1963. *Cooperation in Change.* New York: Russell Sage.

366 Harris, Sydney J. "Innovation and incompetence." *Miami Herald*, 7 August 1969.

367 Hoebel, E. Adamson. 1961. *The Law of Primitive Man*. Cambridge: Harvard University Press.

368 ———. 1966. "The future of the world." In *Anthropology: The Study of Man*. 3d ed., rev. New York: McGraw-Hill.

369 Hollingshead, August B. 1957. "Two factor index of social position." Mimeographed. New Haven: Yale University.

370 Huxley, Julian S. 1955. "Evolution, cultural and biological." *Yearbook of Anthropology*. New York: Wenner-Gren Foundation.

371 Lewis, I. M. 1961. *A Pastoral Democracy: A Study of Pastoralism and Politics Among the Somali of the Horn of Africa*. London: Oxford University Press.

372 MacLeod, Robert B. 1957. "Teleology and theory of human behavior." *Science* 125: 477-80.

373 Maruyama, Magorob. 1965. "The second cybernetics: deviation amplifying mutual causal processes." *American Scientist* 51 (2): 164-79.

374 Meehan, Eugene P. 1968. *Explanation in Social Science*. Homewood: Dorsey Press.

375 North, C. C., and Hatt, P. K. 1947. "Jobs and occupations." *Opinion News* 9 (4): 3-13.

376 Odiorne, George. 1969. *Green Power: The Corporation and the Urban Crisis*. New York: Pitman.

377 Polanyi, Michael. 1957. "Scientific outlook: its sickness and cure." *Science* 125.

378 ———. 1958. *Personal Knowledge: Towards a Post Critical Philosophy*. Chicago: University of Chicago Press.

379 ———. 1968. "Message of the Hungarian revolution." *Psychology Today* 1 (12): 62-64.

380 Radin, Paul. 1926. *Crashing Thunder: The Autobiography of a Winnebago Indian*. New York: Appleton.

381 Sahlins, Marshall D. 1961. "The segmentary lineage: an organization of predatory expansion." *American Anthropologist* 63 (2): 322-45.

382 Sahlins, Marshall D., and Service, Elman R. 1960. *Evolution and Culture*. Ann Arbor: University of Michigan Press.

383 Siegel, Sidney. 1956. *Non-Parametric Statistics for the Behavioral Sciences*. New York: McGraw-Hill.

384 Teilhard de Chardin, Pierre. 1959. *The Phenomenon of Man*. Translated by B. Wall. New York: Harper.

385 Warner, William Lloyd. 1960. *Social Class in America: A Manual of*

the Procedures for the Measurement of Social Status. New York: Harper.

386 Weaver, Warren. 1963. "The imperfections of science." In *Selected Botanical Papers*. Edited by Irving W. Knobloch. Englewood Cliffs, New Jersey: Prentice-Hall.

387 Werner, Ernest. 1966. "Protestant transformation." *American Scholar* 35 (3): 443-57.

388 White, Leslie A. 1949. *The Science of Culture*. New York: Farrar, Straus.

389 ———. 1959. *The Evolution of Culture*. New York: McGraw-Hill.

390 Wilson, Godfrey. 1945. *The Analysis of Social Change Based on Observations in Central Africa*. Cambridge: Harvard University Press.

Index

Luther P. Gerlach is a graduate of the University of Minnesota and the University of London. An associate professor of anthropology at the University of Minnesota, he lectures frequently to government, religious, and social activist groups. In cooperation with the University of Minnesota Audio-Visual Service, he produced the film, *People, Power, Change*, which was released in 1968. He is currently studying trends indicating that political and social responses to the ecological crisis may develop into a major mass movement of the 1970s.

Virginia H. Hine received her academic degrees from the University of Minnesota, where she was a key member of the staff of ten which assisted Professor Gerlach in his field studies of the Black Power and Pentecostal Movements. At present she is a research assistant in the autoecology of marine algae and synecology of marine plant and animal relationships at the University of Miami's Institute of Marine Science.